Casa da
Arquitectura
—
Lars
Müller
Publishers

Lars Müller Publishers

POWER / ARCHITECTURE

POWER ARCHITECTURE AT THE CASA DA ARQUITECTURA

José Manuel Dias da Fonseca
Nuno Sampaio

Power Architecture marks the opening moment of *Casa da Arquitectura*'s inauguration as *Centro Português de Arquitetura (Portuguese Centre of Architecture)* by calling for a reflection on the ties between Architecture and society. It opens itself to public debate and the media, reveals itself in the collective interest and the common good, and places itself politically in the built environment, from the building to the city and the territory.

At *Casa da Arquitectura*'s behest, Jorge Carvalho, Pedro Bandeira and Ricardo Carvalho propose this debate around a far-reaching and cross-cutting set of pre-identified "powers": Collective, Economic, Regulatory, Ritual, Technological, Media, and Cultural powers, as well as Counterpower itself.

Two sets of contents coexist in this event through two autonomous supports, independent from and complementary to each other. On the one hand, the contents of this book, more specialised, perhaps more lasting in time; and, on the other, the contents of the exhibition, the first to be held in the new premises of *Casa da Arquitectura*, certainly more intense as it is open to different publics, to all who are interested in Architecture, to all those who build and inhabit the city and the territory. Both sets of contents and supports can be said to be directly inscribed in *Casa da Arquitectura*'s core objectives, not least because they promote complementary readings about the field and decode it for the greater and better understanding of society as a whole.

As a place for the creation, promotion and dissemination of knowledge, or for research and storage of documentation and information, or for meeting and social mobilization, *Casa da Arquitectura* now opens up a new stage and an extraordinary opportunity for Architecture – both within and outside of the country –, searching for it in critical reflection and debate, urging on its reality-anticipatory and reality-transforming powers, always with the perspective of improving the built environment and the life of the citizens – as inseparable from the democratic exercise of Power as from Democracy itself. With Architecture, we aim to make this world a better world for all.

Contents

POWER/ ARCHITECTURE

Jorge Carvalho
Pedro Bandeira
Ricardo Carvalho

When we began organising the book *Poder Arquitectura*, we thought that there was a place in the contemporary debate on Architecture for reflecting on the meaning of the powers that influence and constrain its activity today. Perhaps that is why one of the first diagrams we drew turned out as a set of lines which contain the various powers acting – from the inside out and from the outside in – in the field of Architecture. The result is a system of overlaps, clashes and mergers and deadlocks, the likes of which we find, for example, in the diagrams of a city's underground raillines. On the one hand, this sort of diagram reflects a real, tangible geography, a systemic desire and a circuit; on the other hand, the diagram is an abstraction that reinvents a certain cartography. *Poder Arquitectura* is also a mental map, rhizomatic rather than systemic in its final version. It is this map what guides us in the relations between the works presented in the book, and a given reality that they transform.

Outside its domain, Architecture is traditionally perceived as a practice which above all represents an institutional Power – or, in the contemporary world, the Power of the global financial system – which tends to render relative the specific and the concrete and, instead, place value on a global uncritical action. But the field of Architecture has always been the one coming up with necessary syntheses so that, even when working for and with a specific power, it was able to critically transform a certain reality – to project is to anticipate a reality with various degrees of limitation. In this sense, the idea of critical transformation calls for another notion of representation. This is the sense of *working with the projects* that the book addresses.

Architecture, we know, is not just the expression of a single power. It reflects, and works from, various powers. We have therefore decided to isolate those powers who help clarify this complex cartography. Thus we have collective, regulatory, technological, economic, domestic, cultural, media and ritual powers. They were all present in the history of civilization and are still determining forces in the course of events on a global scale. In the long struggle between Man and Nature, Culture and Technology, these powers exerted influences of variable intensity in the production of architectural artifacts and in the design of the city and the territory. Today, faced with a political impotence that excuses and validates decisions that harm the public good and the meaning of communities, there seems to be room for a new reflection on power against impotence. Or, to put it another way, about the various powers in the face of widespread impotence.

Poder Arquitectura presupposes another notion of representation, which requires us to immerse ourselves in the architects' work and interpret their relationship with the brief, regulation, and social and ideological contexts. Before the design process begins, much information is drawn *a priori*, a fact the book tries to make apparent. Working the complexity of the various powers present therein does not presuppose a denial approach. A power is in itself neither negative nor positive. Sometimes powers cancel themselves out, sometimes they create synergies, sometimes they instigate counterpowers.
This book is also a document that stimulates a reading of the consensuses that create a certain work of Architecture. This process is usually excluded from a work's ultimate understanding once it has been delivered to its community or residents. The process, however, radically configures the outcome of a project. In this way, a work of Architecture represents the various actions of internal and external actors in a process, that is, it represents a way of functioning of the world, and in the world.

The selected works seek to reveal, in their absolute heterogeneity, this complexity of performance of architects and multidisciplinary teams. Working from very different contexts (from the social, geographic and economic point of view), points of contact are created between practices and issues, and it is this book's aim to lift the veil on them, as it were, and make them known.
To that effect, we favoured works to the detriment of authors. It seems more operative to reveal in the chosen works – with a multiplicity of functional programs –, forms and modes of overlap and convergence, unexpected encounters, dialogue

with the various actors present, the richness of the work process; and the analogy, synchronous and diachronic, with other works and processes. Perhaps that is why some of the chosen works can be read in the context of various powers and not just the one they're attributed to. We always understand the book in this sense – an open narrative, a process. It is also intended to bring together works and authors that do not usually appear side by side – hence the novelty of this cartography of powers.

The book's structure corresponds to a desire to work on the overlaps between powers and the theme's complexity. The introduction to the theme set of powers is made by a set of essays of several guest authors. The graphical content offer a solid atlas-like structure that contains drawings, images and references.

We have found a limitation to this cartography of powers, however: The representation of counter-power. In *Poder Arquitectura*, we knew that the inclusion of counter-power was necessary, but an impossibility a the same time – because the curatorial act itself *is* already a manifestation of power. Counter-power may be understood as resistance or ridicule, thus we can hardly incorporate it into an institutional discourse. To include it in the exhibition would immediately cancel its value as real counter-power. We can assume that, in the face of the generalized imposition of the global market, Architecture itself can function as a disciplinary stronghold of counter-power, as opposed to the banality and lack of meaning of generic construction. Or perhaps we might conclude with a neologism by Antonin Artaud, that of the need for *l'impouvoir*, for powerlessness.

MAPPING POWER/
ARCHITECTURE

Bruno Figueiredo

DOMESTIC

ECONOMIC

TECHNOLOGICAL

The cartography of Power / Architecture we present here was conceived as an installation of a spatial structure. This suspended installation, whose formal layout is created through the interpretation of the data at the core of Power / Architecture's project selection, is generated in a similar way to *data visualization* processes.

The spatial structure consists of a suspended web, from which the edges of 36 inverted pyramidal prisms of different sizes jut out. Each of the vertices of these pyramids represents a project in space. The configuration of the web, the spatial location of the prisms and their size, all are the result of a formal generation process, whose algorithmic principles take into account eight types of representations of power, to which the architectural projects in the exhibition are associated. This cartography establishes a possible version of this ideally dynamic spatial structure.

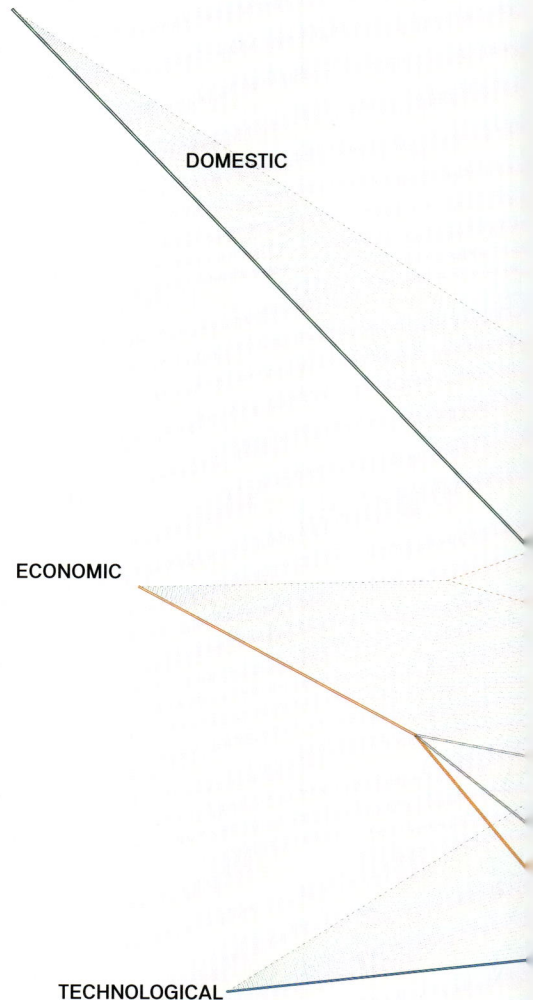

1 Anastasis Church, St Jacques-de-la-Lande, Rennes, France
2 Bait Ur Rouf Mosque, Dacca, Bangladesh
3 Baitul Mukarram Mosque, Lisbon, Portugal
4 Santa Luzia Church, Maia, Portugal
5 Warwick Junction, Durban, South Africa
6 Cologne-Bonn Airport Terminal 2, Germany
7 Cruise Terminal, Lisbon, Portugal
8 Mariposa Land Port of Entry, Nogales, Arizona, USA
9 Svalbard Global Seed Vault, Norway
10 Arena do Morro, Natal, Brazil
11 Granby Four Streets, Liverpool, United Kingdom
12 Galkadawala Forest Lodge, Habarana, Sri Lanka

13 SESC 24 de Maio, São Paulo, Brazil
14 Fish Market, Besiktas, Turkey
15 Lubango Centre, Lubango, Angola
16 De Rotterdam, Rotterdam, Netherlands
17 Data-Center, Covilhã, Portugal
18 Winery Gantenbein, Flash, Switzerland
19 Tua Dam Building, Portugal
20 Fovam Ter Subway Station, Budapest, Hungary
21 Shaekespeare Theatre, Gdansk, Poland
22 Showcase over the Camp Commander's House, Westerbork, Netherlands
23 Astley Castle Renovation, Warwickshire, United Kingdom
24 Alhambra New Gate / Puerta Nueva, Granada, Spain

25 Bridge, Mont Saint Michel, France
26 Performing Arts Centre, Taipei, Taiwan
27 Pôle Museal, Lausanne, Switzerland
28 Pavilion of the Architecture Triennale of Lisbon 2016, Portugal
29 Amager Resource Centre, Copenhagen, Denmark
30 Mulhouse Neppert, France
31 Star Apartments, Los Angeles, USA
32 Building A, Mehr Als Wohnen, Zurich, Switzerland
33 Maulee de Seram House, Colombo, Sri Lanka
34 Bern Heim Beuk House, Belgium
35 De Lork Assisted Living Residences, Brussels, Belgium
36 Quinta da Tília, Ponta Delgada, Portugal

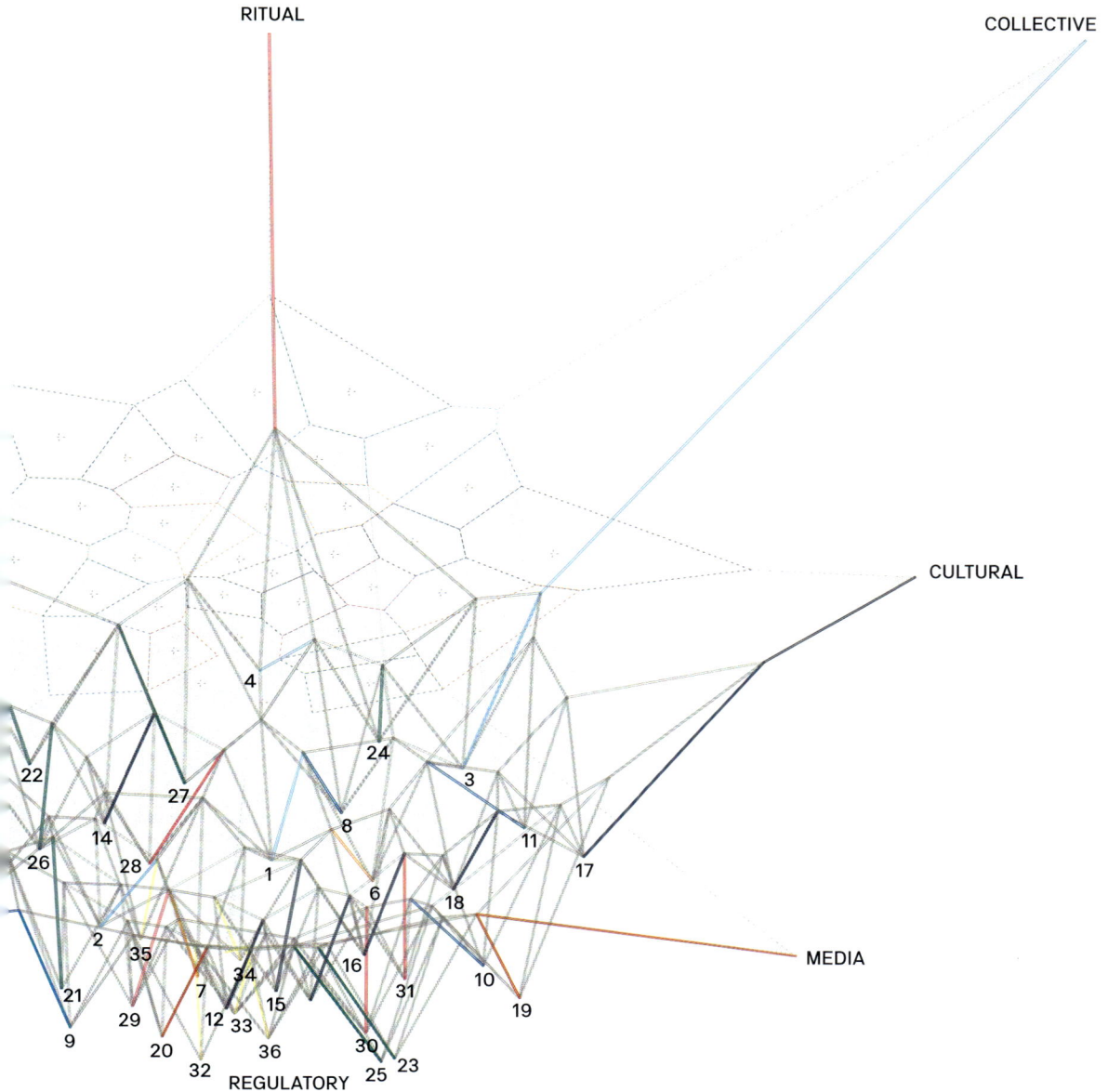

RITUAL

COLLECTIVE

CULTURAL

MEDIA

REGULATORY

ARCHITECTURE AND COLLECTIVE POWER

Guilherme Wisnik

São Paulo, 2001–04

In the early 2000s, a significant set of 45 state schools, called *Centros Educacionais Unificados* – CEU (Unified Educational Centres), were built in São Paulo's peripheral neighbourhoods. Conceived during the administration of Mayor Marta Suplicy (2001-04), who inaugurated the first 21 units, the CEU project was of great importance in the fields of education, architecture and urbanism. The project not only created new schools in underprivileged areas of the city, but mobilised real social and cultural mechanisms as a unifying force in local life, re-interpreting the concept of "social cohesion" in the context of the periphery of São Paulo of the years 2000. This concept was formulated during the constructivist experiments of the Soviet Union of the 1920s and 1930s.

The peripheral areas of São Paulo are marked by unlawful land use and thus open the way for unauthorised occupation, such as the *favelas*, as well as large housing estates built by the State. These are regions with many risk factors, environmental problems and situations of violence associated with crime and drug trafficking. Yet, these are also areas of great social mobilisation, where social movements, non-governmental organisations, cultural collectives, and various forms of political and artistic expression take place. Thus, these are places where social and urban precariousness contrasts with the multiple forms of resistance and creativity generated by active social consciousness.

The CEU project was developed by the *Departamento de Edificações da Prefeitura* – Edif (The Municipal Buildings Department), under the coordination of Alexandre Delijaicov, André Takiya and Wanderley Ariza. Conceived as "facilities built around a square," the school comprises three programmatic buildings: 1) a rectilinear school pavilion with classrooms, canteens, a library and exhibition and play areas; 2) a child care centre in the shape of a disc and raised above ground level; 3) and a compact volume for a theatre, sports facility and music room. There are also spaces for outdoor activities that include swimming pools. The simple and modular nature of the geometric volumes offer a flexible construction system which adapts to the topographical and contextual particularities of the different terrains at the sites.

In consideration of the principle of constructive rationality as well as the need for rapid construction of a significant number of building units, pre-fabrication was a clear choice, and so pre-cast concrete elements and metal stairs were used. In this aspect the experience was similar to the project for the *Centros Integrados de Educação Pública* – CIEP (Integrated Centres for Public Education), built in Rio de Janeiro between 1983 and 1987, an Oscar Niemeyer design and the *Centros Integrados de Atendimento à Criança* – CIAC (Integrated Centres for Child Assistance), a design by João Filgueiras Lima, Lelé, built in 1991 by the federal government but soon deactivated.

Flying over the immense expanse that is today's City of São Paulo, looking down on the outlying areas built so haphazardly, we occasionally notice the presence of the CEU projects as facilities visibly etched into the territory, like large geometric volumes organising an area that is clearly set apart from its immediate context. Yet, this distinction is defined by contrast rather than by negation. Placed in disadvantaged areas characterised by low rise and irregular housing, the CEU projects create cores of local urban life, hosting recreational and cultural activities that extend the school's service into the weekends and open them up to the local residents by acting as a type of community centre. From this perspective, it is very important that the architecture sought an opening to the surrounding areas as opposed to a closure, examples of which are the large open-circulation balconies of the school pavilions and the broad windowed façades.

From a pedagogical perspective, the direction taken by the CEU follows the educational model idealised by an educator from Bahia, Anísio Teixeira, a pioneer in supporting state-run, secular and free schools in Brazil and creator of the "Escola Nova" movement.[1] A disciple of John Dewey, Teixeira envisioned education as extensive and dynamic learning, a permanent process of reconstruction

CEU Butantã, São Paulo, Brazil. Alexandre Delijaicov, André Takiya and Wanderley Ariza (coordination). © Nelson Kohn

1 See Simon Schwartzman, Helena Maria Bousquet Bomeny and Vanda Maria Ribeiro Costa. *Tempos de Capanema*. São Paulo: Paz e Terra, 2000.

and reorganisation of experience. Based on this premise, he developed an educational project in which formal instruction should be complemented by other important activities, such as physical education, the arts, and social and industrial education. This idea is projected spatially in the distinction between the 'classroom-schools' and 'park--schools' in buildings that are formally differentiated and frequented by children who attend at different timetables.

This concept was put into practice during a revolutionary period in education and educational architecture in São Paulo between 1949 and 1954, which is known as the *Convênio Escolar*, This coincided, not by chance, with the city's great cosmopolitan leap forward, which used industrial development to transform its economical hegemony into urban and cultural prominence, resulting in the creation of its most important museums and cultural institutions – under the aegis of the so-called *Arte Concreta* – and the support of advanced industrial design concepts. São Paulo, preparing to celebrate its 400th anniversary in 1954, was finally emerging from a decades-long period of provincialism.

In this context, the *Convênio Escolar* was a broad program, aimed at reducing the shortage of state schools in the city during that period, which resulted in the construction of more than 100 new buildings, including libraries, health centres, theatres, playgrounds and rural schools.[2] The architect responsible for the coordination of these projects was the Rio native, Hélio Duarte, who had developed important work in educational projects in Salvador, Bahia, alongside Anísio Teixeira, in 1947.[3]

According to Duarte and Teixeira's concept, the school should be at the service of the child, meaning that the school's characteristics should incorporate a "childlike spirit," rather than based on the hierarchal discipline that characterised the school buildings idealized during the First Republic (1889-1930), which were symmetrical and imposing. According to Duarte's concept, the school space should stimulate pleasure and growth, as well as the child's free movement when engaged in outdoors activities. In addition, the school started to be understood as not just an autonomous building but as an urban facility for unifying the local community and offering new experiences, open in the evenings and during the weekends. In each neighbourhood, the school started to be seen as a place for parents' meetings, courses, dances, cinema and educational theatre, as well as being the location for the public library.

[2] "The 'Convênio Escolar' was an agreement between the city government and the State, which came together at that time to comply with the provisions of the 1946 Constitution which obliged the federal, state and local governments to invest a minimum percentage of their revenues in primary education. According to this agreement, the city government would commit to constructing school buildings to cover the existing deficit in the sector, while the state government would be responsible for teaching." Avany de F. Ferreira, Maria Elizabeth P. Corrêa, Mirela G. de Mello, *Arquitetura escolar paulista: restauro*. São Paulo: Fundação para o Desenvolvimento da Educação, 1998, p. 27.

[3] Hélio Duarte graduated with a degree in Engineering and Architecture from the Escola Nacional de Belas-Artes (ENBA) in Rio de Janeiro in 1930. This came before the historical reform promoted by Lucio Costa at the institution. See Hugo Segawa, "Hélio Duarte (1906-1989): moderno e peregrino", *Revista Projeto #131*, May 1990, p. 51.

Thus, Hélio Duarte and the architectural team of the *Convênio Escolar* took apart the traditional school monoblock, which was the main spatial model for schools at the time, dividing it into an assemblage of units, articulated by windowed balconies, walkways and ramps linking garden areas, forms which are largely characteristic of the modern architecture in Rio de Janeiro. These units contained separate programmatic areas for teaching, administration and play, where the latter was divided between a sports court and a covered area for recess. The emphasis on the students' socialisation with each other and with the local community is demonstrated in the shape of the covered play areas where platforms indicate that these spaces may be used to stage theatre performances.

CEU Butantã, São Paulo, Brazil. Alexandre Delijaicov, André Takiya and Wanderley Ariza (coordination). © Nelson Kohn

From an architectural point of view, the group of schools built by the *Convênio Escolar* have a very distinct general physiognomy, even though these do not use standardised construction systems. The most noticeable characteristics are the vaulted covered areas made of pre-cast concrete arches, placing the children's playground within a covered and yet open environment, and the separation of the classroom and administrative programs in different units, often arranged orthogonally, with the second being hierarchically subordinate to the first.

Approximately a decade later, the paradigm of educational architecture in São Paulo experienced great change. I am referring to a period in which the *Plano de Ação e Desenvolvimento Integrado* (Integrated Action and Development Plan) was introduced during the government of Carvalho Pinto, between 1959 and 1962.[4] Unlike the *Convênio Escolar* in which the local government appointed a team of architects to develop the projects within the framework of public functionalism, during the Action Plan a series of independent architectural firms were hired to carry out the projects individually. In this context, approximately 600 schools were built in numerous cities across São Paulo State within four years.

Reflecting on that period, the architect Vilanova Artigas observed that from that moment onward "society acknowledged the existence of the heritage present in the images of São Paulo architecture".[5] In a complementary way, Paulo Mendes da Rocha noted that "the need for a unified voice on the school problem" ended up creating "a working group which truly collaborated and shared information," and that the resulting projects "revealed in general how professional practice in our field had notably advanced."[6]

4   "The PLADI, 'Plano de Ação e Desenvolvimento Integrado' – Integrated Action and Development Plan, or 'Plano de Ação' – Action Plan – as it was known, developed during the government of Carvalho Pinto, described the situation at the time: deemed necessary was 'the construction and equipping of schools, 683 classrooms in total, for approximately 55,000 students, who at the moment attend classes in sheds or inadequate classrooms. The construction and equipping of schools, 2,298 classrooms in total which will keep the students on the school grounds for 4 hours, whereas they currently attend school for only 2.5 or 3 hours daily. The construction of 4,000 new classrooms at new school. Vilanova Artigas, "Sobre escolas" [1970], in *Caminhos da arquitetura*. São Paulo: Cosac Naify, 2004, p. 130.

5   Vilanova Artigas, 2004, op. cit., p. 130.

6   Paulo Mendes da Rocha, "Edifícios escolares: comentários", *Revista Acrópole #377*, September 1970, p. 35.

CEU Rosas da China, São Paulo, Brazil. Alexandre Delijaicov, André Takiya and Wanderley Ariza (coordination). © Nelson Kohn

The practical consequence of this process became, to a large extent, the formation of what came to be called the Paulista School of Architecture, or "brutalismo paulista" – São Paulo Brutalism.

Its main characteristics consist of assuming a daring structure as form-defining, the broad use of reinforced or pre-stressed concrete, the compact volumetry set under a luminous roof in the form of a skylight, the predominance of blind gables to hinder a more forthright relationship between the interior and exterior of the building, and the emphasis on creating a continuous internal spatiality. A spatiality, made of patios, gardens or large empty spaces that can bring the landscape features of outdoor spaces inside the building.

Originating in the schools that Artigas designed for Itanhaém (1959) and Guarulhos (1960), in the context of Carvalho Pinto's Action Plan, these characteristics reached their apogee in a project that Artigas designed for the Faculty of Architecture and Urbanism of the University of São Paulo in 1961, a building that expresses not only a specific architectural vision but also a conception of university teaching, understood as knowledge to be shared amongst everyone and thus necessarily interdisciplinary in nature.

Built in a city devoid of evident natural beauty which grew very rapidly under the predatory force of real estate speculation, the buildings that were dubbed *brutalismo paulista* turned their backs on the urban fabric, looking to reconstruct spaces internally with a new sociability, which was collective and more austere, as if these were cities conceived in a laboratory. In this sense, they exchanged the elementary composition of independent units of the *Convênio Escolar* buildings for a stronger sense of volumetric unification, where all the school's programmatic areas would be gathered under a single roof. Simultaneously, there was a sensitive closure in these buildings with respect to their urban surroundings as they sought to direct their environment toward the large internal open space which featured natural light. The windows or glass façades, were replaced by blind gables.

But returning to the present context: although educated within the architectural tradition of *brutalismo paulista* – Alexandre Delijaicov who worked for 10 years with Paulo Mendes da Rocha and is a professor at FAUUSP – the architects that designed CEU preferred to once again take up Hélio Duarte and Anísio Teixeira's example, following the exteriorised model of "park-schools" rather than the introverted "temple-schools" model. This was clearly a pedagogical option, combined with a firm positioning in relation to the role of a public facility of this scale in the periphery of São Paulo. Opening up to its surroundings as "facilities built around a square," the CEU adopted a more optimistic position in relation to the transformation of the neighbourhood as based on an exemplary and synergetic reference. The intention was not to create an isolated laboratory of a new and utopic social structure, but to activate the excellence of an existing reality, recognised as such. More than an architectural gem, the CEU is a great social and urban accomplishment. Its success with the public, which goes beyond the political disputes of any given moment, is the great evidence of this.

CEU Butantã, São Paulo, Brazil. Alexandre Delijaicov, André Takiya and Wanderley Ariza (coordination). © André Rosso

Natal 2011–14

At the beginning of 2010, twelve new stadiums (called arenas) were built for the 2014 World Cup in Brazil.[7] This was indeed a significant number, which certainly reflects the continental scale of the country, but also an enormous political arrangement between the different states and their capital cities, which competed with each other to host the event. Despite Brazil's well known football tradition, at least one-third of the host-cities selected to hold the event were unable to justify such an investment due to the fact that they no longer had football clubs nor local championships that could sustain the maintenance of such large stadiums.[8] The high construction costs of such projects, added to a lack of clarity about the true legacy of the event and the general feeling of discontent regarding FIFA's onerous demands (which seemed to be a repeat of neo-colonial intervention whose role had previously been played by the IMF) provided the fodder for a popular uprising, with citizens taking to the streets of the main Brazilian cities in June 2013 during the Confederations Cup. These mass demonstrations, in a clearly ironic statement, appealed primarily for more affordable public transport, along the lines of the "FIFA standard."[9]

A case in point is in the city of Natal where the Arena das Dunas was a controversial stadium erected for the World Cup, an imposing urban facility that cost the public treasury around 400 million Reais and which in fact has little year-round occupancy, although it included a relatively small sports gym built in a poor area called Arena do Morro.

7 Even the stadiums that were originally reformed, were eventually almost entirely rebuilt according to the "arena" model.

8 I am referring to the Arenas de Cuiabá, Manaus, Brasília and Natal.

9 See Andrew Jennings et al. *Brasil em jogo: o que fica da Copa e das Olimpíadas?* São Paulo: Boitempo, 2014.

This was a modest project, which by a curious twist of fate, was designed by the Swiss team of Herzog & de Meuron, the architects who designed the celebrated Allianz Arena (2001-05) in Munich built for the 2006 World Cup, and The National Stadium of Beijing (2002-07) built for the 2008 Olympics. The temporal and semantic coincidence – the shared name of "arena" – is in fact very significant. For if the 2014 World Cup arenas were not brilliant architecture projects and neither were their architects selected with clear criteria, this small sports project, connected to a school and a community project, proved extremely successful for its local impact, becoming a catalyst for a set of important positive changes in the neighbourhood.

When it emerged on the international scene in the transition from the 1980s to the 1990s, with its laconic asepsis and geometric rigour, the architecture of the so-called "Swiss rationalism" represented an evident contrast in relation to the already decadent and extravagant formalism of a certain post-modern architecture which was dominant up to that stage. With its compact boxes, directly revealing the expressiveness of materials, it affirmed an economy of means, which was nevertheless distinguished from a scarcity of resources. This poetic and constructive direction of Herzog & de Meuron's work underwent a great transformation, however, after the success of their project for the Tate Modern (1995-2000) in London, which brought a new set of clients and assignments to the firm. In Jacques Herzog's words, in the early 2000s, there was an important change in the office's work. Their early buildings built in Switzerland were of smaller scale and their relationship with the clients was based on strong dialogue, whereas when they started designing large scale works for authoritarian regimes, such as China and Russia, "dialogue" was replaced by "logo," that is, with buildings of emblematic and sculptural shapes, such as the aforementioned Munich and Beijing stadium projects. Thus, according to Herzog "if art and architecture are now more than ever political instruments, it is because they are closer to the branding universe than ever."[10]

Returning to the Brazilian context, we note a significant reversal of expectations, as mentioned above. Whereas architects with little work on the international scene designed great arenas built all over the country, Herzog & de Meuron designed a modest building of only 1,800 m². The project was a philanthropic gift to the community by the Ameropa Foundation, a Swiss company of cereals and

10 Luis Fernández-Galiano, "Diálogo y logo:
Jaccues Herzog piensa en voz alta",
Arquitectura Viva n. 91. Madrid: 2003, p. 26.

fertilisers, in partnership with the Centro SócioPastoral Nossa Senhora da Conceição, a religious entity that is very active in the Mãe Luiza neighbourhood of Natal where the gym is located, integrating the existing building complex of the Escola Estadual Dinarte Mariz. In fact, the gym is only a small part of a larger urban proposal by the Swiss firm, called "A Vision for Mãe Luiza," which is a proposal that extends over a linear axis for future development that nearly reaches the beach line to include existing areas and new cultural and educational facilities. This urban extension has unfortunately not materialised to date because its cost would require co-financing from local public officials.

Although close to Natal's historical centre and coveted seafront, the Mãe Luiza community, where the Arena do Morro is located, is traditionally one of the poorest and most violent areas of the city. According to the physician and activist Ion de Andrade, at least one murder per month was recorded in the community up to 2013, which represents 38.5% of the total number of homicides in the Eastern Zone of Natal.[11] Ion de Andrade's data showed that this situation changed significantly after 2014 with the inauguration of the sports facility, with a significant reduction in the number of homicides in Mãe Luiza, at a rate four times higher than in the rest of the city. Is this a mere coincidence? Clearly it seems not, as similar recent events in Medellín, Colombia have reflected, where a series of projects and facilities for public mobility were successfully implemented, showing that the most intelligent and effective way to fight urban violence is not to build up the security apparatus but to build places for daily use which can become truly embraced by the local communities. That is the real "collective power" that architecture can help materialise in cities: to serve as a catalyst for real social interactions.

Since it was inaugurated, the Arena do Morro has had a use that extends beyond the practice of sport. Not only because it has multi-purpose spaces – for education, performance, culture or recreation activities – but also because it remains open during the evenings and weekends, making it a real community centre of shared management. It is a unifying centre for both the neighbourhood and the city, where the population has meetings and parties, and groups linked to social movements can meet to discuss matters essential to the city. It is not by chance that the preparatory meetings for the drafting of "Carta de Natal" – an important document

11 See Ion de Andrade, "Ginásio Arena do Morro derruba os números da violência em Mãe Luiza", *Jornal Fala Mãe Luiza*, 09 November 2015. http://jornalfalamaeluiza.blogspot.com.br/2015/11/gunasio-arena--do-morro-derruba-os.html

Arena do Morro, Natal, Brazil. Herzog & de Meuron.
© Leonardo Finotti

that presents a synthesis of the popular claim for the decentralisation of investments in the city, extending the role of the State to the peripheries – took place in the Arena do Morro in 2015.[12] In this context, Ion de Andrade, the main coordinator of the movement which resulted in the Carta de Natal, observed that the gym Arena do Morro is in itself an exemplary paradigm of the transformation that is intended for the city, as it "points towards a new model of public presence in the communities that causes a rupture with the excluding logic of the current model."[13]

In conclusion, it seems possible to state that there are significant similarities between the two situations analysed, which are present in two different Brazilian capital cities and developed a decade apart. Even though the Arena do Morro is an isolated project on much smaller scale, it enjoys some of the vitality created by the CEUs, which took place ten years before, reviving the theme of "facilities built around a square" managed both by the public officials and the local community. Praise is not only due to the important action of the *Centro Pastoral*, the financial support of the Ameropa Foundation, or the media--friendly architects, but also and more fundamentally to the constructive and spatial qualities of the building. They personify Swiss rigour, which seemed to have waned in the transformation from "dialogue" to "logo" in the previously mentioned work of Herzog & de Meuron but which here have succeeded in establishing a profound dialogue with the local reality, addressing the concept of place, the people involved and the architectural tradition in Brazil with a covered, open and translucent building, made of pre-fabricated components (metal structure and concrete blocks) and fluid spaces that invite creative uses, opposing notions of enclosure and privacy. Given the educational character revealed in the different uses of the Arena do Morro, strengthening the urban and political consciousness of social movements in Natal, one can say that the project– in articulation with the "classroom-school" Dinarte Mariz – merits the designation as a real "park-school."

12 See Ion de Andrade, "A Carta de Natal: o documento completo", *Jornal GGN*, 27 April 2015. http://jornalggn.com.br/blog/ion-de-andrade/a-carta-de-natal--documento-completo

13 Ion de Andrade, "A caminhada de Mãe Luiza e o desenvolvimento local em Natal", *Observatório das Metrópoles – Instituto Nacional de Ciência e Tecnologia*, 09 April 2015. http://www.observatoriodasmetropoles.net/index.php?option=com_k2&view=item&id=1161:a--caminhada-de-m%C3%A3e-luiza--e-o-desenvolvimento-local-em--natal&Itemid=164&lang=pt#

ARCHITECTURE AND REGULATORY POWER

João Belo Rodeia

Casa da Arquitectura - Centro Português de Arquitectura
decided to include in the inaugural program of its new
facilities the exhibition *Poder Arquitetura*, centred "on the
critical reading of the various manifestations of Power in
the field of Architecture". Within this wide scope, I accepted
the task of trying to outline its "regulatory power", and I
was soon confronted with two paths to that effect: either
I would try to talk about the "external regulatory powers"
of Architecture, which I believe were the main subject
of interest; or I would talk about its "internal regulatory
powers", perhaps less obvious.

In Portugal, and in the European Community, external
regulatory powers are well identified – namely, legislative,
normative, administrative, and security powers of every
sort. These forces are ever profuse, robust and wide-
-reaching, as well as disparate or even incompatible with
one another. They discombobulate – sometimes even
design – the *doing* of Architecture, entailing intrusions
in the technical, aesthetic and ethical (and economic)
aspects of the work, with harmful incidence in the
quality of building and construction, in the organization,
humanization and improvement of the built environment
and even in the very coexistence of shared space –
and also, it must be said, an insistence on replacing
the architect's creative dimension with a mere more or
less financial scope of services. It is an inexhaustible
bureaucratic abyss, and it is paradoxical that, at a time
when the public notoriety of Architecture (and architects)
is so celebrated – as *Casa da Arquitectura* itself well
testifies –, such regulatory powers tend to disregard
it even in its own core.

Still, this was not the path I took. I have been more
interested in the regulatory powers of Architecture itself,
especially those (or those parts of them) that, while

internal, go beyond its confines – all the more when we consider that it was the architects' own devaluation of, or at least distraction from these powers, what contributed to this state of affairs.

Now, to begin with, by "Power" I mean not the authority to command, but the authority to do; that is, being able to create the possibility of a force of positive transformation. And "Regulatory" means more as an assertive force than a normative (or repressive) one. Having defined both of these terms, I must now talk about what I want to talk about.

I have always said – and I don't believe that there is any novelty in this – that the origins of Architecture are deeply enmeshed with the genesis of the human adventure, and that, in addition to its identitary function, Architecture emulates Man as a human being, as a being-in-project; that is to say, a being that lives not only for the present, but for the future as well. In my view, the most determining part of the internal regulatory powers of Architecture comes from both these aspects.

At its origin are Spatialisation, Construction and Comfort. Not so much shelter, common to most species, but the *intentionality* of shelter, something that already goes beyond mere refuge. Perhaps around the fire, in a shared circle, as Man became aware of the space between centre and circle and their associated form, later configured with a protective wall and ceiling – already as Construction, as building, as house. Architecture was thus born of the will to protect against the discomfort of nature, less as opposition and more as correction. And this birth was simultaneous to the shell of the home, that is, to the dwelling. By this I mean that Architecture and dwelling are inextricably linked by ancestral ties, and it can thus be said that the latter is a foundational root of the former. So we come to one of the main regulatory powers of Architecture – associated as it is with a primordial, almost restorative necessity, and because most of what was and continues to be built is housing.

However, the origin of Architecture is far from being exhausted in the primordial house, just as the genesis of the human adventure reaches far beyond the protection of the home. From an early age, human beings became aware of what surrounded them, that they lived in a land. And, as they inhabited it, they marked it as their own, recognized and spatialized it and themselves in it. Not so much in their initial naming of things in sight – when faced with the particularity of a mountain, a rock or a tree, among many such others, celebrating them in their interaction with themselves – but more in the organisation and combination of named things in fields of spatial recognition. Or in translating the horizon as a circular boundary, first around an object stuck to the ground and then recreating this boundary from new objects, generating successive circular spaces. Or even in the celestial declension, by taking hold of the heavenly dome, of the solstices, the apparent solar movement or cardinal points. Alignments, geometries, composition and harmony were created. And nature was simulated in a more or less abstract order. This is also where Architecture comes from, from the wonder or fear of nature, sublimating it into protective fields and appropriating it in primitive territorialisation. To get to the city took only a step, a great step, in which housing and territorialisation were consubstantiated. By this I mean that Architecture and territory are also linked since primeval times, and, this being the case, it can be said that territory is a foundational root of Architecture, from which another of its principal regulatory powers stems. Not only because it is associated with the primordial necessity of common dwelling, of living in common, of common space, but because, by reverberating in the city – possibly the most extraordinary invention of the human adventure –, it associates the greatest number of people with the greatest amount of edification, thus foreshadowing an extraordinary possibility of redemption.

Now, the intentionality of both these roots – house and territory – is associated with a specific *thinking*, which allows us to speak of Project. It was this *thinking*, always associated with the continuous experience of building, which generated self-contained, autonomous knowledge from which the *arkhitektôn* – to the letter, the principal constructor or builder, the one who directed the *Arkhitektoniki*, i.e. the main construction or building – emerged, which immediately denotes the pre-eminence of the Mediterranean basin in the gestation and emancipation of what we still call Architecture today – juxtaposing learning and synthesis since then and until today, a major component of what we call architectural culture. However much we may wish otherwise, there is no room here to speak of this very extensive heritage, which also legitimises Architecture (and is a regulatory power in itself), although it is important to take note of it with regard to the Project.

The Project, as we now see it, is relatively recent, but not less important for that. It was during the Transalpine Renaissance, under direct induction from the Roman Empire of the East (and the Arab world), that the Project separated itself from the work in specific ways of *thinking* and *doing*; duly recorded in individual elements, drawn and compatible among themselves, a very important conceptual rupture compared to the project which happened simultaneously to the work, fragile and ever--changing. A new chapter. And these ways of *thinking* and *doing* implied researching beyond the strict purpose in the then-invoked Classic Antiquity, since it had to be studied and reinvented. The Project became thus a powerful resource, not only as a legitimator of the work and the autonomy of the architect as creator, channelling and conveying other knowledge, but above all because it implied research, and anticipated in a concrete and realistic manner what had not yet happened but could very well come to pass. By binding together research and anticipation, Architecture allowed for proposals beyond commission work and the contingencies of reality, imagining in time and beyond time worlds better than our own. The ideal city of Sforzinda (1460-64) by Antonio di Pietro Averlino (c1400-1469), better known as Filarete, never left the paper. He could not even imagine getting it off the paper. However, over a hundred years later Vincenzo Scamozzi (1548-1616) was able to design and build Palmanova (1593), which serves as a faithful testimony to this regulatory power of Architecture.

This transformative force has shone with special splendour since the late eighteenth century, most insistently between the late 19th century and the sixties of the 20th century. And it has shone because Architecture, stimulated by mechanization, new materials and constructive systems, and by new aesthetic (and ethical) orders, went step by step back to its foundational roots — that is, it once again embodied housing and territory, now under authorship and in unprecedented scale and intent, in the face of the greatest number of people living in misshapen cities without adequate housing. We know what happened after the First World War. In an eagerness and conviction of Project, so often without certainty of work, the purpose of housing was researched, in the whole and in each of its constituent parts; spatiality, constructive systems, materialities, facilities, equipment and even furniture were all reconsidered and rethought. And from housing to collective equipment, and from these to productive, commercial, administrative, educational, entertainment or institutional facilities. From all of these to the "voids", from circulation to spaces of leisure. The city was redesigned by the dwelling, and the dwelling was redesigned by the city. Everything detailed and discussed, in between intense restlessness, reflection and, above all, research. And everything designed, of course, with the characteristic power that only simulating the future has – sometimes with the awareness of impossibility, some other times with the awareness of provocation, but always believing that transforming the state of things was possible, starting with better housing and a better city for all, perhaps a better world. Some results of this research, much more positive than negative, are known from even before the Second World War, when extensive and extraordinary housing and city reform programs were made possible in some European countries. Even today, coming face to face with projects like Ernst May's *Neue Frankfurt* (1886-1970) or Martin Wagner's *Neue Berlin* (1885-1957) is astounding, if not moving. We then know of the results after the catastrophe of the war, and how Architecture was prepared for the efforts of reconstruction. And reconstruction was done. Not everything went smoothly in the face of urgency, but much of it went well and in many cases very well indeed, as shown even today – especially when compared with later analogues – many of the rebuilt (or new) areas in the UK, Germany, France, the Scandinavian countries and even in Italy, not to mention other parts of the world.

However, as luck would have it, in one moment, and from moment to moment, Architecture did not take due account of what it had done well, and held itself in contempt in the face of what had failed. Scorned by criticism from non--architects, sometimes rightly and sometimes not so much, Architecture lost itself in its own critical voracity and even in nihilism without coming up with meaningful alternatives, subjecting itself too much to other fields of knowledge without identical capacity for anticipating the future, and gradually dissipating its most meaningful internal regulatory powers.

The consequences came. Architecture as a great narrative collapsed. It stopped researching and imagining the dwelling that could happen or come to happen from the architects' *doing*, and the city as well. Both collapsed as possibilities for a positive, assertive, and workable force on a large scale. And, through the fissures, there came the external bureaucratic powers, appropriating research, if not the invention, in regulation and quantification. Almost without anyone noticing it, Architecture and architects were again relegated – or left to relegate themselves – to *petits récits*.

And yet, there continues to be excellent architecture and excellent architects in and out of the so-called and oft-berated *star-system* which, in itself, by the way, is not even something new; for the firm notoriety of some, for all the pride or contempt of others, has always been part of the history of the craft and the profession of the architect, as in any other craft and profession. I speak of those – I insist, outside and within the *star-system* – who are intensely committed to their own *doing*, who persist in researching and presenting their research, who maintain critical concern for the contingencies of reality, and that, in every project and every work, even in the face of many an adversity, manage to overcome them by the audacity of their "creative spirit", favouring the common space, generating intense syntheses and greatly improving all situations they encounter. It is them, just as it is the best Architecture, that, nevertheless, make or may come to make the most evident and noticeable *pièces à résistance* in this world.

Now, Architecture can and should be conjugated in Construction (in the sense of Baukultur), its indissociable condition; it can be objectified in Functionality (in the sense of rationalization of use), its inescapable premise; it can ambition Beauty (in the sense of Intentionality, and aesthetic intensity), perhaps its obligation; and it may even be iconic – there is room inside of the city and out – provided it does not incur the risk of losing itself. Architecture can make itself into *Agit-Prop*, more or less iconoclastic, and it can strive for Participation, palliatively taking care of the world's pains, as long as neither incurs the risk of making it lose itself outside of itself, and it does not give up everyone's right, from poor to rich, to excellent architecture.

However, Architecture's most determining regulatory power, if not *the* Power of Architecture, capable of a positive and assertive force of transformation in the world, comes from where it always came from – that is, from house and territory, even more so when they're embodied in the city.

And in the face of so many increasingly misshapen cities and the lack of dignified housing, it is easy to understand Architecture's latent range on the one hand, when more than half the population lives or survives in cities; and, on the other hand, the stimulation of new conditions, which include, in addition to climate change, self-production of food, energy and water self-sufficiency, and material and waste recycling. In addition, of course, to many inherited conditions which continue to make sense in our day.

That is to say: as long as Architecture – between research and invention, from the architects' *doing* – hasn't a proper, pertinent and purposeful voice in the dwelling and in the city; as long as it is not able to anticipate in its contrived plausibility what has not yet happened but may come to happen; as long as it is not allowed to imagine, in time and beyond time, worlds better than our own; as long as it doesn't ambition itself as redemptive, it will never become as determinant as it once was. It remains to be seen whether it wants to be so again, and whether there are architects up to the challenge. It is not easy, but History proves that it is not impossible.

In short, it can be said that this is a radical perspective of Architecture and its regulatory powers, for it delves into its primeval roots. But as Sophia de Mello Breyner Andresen would say, "os clássicos implicam-nos e explicam-nos" ("the classics concern us and explain us"). We must return to the human adventure and, like Ulysses, go on a new journey to return to the starting point.

TECHNOLOGICAL POWER. THE ARCHITECTURE OF REDUNDANCY

André Tavares
Ivo Poças Martins

The Power of the Black Box

Information is power. When information is digital, storing it is an act of power. The cloud is thus a contemporary space of power. What is the architecture of the cloud? Close to Serra da Estrela mountains in the city of Covilhã, the recently completed Portugal Telecom (PT) Data Center embodies an ambitious program of hosting data.[1] Designed by João Luís Carrilho da Graça, the building is a massive cubic form surrounded by a reflecting pool around which are low, skewed slabs of offices. It marks a metaphysical presence on the landscape. The cloud is embodied as an inaccessible black box.

Its most fascinating characteristic is that it has no solid walls. Despite its massive appearance and its solid concrete structure, the building's performance relies on environmental fluidity. Its walls are massive air filters, giving the impression that the computers within the core of the building are standing free in the air. The walls are not meant to enclose but rather to mediate between the interior and the exterior; the massive cube is just a membrane that protects the hardware.

The Data Center's main objective is to safely store data. Both physical and digital safety are key to every decision. Large, flexible office areas surround the box, and they welcome ever-changing technology to monitor the sacred core of the building. The architect deploys a very simple concrete structure, with freestanding, fully transparent façades built with standard aluminium framing. Looking down from Portugal's highest mountains, the building looks like a slick fortress that has just landed from outer space (it helps that it was built on the runway of a former airport). As if the building was a medieval fortress, the office slab is laid out around an

1 Marco Mulazzani, «Architetture topografiche» in *Casabella*, n.° 857, Milano, January 2016, p. 39-49.

interior court filled with water. Between the cube and the reflecting pool there is a gap, much like a castle moat, providing an additional physical obstacle between the outside and the hard core. A single door gives access to the cube, where sophisticated devices guarantee that every person's identity is checked and that no undesired intruders are allowed access. Despite the seemingly plausible ways that spies in action films succeed in entering such a stronghold, here no ninja could ever elude every sensor, every guard, and every architectural obstacle to reach the computers (and the data) stored within the cube. The same applies to the cyber pirates and hackers who must elude digital security permanently working within the neutral architecture of the office space.

© FG+SG

The computers' safety relies on a constant energy supply and the evenly regulated temperature of the environment. Hence, the Data Center uses a substantial amount of energy to keep the hardware both running and cool. As for the space's physical safety, there are redundant safety schemes to ensure the hardware's energy supply and proper temperature. The building is connected to the main energy network, but in case of failure, there are diesel-powered back-up generators at the ready (housed under the reflecting pool), and a solar energy plant to power the building should the grid become non-operational.

Data Center, Covilhã, Portugal.
João Luis Carrilho da Graça.
© Rita Burmester

To further guarantee continuity and generator output should any interruption in the public energy supply occur, the cube's ground floor is packed with eco-friendly batteries to aid in the transition phase. The hardware's energy feed is secured by quadruple redundancy.

While working, the hardware generates a considerable amount of heat, so much so that it must be constantly cooled down. Thus, the pool is vital as it helps to generate a microclimate up to 5° C below the average ambient temperature. Given the region's already moderate climate, the building can maintain an appropriate uniform temperature nearly all year round. This enables the solid walls to be replaced by a metallic grid, which can serve as air-filters whose the main function is to pull in the outside air and expel the heat generated by the hardware, leading to a significant level of energy economy. However, when it is too warm in the summer, the wall uses the water from the pool to help lower the temperature of the incoming air by a few degrees. If that "free-cooling" system does not lower the temperature sufficiently, then a standard air-conditioning assumes the hardware's environmental safety. In the winter, the heat generated by the hardware is stored, to be re-injected into the building after being mixed with the cooler outside air. Maximum security is achieved by redundant mechanical systems that build up the architectural reasoning underlying the concept of the building.

The PT Data Center features two architectures: one for data (the cube) and one for humans (the office spaces). The latter is an architecture of redundancy as well as an architecture equipped to respond to disaster. If a client experiences a failure at their facilities, these spaces are available to aid in maintaining "business continuity" with its most precious asset: information. The offices are conceived to physically host the client company's work force and can be set up within a few hours. Unlike the cube, the glazed office building employs architecture that is not constrained by issues of energy consumption; the regular spacing of the air-conditioning units, 10 meters apart, balance the façade's environmental performance. And in the final accounting, the amount of energy required to temper the office environment is but an infinite fraction of what the data building consumes.

The cube is no more than the most effective construction to build up a material-less wall whose function it is to filter the multiple alternative and redundant systems to secure the building's core environment. Whereas its energy redundancy has little architectural expression (the generator rooms being hidden below the pool), the cooling and warming systems take material shape in the gigantic filter that keeps the hardware as close as possible to the outside environment, and yet as protected as possible from the same environment. Those who manage to be swiftly connected and highly protected control the power. This architecture symbolizes such power, simply transcribing in material forms the redundant systems required to secure the fragile nature of its digital permanence.

Mutant Cloud

From the user's perspective, the Internet is an ethereal, omnipresent entity, and the idea of heavy, remote satellites orbiting the planet reinforces the metaphor of the cloud.

However, information technology operates in the physical realm: data is stored in computers housed in buildings and wired into a material network. This territorial existence also performs through redundancy, a web of hubs managing information without hierarchy, each hub connecting to its surroundings through multiple links; and the failure of any link is counteracted by an alternative route within the homogenous system. Once more, redundancy is key to performance and safety. For the sake of speed, safety, and liability, the networks are linked via high debit bandwidth fibre optic cables, often laid out near heavy infrastructure such as roads, highways, railways, high--voltage electric wiring, water or sewage systems. The information networks often overlap existing infrastructure and enhance the territorial hierarchy already in place, serving activities where they are already installed and operating upon the development and transformation of existing urban models and hierarchies. Unlike the early Industrial Revolution in the eighteenth or nineteenth centuries, when mining and manufacturing carved a new landscape and territorial system supported by innovative railroad or canal systems, present-day information networks are more likely to colonize existing infrastructure, mutating its performance to serve its own purposes. Information networks are not the idyllic rhizomatic liberation of heavy infrastructures, but rather the mutation of heavy networks and apparatus to further foster territorial inequalities.

Cloud architecture

We live in a material world. Few buildings have made more of such an assertion than Diller Scofidio + Renfro's "Blur" built over Lake Neuchatel for the Expo 2002.[2] It stands as the most literal take on a cloud architecture.[3] It was a "building of atmosphere," its authors said, relying on rather simple devices: water pumped from the lake was sprayed through tens of thousands of high pressure nozzles. The water sprays immersed a circular platform in a white mist. As an exhibition space, it housed nothing but its own atmosphere – a borderless space filled with emptiness.

    As extraordinary as the experience of this ephemeral architecture was, the original concept – which was not fully completed due to lack of funds – was even more

2 Ashley Schafer, «Designing Inefficiencies» in *Scanning: The Aberrant Architecture of Diller + Scofidio*, New York, Whitney Museum of American Art, 2003, p. 93-102.

3 Its most direct predecessor was an intervention by Experiments in Art and Technology on the 1970s Osaka Pepsi Pavilion, designed by Tadashi Doi. The artist Fujiko Nakaya (who also collaborated on the swiss Blur pavilion) and the physicist Thomas Lee, transformed the concrete polyhedron designed by Tadashi Doi for the Pepsi Pavilion in the 1970 Osaka exhibition into an elusive misty cloud.

Blur, Expo 2002, Neuchatel Lake, Switzerland. Diller & Scofidio + Renfro. © www.dsrny.co

ambitious. The aim was to "weave together architecture and electronic technologies," creating an immersive environment where the visual and sonic connections to the surroundings would be whited-out and the space filled with image projections, sound and interactive digital technology, as if it were a three-dimensional and physical representation of the Internet. Anticipating the invention of social media platforms by a few years, the visitors would wear a technological prosthetic – a white raincoat in which the user's personal information was stored, which in turn would interact by illuminating in warm red when coming close to another person with common interests or blue--green when in the proximity of someone with opposing ones. This wearable piece of technology, the "Braincoat," was meant to allow for a more complete immersion in the Blur, protecting both against moisture and enabling a connection to a visible network consisting of a passing group of visitors.

Like the numeric showers often portrayed in science--fiction movies to represent the digital realm, the Blur has become a powerful symbol of architecture within an immaterial age of digital data. It created an anti-architecture, one that disappears, a transient, atmospheric experience complementing our ephemeral experience of life. Following Reyner Banham's proposal to consider architecture as a device to produce well--tempered environments,[4] and focusing on ways to choreograph the movements of various invisible fluids through solid enclosures and mechanical apparatus – becoming hot, cold, dry, moist, clean, dirty – the Blur was a radical expression of the domestication of the non--palpable. Technology and architecture expressed the environment itself. Beyond the dichotomy of solid and void or volume and space, architecture could deal with "organizing matter," be it solid, fluid, energy or information. Architecture was software and hardware, and one was by no means lighter or less physically imposing than the other. This immateriality incarnated the spirit of our coming digital age, finally reaching an era where "everything that is solid melts into air." Instead of the romantic self--destructive quest for progress, progress can be achieved by the peaceful evanescence of our harsh material legacy.

Alas! Life is more banal than architects like to make it appear. Information can be easily stored in ordinary architecture, and it often becomes a squatter in existing buildings the same way it may hitchhike onto

4 Reyner Banham, *The architecture of the well-tempered environment*, London, The Architectural Press, 1969.

other existing infrastructures. It might be the greatest form of disappearance, mingling with the generic built environment. The physical manifestation of digital data is easier to disguise within ordinary architecture. Data centres and communication hubs are often erased from maps, and when attempting to google their locations they are often concealed: "For security reasons this is not the exact location of the data centre." Instead of their rhizomatic dispersion, concentration is more frequent.

A radical example of hard infrastructure resilience can be found in the Los Angeles Corporate Square at One Wilshire, a thirty-story-tall office tower built in 1966 for law firms and designed by Skidmore, Owings & Merrill.[5] A dull, giant white box, it is an archetype of banal corporate architecture, never intended to become a major player in telecommunications as it gradually did. As lawyers were no longer the main tenants, this opened the way to telecom companies and data storage hardware, and now miles and miles of fibre optic cable occupy a significant area of the building. It is now a colossal hub in the American network, a crucial exchange point between underwater cables coming from the Pacific and those crossing the mainland. It is also a place where networks from different carriers are physically connected in the appropriately named "meet me rooms." Not surprisingly, this rather anonymous building has become one of the world's most expensive properties; it currently deals with the most valuable commodity. Unlike the redundant architecture of Covilhã's black box, One Wilshire is a mutant building that takes advantage of its pre-existing location within the unbalanced network.

One Wilshire, Los Angeles, USA. S.O.M.
© Dave Greer

Standby Architecture

As buildings, One Wilshire and the Blur could not be more different. Where one is sheer mass, hierarchy, and heavy concentration, the other epitomises lightness and ethereal immateriality. As Guilherme Wisnik has pointed out,[6] "contemporary architecture is experiencing the passage from mechanical form to performative behaviour." In the context of contemporary afflictions tragically affecting society (climate change, armed conflicts, waves of migration, etc.) architecture has been seeking out new hierarchies to replace the classical relationships

5 Kazys Varnelis, «Centripetal City» in Cabinet, n. 17, Spring 2005 (online ed. consulted January 2017, www. cabinetmagazine.org/issues/17/varnelis. php).

6 Guilherme Wisnik, «Inmersión contra imagen: desenfocando el mundo» in Plot, n.º 32, August-September, Buenos Aires, 2016, p. 10-12.

of construction processes (for example, blurring the distinction between structure and enclosure). New design and building technologies are contributing to this change. The idea of a society inhabited by a diffuse data cloud pervades every aspect of life, and it could not be a more appropriate metaphor for the passage from mechanics to performance.

A sharp synthesis for this argument can be found in the "cross-fertilization" experiments conducted by Made In studio in their Zurich academic programs.[7] Their architecture combines issues of territory and politics. For instance, Christopher Metz and Elisabetta Mini designed a databank carved into the Swiss Alps. The design is located below the Linth-Limmern Power Stations; its door opens into the hillside, the effect suggesting the water intake towers of the Hoover Dam in Nevada. The image combines European and American heavy hydroelectric infrastructure, evoking mechanical forms of electric power production. Inside, a grid of computers fills a rather neutral space, contrasting the primitiveness of the rock-cut cave with sophistication of high-tech computer racks. The heat produced by the hardware is removed through a series of ventilation chimneys proudly displayed as if organ pipes in the monumental entrance. One might well imagine the ventilation operating as a gigantic musical instrument, the vanished architectural space overtaken by digital technology transformed into soundwaves. It seems architecture is disappearing and becoming a performance, the power of the architects being solely to represent the negotiation between digital bytes and space.

Despite this "cross-fertilized" databank powerful symbolic portrait, a technical assessment would dismiss it as a plausible response to the technological requirements to be the architecture for the cloud. It is not a redundant architecture. From a material perspective, it would be too hot. Is information just a heater for the digital circuits through which power moves? If so, architecture's power seems to reside in cooling the hardware where such power circulates. Is there any architecture left when walls are meant to disappear? If the cloud metaphor took over the imaginary of our digital age, its actual architectural counterpart could not be more distinct from the ethereal building. The random and adaptable structure of the formless cloud requires a precise and heavy infrastructure that, although it might shift places and time, requires a

Data bank, Linth- Limmern, Switzerland.
Portraits II – Made in ETH Zurich (2012)
Photomontage: Christopher Metz and Elisabetta Mini

7   François Charbonet, «Portraits» in AA Files, n. 67, London, November 2013, p. 147-157. See "Cloud Formation, Databank, Threshold," project by Christopher Metz and Elisabetta Mini for Portraits II, Territory/Politics, 2012.

pre-existing and pre-determined set of qualities to be effective. Facing the power of technology and the power of established systems and networks, architecture seems powerless to address the territorial ossification that digital technology is performing. In our technological era is there any power left for architecture? Are architects doomed to merely find symbolic representations of redundancy? Or will they merely find solutions to technical problems?

© Rita Burmester

Data Center, Covilhã, Portugal.
João Luis Carrilho da Graça. © FG+SG

ECONOMIC POWER. AGAINST CYNICISM

Alexandra Vougia

"Technologically sophisticated, the curtain wall becomes the universal symbol of the corporate look: self-confident, professional and anonymous."[1]

The words above, written by Charles Jenks early in the 1970s, emphatically asserted the new conservative psyche of the (postmodern) architectural discipline. These words openly defended a new relationship between architecture and the representation of political power, one that, although not yet fully asocial, transformed architecture from the practice of a largely critical project[2] to one of an unconditional surrender to the dominant political and ideological forces of financial capitalism. Along these lines, architecture's ideological and material engagement was reduced to the symbolic value of a single architectural element – in this case the curtain wall – while the communication and proliferation of any dominant diagrams of power could be maintained through the element's repetitive rhythm, constructing many of the urban landscapes we experience today on a global scale. This new relationship between architecture and political power initially pointed to a shift occurring in the institutions that used architecture to project such a power, from the wide predominance of state or other publicly funded production to the private sector and other institutions of corporate capital. More importantly, however, in my view, the words above confirm a transformation that occurred in architectural discourse during this time, a deviation from a certain critical awareness of the architect's historical role to an unapologetic indifference that becomes the modus operandi within architectural discourse from the 1970s onward.

It is this unapologetic indifference and unconditional surrender to the political and social forces of the financial market that Peter Sloterdijk identified as the dominant operating attitude emerging during that era and which became a central feature of the postmodern condition

[1] JENCKS, Charles – *Modern Movements in Architecture*. 2nd ed. London: Penguin Books, 1987. ISBN 13: 978-0-1402-3005-5. p. 201. Jencks reflects here on buildings such as the 1953 Alcoa Building in Pittsburgh by the American firm Harrison & Abramovitz.

[2] Here I use the term 'critical' project in a rather direct manner. I have borrowed the term 'critical' from Peter Bürger and his assertion that a critical judgment is in the interest of "the production of cognitions". "Criticism," Bürger continued, "attempts to separate the truth of ideology from its untruth – the Greek word for criticism, *krinein*, means 'to part,' 'to separate'." (In BÜRGER, Peter – *Theory of the Avant-Garde*. Minneapolis, MN: University of Minnesota Press, 1984. ISBN 13: 978-0-8166-1068-6. p.8) A project of "cognition" is then, first and foremost, an intellectual operation (as opposed to one requiring the faculty of sensibility), that is, it is opposed to any feeling derived from a mere contemplation of the work of art, or in this case architecture. Cognitive function requires understanding and reasoning, demanding the construction of an awareness based on knowledge that the subject already possesses independently of the content of the object. Along these lines, a critical project is one that demystifies the ruling ideas at a certain historical moment, one that uncovers the historically specific essence of things and events masked and silenced by the "eternal laws" of the then dominant ideology.

of the 1970s and 1980s. While not directly addressing the discipline of architecture, Sloterdijk in his *Critique of Cynical Reason* associated this attitude – appearing on both institutional and individual levels – with the figure of the 'cynic.' The cynical indifference and amoral ethos ultimately represent how institutions of power and individuals correspondingly determine and participate in the collective sphere whereas an apparently (bluntly) rational – or "enlightened" to use Sloterdijk's words – way of seeing things is interpreted as a form of contemporary intelligence. Sloterdijk writes:

"Today the cynic appears as a mass figure [...] not only because advanced industrial civilization produces the bitter loner as a mass phenomenon. Rather, the cities themselves have become diffuse clumps whose power to create generally accepted public characters has been lost. The pressure towards individualization has lessened in the modern urban and media climate. Thus, modern cynics are no longer outsiders. [...] The person with the clear, 'evil gaze' has disappeared into the crowd; anonymity now becomes the domain for cynical deviation."³

It is difficult here not to return to Jencks' opening quote to draw some parallels between the former's blunt assertion of the discipline's status and Sloterdijk's evaluation of postmodern cynicism. Jencks candidly confessed to architecture's destitution of any critical function and its submission to the dominant power structures; the proliferation of "self-confident" and "anonymous" façades affirms the very magnitude of ideological surrender.

Where do we stand today, however, three decades after Sloterdijk's *Critique of Cynical Reason*? I argue here that we are still very much embedded within the conditions of cynicism that the former suggested. More specifically within architectural discourse, this cynicism continues to be the glorified operating attitude of prominent architectural practitioners and theorists as it has permeated not only the production but also the reception, analysis and evaluation of the built environment and the architectural objects that constitute it. Contemporary cities themselves, besides being the arena where the existential forms of cynicism are being manifested and reproduced, are shaped by anonymous, alienating objects manifesting the universal authority of institutions linked to global financial capital. One of the most familiar urban typologies – familiar by virtue of its function to project

De Rotterdam, Rotterdam, the Netherlands. OMA.
© Charlie Koolhas / OMA

3 SLOTERDIJK, Peter - *Critique of Cynical Reason*. Tran. Michael Eldred. Foreword by Andreas Huyssen. Minneapolis, MN: University of Minnesota Press, 1987. ISBN 13: 0-8166-1586-1. p.4.

De Rotterdam, Rotterdam, the Netherlands. OMA.
© Ossip Van Duivenbode / OMA

4   In the presentation of the project in the
    architectural journal A+U, OMA expressed
    the design treatment of the urban context
    with the following platitude: "the clustering
    of these blocks into functioning ensemble
    creates a seemingly random composition
    that allows the building to blend into its
    context and yet maintain a distinct look."
    In: MAB-Tower, Rotterdam. A+U: OMA@Work
    1972–2000, Japan (March 2000). ISBN 13:
    978-4900211537. p.67.

5   Of course, the work of OMA and De
    Rotterdam is only a symptomatic example of
    that attitude; that is, it is both specific and
    generic at the same time but nevertheless
    manifests this general ideological shift
    towards a disciplinary cynicism.

6   There are other architectural gestures
    that assign socially alienating features
    to De Rotterdam, one example being the
    use of the platform that operates against
    OMA's original intention for a contextual
    integration of the project. In fact, the very
    classical element of the platform isolates
    and objectifies architectural production,
    affording the objects placed on top more
    prominent visibility from a distance. In the
    case of De Rotterdam this objectification
    is further accentuated by the physical
    distancing provided by the river.

the unmediated power of such institutions – is that of the high-rise. Instead of addressing, however, the largely "unauthored" production of high-rise architecture, I would like to concentrate on the work of the Office for Metropolitan Architecture (OMA), whose discourse has been largely associated with the theorisation of that typology since 1970s.

Indeed, within OMA's body of work, the typology of the high-rise occupies a prominent yet frail position. Largely theorised by Rem Koolhaas and recurrently studied and designed by the Office, only a few projects have been carried out. After more than a decade in the making, OMA's third high-rise to be built, De Rotterdam, was finally completed in 2013 as part of the redevelopment plan for the city's old harbour district. The lengthy time frame for executing the project – the original study dates to 1997 – can trace the conceptual and ideological shift in the Office's work; beginning with the more critical variations on the vertical cities motif (such as the studies for Boompjes of 1980 and the C3 Maastowers of 1994) and moving to the unapologetic indifference and cynicism of De Rotterdam is of significance here. Again, this indifference is not expressed necessarily against the physical context[4] but is mostly understood as a political and ultimately asocial ethos of cynicism.[5]

Although De Rotterdam is a project that has undergone quite a long process of development, its basic compositional idea has remained very similar through the past decades. The building integrates diverse uses in pursuit of a relative programmatic autonomy in line with the genealogy of the "vertical cities", common in the writings of Koolhaas and the work of OMA: De Rotterdam includes commercial, working and residential spaces (restaurants, cafés, conference facilities, municipal and corporate offices, private residential units and a hotel). All functions are accommodated within a complex of rectangular volumes that are horizontally sliced and slightly shifted, while they are standing atop the unifying platform of the car park that sits on the riverbank.

It is useful to once again return to the symbolic value of the corporate anonymous façade that envelops this project as well, an element which is explicitly associated with the dominant institutionalised powers of financial capitalism.[6] Indeed, one immediately perceives De Rotterdam as wrapped within such an envelope, in fact, within its "theoretical envelope," to use Rem Koolhaas' own words.[7] On the one hand, however, OMA attempted to break from the volume's theoretical envelope by the slicing of the tower masses both horizontally and vertically. This slicing operation resulted in the fragmentation of the original volumes into a series of boxes differentiated in size and seemingly randomly placed that challenge the familiar lean proportions of a tower building. That very same operation has produced a further sculptural effect. Each of *De Rotterdam*'s elevations is quite unlike any other; the building at times constructs a wall, that is, a single continuous mass, at times a complex of 2 or 3 individual volumes.

In addition to its formal virtues, however, the building still confirms the consolidation of a cynical attitude of contemporary architectural production, a production which has unconditionally surrendered to and continually glorifies corporate power by internalising – now through its own discourse – the conditions of its own submission. A second and more advanced stage of architectural cynicism, even more empowered by the internalisation of this corporate power, is thus achieved. This time, it "no longer sees any reason to expose itself aggressively and spectacularly" as Sloterdijk again writes. A cynical attitude that "has withdrawn into a mournful detachment that internalises its knowledge as though it were something to be ashamed of, and as a consequence, it is rendered useless for taking the offensive."[8] Along these lines then, any opportunity to express criticism thus appears in vain.

To conclude, I would like to bring forward another condition, this time used as a narrative device that could counter-balance contemporary cynicism and perhaps open the way for architectural criticism: the device of irony,[9] which is, in fact, very present in the early writings of Rem Koolhaas. Irony as a literary technique has always been used for its powerful subversive function as it reveals an indirect narration, and though it is delivered via a pseudo-ignorant voice, the latter operates as an intentional concealment of actual knowledge. This ironic dimension – evident and influential during the earlier OMA studies and designs – to my view, is an element which we could recover from the Office's discourse and adopt again broadly within our disciplinary field as a form of subversive reasoning and production. It is the criticality associated with the device of irony, whose purpose is to reveal and to unearth the true workings of architecture as a historically specific aspect of human production which should be

De Rotterdam, Rotterdam, the Netherlands. OMA.
© Ossip Van Duivenbode / OMA

7   Koolhaas theorised the concept of the "theoretical envelope" in *Delirious New York*. With the concept of "the theoretical envelope," he referred to the maximum possible buildable volume of a certain plot which, at the same time, since it exceeded any perceivable limits of mass, it could no longer indicate the functions included in its interior spaces. In KOOLHAAS, Rem – *Delirious New York: A Retroactive Manifesto for Manhattan*. New York, NY: The Monacelli Press, 1994. ISBN 13: 978-1885254009. p.86.

8   SLOTERDIJK, Peter - *Critique of Cynical Reason*. Tran. Michael Eldred. Foreword by Andreas Huyssen. Minneapolis, MN: University of Minnesota Press, 1987. ISBN 13: 0-8166-1586-1. p.6.

9   In their dictionary, Liddell and Scott indicate as the primary definition of irony (εἰρωνεία): "dissimulation, i.e. ignorance purposely affected to provoke and confound antagonist, a mode of argument used by Socrates against the Sophists: generally, mock-modesty; sarcasm; understatement." In LIDDELL, Henry George; SCOTT, Robert – *A Greek-English Lexicon: Volume I* α-κώψ. Oxford: Clarendon Press, 1925-40. s.v. "εἰρωνεία".

De Rotterdam, Rotterdam, the Netherlands. OMA.
© Charlie Koolhas / OMA

emphasised here, architecture as an instrument of power, on the one hand, but primarily as a general indication of the discipline's relationship – whether subversive or submissive – to the dominant political and social forces that shape the production of subjectivity.

DOMESTIC POWER. A NEW AGENCY

Andreas Ruby
Ilka Ruby
Yuma Shinohara

Let's start by talking about power – or, more precisely, a lack of it. Architects across the industrial world are today feeling a general sense of waning influence. Private commissions are drying up, with more and more of the general building taken over by efficiency- and profit--driven developers. At the same time, a widespread climate of austerity and the retreat of the welfare state have meant a scarcity of public commissions. The prospects for interesting work, much less work that serves the public good, seem to be dimming by the day.

Architects have reacted differently to this sense of powerlessness. Some enter academia, while others cynically embrace free market ideology – and yet some others divest themselves of all social responsibility, shrugging their shoulders and claiming: "It's not my duty!" Perhaps a more hopeful approach would be to direct their attention to a new trend in architecture that has the potential to shake things up.

This trend is the emergence of a new type of client, one who in the last ten to fifteen years has begun to demand more attention in the field of multi--family housing development: the users themselves. Demographic and cultural changes are transforming the modern city-dweller, yet neither private developers nor public housing authorities have managed to keep up. Users are thus beginning to take matters into their own hands, banding together and developing their own housing from the bottom up. This turn of events is not just of consequence for real estate developers, but – as we argue – also contains massive potential for the practice of architecture as well.

A New Architecture of the Collective

The populations of many industrialized nations are currently undergoing a dramatic shift. Our societies are becoming both older and more atomized, meaning that the number of people per household is rapidly declining – indeed, more than 60 percent of private households in the European Union today consist of just one or two persons.[1] The conventional ideal of the nuclear family is rapidly losing importance in favor of a plethora of living situations; the housing market, however, is failing to follow suit with these changes, meaning that many of these unconventional households – such as single-parent- -households or patchwork families, as well as young and elderly singles – remain underserved and frequently affected by social isolation.

Communal meal space in a building for 21 inhabitants, Spreefeld, Berlin, Germany. GmbH Architekten © Ute Zscharndt

In response to this, a number of housing pioneers have taken matters into their own hands, developing new forms of housing through grassroots movements that attempt to rethink the paradigm of the classic single-family home. These projects are collective in nature, either developed out of a collaborative process, funded and managed according to a cooperative model, or designed with new forms of common living in mind. They often feature a willingness to limit private space in order to maximize communal spaces, and demonstrate a commitment to their surroundings through public facilities that can be used by both residents and members of the larger community.

We have described this new phenomenon – which we term the "new architecture of the collective" – with regards to its historical, social, and financial aspects in detail elsewhere.[2] For the purposes of this article, however, we would like to shift our focus toward what implication this phenomenon has for the practice of architecture in particular.

Simply put: the new architecture of the collective redefines the role of architectural expertise in a way that ultimately imbues the discipline as a whole with a new agency.

Certainly, projects for common living in themselves can and do occur without the assistance of architects – one need only look at informal arrangements such as shared flats or squats for proof of this. Yet what sets this new wave of housing experiments apart is the search for architectural solutions to express the new culture of collectivity, which opens the door to ever more innovative building typologies. One of the most significant examples of this is the so-called

1 Eurostat, *People in the EU: Who Are We and How Do We Live?* (Luxembourg: Publications Office of the European Union, 2015), 45, found online at: http://ec.europa.eu/eurostat/documents/3217494/7089681/KS-04-15-567-EN-N.pdf/8b2459fe-0e4e--4bb7-bca7-7522999c3bfd.

2 See, in particular: Mathias Müller, Daniel Niggli, Ilka Ruby, Andreas Ruby, "Together!: On the Renaissance of the Collective in Contemporary Urban Architecture," Introduction to *Together!: The New Architecture of the Collective*, ed. by Mateo Kries et. al., exhibition catalogue (Weil am Rhein, Berlin: Vitra Design Museum & Ruby Press, 2017), 37–42; as well as the exhibition catalogue as a whole.

Residential building, Mehr als Wohnen, Zurich, Switzerland. Plant-type. Duplex Architekten © Duplex Architekten

3 The *Baugruppe* (literally, "building group") is a housing development model whereby private individuals join together as a cooperative organization (in Germany, often as a *Gesellschaft bürgerlichen Rechts*, or private corporation), pool money together, and fund the development of an apartment building from the ground up. While the group acts as a unitary commissioning client during the process, the buildings are divided up into private condominiums once construction is finished. The model, which has established itself over the last two decades in Germany, is popular as a way to develop private apartments that are relatively affordable (because the middleman of the developer is cut out) and individually tailored to residents' needs; see, for example: Barbara Eldredge, "Could This German Affordable Homebuilding Plan Be a Model for the U.S.?", *Curbed*, 7 April 2016, accessed 26 June 2017, https://www.curbed.com/2016/4/7/11376622/baugruppe-housing-cohousing-german--development-home.

"cluster apartment," which has its origins in Swiss cooperatives but has quickly spread to projects in Germany and Austria as well. This consists of a number of small apartments of about 20–35 square meters, each with a bedroom, small kitchen, and small bathroom, all of which are organized around a shared living environment with a generous living room and large kitchen. One ought to think of this as a further evolution of the classic shared flat, providing a solution to a persistent problem that has faced anyone who has ever lived with roommates in the past: sometimes, you just have days when you don't want to be social. By providing each of the small apartments with a kitchen and bathroom, the cluster apartment affords residents the opportunity to retreat when needed, even while giving them all of the benefits of shared living: a sense of community, the security of the large group, and the opportunity to use a kitchen and facilities that you would have a hard time justifying if you just lived alone.

Besides developing new typologies, architects play an important role in collaborative projects by contributing their expertise in visual thinking and relationship management to facilitate communication between multiple stakeholders. R50, a *Baugruppe* project in Berlin, provides a good example of this.[3] The architect collective responsible for the building, a collaboration between Heide & von Beckerath with ifau (*Institut für angewandte Urbanistik*, or Institute for Applied Urbanism) and Jesko Fezer, were not only involved in defining the appearance and structure of the building, but also in managing the collaborative design process for the individual apartments. To this end, they coupled their organizational role as mediators between the various resident parties with their design capabilities, implementing questionnaires regarding residents' wishes and translating the answers into easily understandable charts and diagrams. These so-called "Living Reports" (*Wohnreporte*) functioned as crucial mechanisms for internal communication, helping to make the diverse imaginations of the residents legible and turning them into concrete documents that could be discussed and debated in meetings.

The new projects of the collective sometimes demand architects to do more than just deliver a building design. For another example, let us turn to the Apartments with the Small Restaurant in Tokyo, a small-scale project composed of a restaurant in the ground floor, a co-working space in the basement, and five live-work units across two upper floors. The architect, Toshiharu Naka of Naka Architects Studio, developed the project in close collaboration with the client (the building was privately developed), future tenants, and members of the local community. Besides the physical design of the building, the architect was also involved in the project's "social" design: namely, optimizing the ways in which residents and users can meet, interact, and support one another. To this end, the project features a sustainable system of social and monetary circulation that links together all three functions of the building (living, working, and eating) – a system given form and, indeed, reinforced by the architectural design. Even now, long after the building's completion in 2014, the architect remains involved in the day-to-day running of the project. Together with the owner and the restaurant chef, he is part of a monthly committee that meets to share feedback from residents, assess the functioning of the project, and make new suggestions (a regular dinner event to get people together, for instance, or a new piece of furniture for the common spaces). The new architects of the collective do not so much *create* their projects as *nurture* them, accompanying them and intervening in them as they grow and evolve in an organic manner.

Residential building with restaurant, Tokyo, Japan.
Studio Naka Architects
© Studio Naka Architects

The new roles taken on by architects for these projects are often incongruent with the traditional image of the architect as an autonomous agent of creativity. In the cooperative housing project La Borda in Barcelona, for example, several of the architects are themselves part of the fifty-person housing cooperative that will be moving into the building (under construction at the writing of this article). The apartment floor plans and the placement of common areas were designed collaboratively, in both general assemblies as well as individual consultations. Residents would sketch in their wishes and desires into blank apartment floor plans, which would then be translated by the architects into a concrete plan. The traditional power relationship between client and architect is thereby disrupted, indeed flattened, as the architects take their place within a larger constellation of equals that – collectively – work to realize a building. In this arrangement, the expertise of the architect is less about originating an idea *ex nihilo* as it is about interpreting and synthesizing the needs of users.

The new architecture of the collective provides architects with an unprecedented opportunity to demonstrate their design and organizational expertise,

Cooperativa La Borda, work meeting.
© Lacol Cooperativa d'Arquitectes

developing innovative, even radical, solutions to the new challenges posed by the return of the collective in housing. Yet, at the same time, this new agency requires architects to relinquish the very myth of autonomy that they had claimed for decades, to take their place as one actor within a larger system of equal collaborators. Giving up autonomy to reclaim agency: what sounds like a contradiction is rather a problem of perspective.

Two Vectors of Power

This brings us back, then, to where we started. Perhaps the feeling of powerlessness felt by the world of architecture today stems from an all too narrow conception of the nature of power and its role in shaping the built environment.

Since the advent of Modernism, the language of architecture has tended to privilege a top-down understanding of power. Power is a finite resource – something that is *held*, and delegated down. The dream of the architect is to gain as large a share of this power as possible, so as to have as much ability to implement a unique vision. This understanding of power, perhaps best exemplified in the character of Harold Roark, the misunderstood architect and individualist in Ayn Rand's *The Fountainhead*, can at times lead to a mythologized vision of the architect as the sole shaper of the built environment. But it is also an understanding that can, paradoxically, lead to a certain dependency: on existing structures of influence and capital, on willing clients and untied purse strings. There may indeed be genius architects, but they need someone to recognize them as such first, and give them the money and power to make their ideas into reality. Otherwise they'll just sit around, twiddling their thumbs, until someone asks them – to which they'll reply: "Well, why didn't you ask sooner?"

The new architecture of the collective makes visible an alternative movement of power, one which might be termed "bottom-up." This is the harnessed power of the crowd, a groundswell of money, expertise, and activity that originates not in one source, but many. This is not a power that is *had*, but rather is painstakingly *created*: through establishing relations between various actors, each of whom may not have enough capital, know-how, or political influence to realize a built project on their own. Architects play a critical role in channeling this energy, diverting it in ways that enhance it, make it more sustainable. They, too, can partake in this power, as crucial facilitators of change, if not – and this is an important point – its sole agents.

If recent developments have shown anything, it's that bottom-up development is more powerful than you might expect. In calling attention to long-neglected demands, these new collective projects have managed to preempt and destabilize traditional top-down forms of urban development. Through the sheer fact that these projects are economically sustainable (and often more affordable than mainstream developments), they produce a rupture in the prevailing consensus that housing developers must maximize private apartment sizes (and thus the amount of rent that can be charged) in order to turn a profit.

In Switzerland, where new collective projects have proved particularly successful and sustainable, there are signs that these projects are themselves changing the way we think about our cities. Take, for example, *Mehr als Wohnen* (literally, "more than living"), a "mega-cooperative" developed out of a collaboration among fifty-five housing cooperatives in Zurich. With the help of the municipality, this cooperative was responsible for transforming the former grounds of the Hunziker cement factory in northern Zurich into a housing development focused on new living forms, sustainability, multigenerational living, and affordable housing.[4] The result is a cooperative development on an unprecedented scale: an entirely new neighborhood, comprising 41,000 square meters, thirteen buildings, and 1,200 inhabitants. The task of designing the buildings – which, besides housing, also contain various commercial and communal spaces – was distributed among five different offices, resulting in an assortment of structures with different shapes and personalities. Here, participatory design, instead of limiting the freedom of the designers, prodded them towards ever more creative solutions to accommodate a variety of different households – from studio apartments to clusters of twelve--and-a-half rooms each.

Mehr als Wohnen is just one example of the new architecture of the collective migrating beyond its small--scale, grassroots origins into ever larger scales. Across Europe, cities are realizing that mixed-use, user-driven housing projects are well-positioned to create affordable housing that can serve diverse populations while also injecting a new vibrancy into peripheral neighborhoods. In cities such as Vienna and Berlin, municipal governments have begun to organize competitive tenders for public

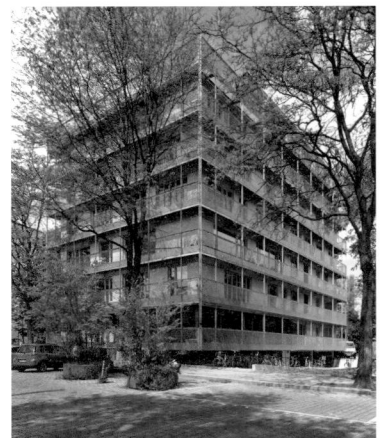

Residential building, Berlin, Germany. R50 – Cohousing / Ifau and Jesko Fezer + Heide & Von Beckerath. © Andrew Alberts

4 "Geschichte," Baugenossenschaft Mehr als Wohnen, accessed 26 June 2017, https://www.mehralswohnen.ch/genossenschaft/geschichte/.

Cooperative residential building, Barcelona, Spain.
Lacol Cooperativa d'Arquitectes
© Lacol Cooperativa d'Arquitectes

Cooperativa La Borda, work meeting.
© La Borda

lands where the main criterion is no longer the amount of the bid, but rather how innovative and socially responsible the housing concept is.[5]

These developments are a testament not only to the achievements of the new architecture of the collective in transforming the discourse, but also to the vast possibilities that lie ahead for this form of development. These possibilities are also those of architecture as a discipline. Harnessing the power of the collective promises not just new jobs for architects, but also ones that are creatively stimulating and socially meaningful. The self-empowerment of users is, at the same time, an empowerment of architecture itself.

Ultimately, architects have a choice: to stay with and reproduce existing structures of power, or actively work to counter them by creating new nodes of power. They can no longer just wait around for opportunities to come their way; they must take the initiative, looking for projects that provide them with new possibilities to exercise their own agency, even if this means rethinking the roles and privileges that they have traditionally been vested with. The new architecture of the collective is thereby a call to arms, an opportunity to finally turn postmodern discontent into positive action.

5   In Berlin, the state-owned real estate management company BIM offers select plots for sale through its "Konzeptverfahren" (concept--based process), which considers the innovativeness of development concepts alongside the offeren buying price; see: "Die Verfahren im Überblick," BIM Berliner Immobilienmanagement, accessed 26 June 2017, http://www.bim-berlin.de/immobilien/verkauf/verkaufsverfahren/; in Vienna, the allotment of housing subsidies are decided through "developer competitions," in which projects are judged according to architectural quality, costs, ecology, and social sustainability, for more details see: Wolfgang Förster and William Menking, eds., *The Vienna Model: Housing for the Twenty-First Century* (Berlin: Jovis, 2016).

THE POWER OF CULTURE IN THE CULTURE OF POWER

Nuno Grande

Cultural creation has been the reflection and instrument of political, religious and economic power throughout history, especially within Western or westernised societies. Even the most radical visions and actions, such as the modern vanguards in the 1910s and 1920s, or the so-called "counterculture" in the 1960s and 1970s, where many creative artists defined themselves as agents of a "counter--power" or an anarchic "non-power," were eventually integrated and instrumentalised by new policies, new capitalist patronage or new exercises in governance. In essence, the transforming power of culture has always nurtured, for both good and bad, an evolution of the culture of power itself.

This question takes on broader visibility in a universe that we call "architectures of culture"[1]: institutional buildings with programmes of a sociocultural nature which in certain decisive historical periods participated in the cultural changes of a society or became eloquent symbols of that transformation. Here we propose to describe, even if briefly, some of those moments and architectures.

From the Renaissance onwards – not to go further back – cultural patronage increasingly gained in importance, remaining firmly in the hands of the Catholic Church for quite some time, mostly due to the actions of the Vatican and the Roman Curia, yet shared with influential aristocratic families with political and economic power in the Italian city-states or Germanic principalities and duchies from the fifteenth to eighteenth centuries. Remarkable urban buildings were erected, such as palaces, galleries, libraries, museums and private " cabinets of curiosities" which enriched the art and architectures of the Renaissance, Mannerist and Baroque periods and

1   GRANDE, Nuno - *Arquitecturas da Cultura: Política, Debate, Espaço*. Coimbra: Doctoral dissertation in Architecture, University of Coimbra (polypectomy), 2009. Web link: https://estudogeral.sib.uc.pt/handle/10316/11786

extended to other governance models in Europe of the *Ancien Régime*. An example of this is the progression from Louis XIV to Louis XVI and the manner in which the power of these successive French courts was expressed in architecture in absolute terms, ranging from manipulating the landscape with sumptuous composite gardens to the edification and ornamentation of royal squares, galleries with art treasures, and several iconic *châteaux*, within and beyond the large cities.

The creation of exclusively public places for cultural fruition would only emerge after the spread of the philosophical and architectural ideas of the Enlightenment – from Voltaire to Rosseau, from Boullée to Ledoux – but particularly following the French Revolution of 1789 when people were given access to the Louvre and the royal collections under the banner of "Liberty, Equality and Fraternity" for all citizens. Its transformation into the Museum of Arts in 1793 would be swiftly instrumentalised by the Emperor Napoleon Bonaparte when nine years later, he christened the Louvre the Napoleon Museum,[2] creating a repository of paintings of his conquests and other countless pieces stolen during his military campaigns. And how fitting that nearly two centuries later, the *Grands Travaux* initiated at the Louvre by then French President François Mitterrand cannot help but reflect this "personalist" character, apparent in the expressive gesture of constructing a majestic glass pyramid for the new entrance to the new museum and commercial complex, a monumental project by I. M. Pei inaugurated in 1993 and erected precisely at the centre of the *Court Napoléon*. Indeed, no other building in modern Europe seems to better symbolise the evolution of cultural power in the context of the culture of sovereign political power than the Louvre.

Louvre, Pyramid, Paris, France. I. M. Pei
© Wikimedia Commons

Opening the royal collections to the general public, a practice which became widespread throughout liberal Europe in the first decades of the nineteenth century, led to the proliferation of a new architectonic programme in the main industrial metropolises - the public museum – also influenced by society's increased cultural interest in the archaeology of ancient civilizations. Invariably built in a neoclassic style, these museums were nearly always inspired by the typological model of the Altes Museum, designed by Karl Friedrich Schinkel and inaugurated in 1830, located at the entrance to Berlin's Museum Island, and built to receive

2 See: MALGOUYRES, Philippe - *Le Musée Napoléon*. Paris: RMN, 2001. ISBN 13: 978--2711839858

Altes Museum, Berlin, Germany.
Karl Friedrich Schinkel.
© Wikimedia Commons

the Prussian collection of Etruscan, Greek and Roman art. These new architectures of culture, along with other eighteenth century typologies, such as public libraries, opera houses, literary associations and "crystal palaces," were dedicated to universal exhibitions or to the large academic art salons. These edifices reflected the social rise of a new urban class – the industrial and commercial bourgeoisie – who viewed their artistic acculturation as the ultimate path to gaining political power, thus definitively supplanting the influence of the Catholic Church and the "cultured" aristocracy.

At the turn of twentieth century, culture exhibited at these exclusive venues became a kind of bourgeois "religion," as noted by the Viennese art historian Alöis Riegl in his 1903 landmark text, "The Modern Cult of Monuments."[3] In creating different value-based definitions for the concept of the historical monument, Riegl came to explain a form of modern sacralization in which monumentality is transposed from the religious to the cultural sphere. Thus, museums became the most popular "temples" of the newly arrived century, during the course of which they would become one of the focal points of the cultural debate amongst the artistic avant-gardes. The debate included analogies between the concepts of "museum" and "mausoleum" developed in various artistic and literary manifestos – the writings of Italian futurist Filippo Marinetti (1909), Russian suprematist El Lissitzky (1923), and French symbolist Paul Valéry (1925), among others – which criticised eighteenth--century museums for being decadent and relegated to the veneration of relics from the past or the works of deceased authors.[4] A common claim was centred on the need to separate museum programmes from the encyclopaedic discourse of academies to take a more "laboratorial" approach, one dedicated to living, active, and culture--bearing creators of the modernity being proclaimed by the new century. Coping with the legacy of World War I, however, and on the eve of continued armed conflict spurred by the rise of conservative dictatorships, Europe delayed the creation of any modern art museums capable of facing the challenges of the emergent cultural avant-garde.

Forging ahead in this area was the United States, where a group of New York philanthropists from the world of high finance supported the founding of the Museum of Modern Art (MoMA) in 1929. Art historian and art critic Alfred Barr

3   See: RIEGL, Alöis - "The Modern Cult of Monuments: Its Character and its Origin", in. *Oppositions Reader*, New York: Princeton Architectural Press, 1998, p. 632, ISBN-13: 978-1568981536

4   Filippo Marinetti referred to Museums and Libraries as "cemeteries" in his 1909 Futurist Manifesto, while El Lissitzky regarded the museum space as a "painted coffin for our living body" in Exhibition Spaces of 1923. Paul Valéry, in his Essay of 1925, *The Problem of Museums*, described the orphanage of painting and sculpture by the death of the architecture of museums. See: NEWHOUSE, Victoria - "The Museum as Sacred Space" in *Towards a New Museum*, The Monacelli Press Inc., New York, 1998, p.48. ISBN 13: 9781580931809

was named director[5] and took the daring decision to create a departmentalised museum where Fine Arts and Architecture would overlap with those disciplines now popularised in the new century, namely Design, Photography and Cinema, the goal being to entice the most experimental and radical creative artists from both sides of the Atlantic. By the time the MoMa opened its new modern facilities on 53rd Street in Manhattan[6] only a decade later, the institution had already become totally instrumentalised by political power, as clearly expressed in President Franklin Delano Roosevelt's inaugural speech which described the MoMa as a symbol of national entrepreneurship and individual artistic freedom, as opposed to the winds repressing modernity blowing across Europe.[7]

This instrumentalisation would continue during the Cold War, with the "MoMA effect" being felt in the USA's political and economic support of its allies, particularly directed toward a Europe in reconstruction. The culture of the "American friend" would arrive in many forms, amongst which was the model for a modern art museum, which rapidly spread across several European nations, particularly those whose capital cities were destroyed during World War II and needed to rebuild facilities in their city centres. It may well be said that in the modern history of European-American relations, there is no building that better symbolises the evolution of the power of culture within the context of political-diplomatic power than the MoMA.

Throughout the 1960s, the agenda of the museum would return to the centre of this debate, now featuring a new generation of artists and essayists for whom modern cultural institutions were no longer avant-garde places for experimentation but rather symbols of a conformist and established political system to be contested. This "countercultural" position, also associated with the affirmation of Conceptual Art and Land Art, led many creative artists to abandon the conventional space of the "white cube" of the modern museum to seek out other fields of artistic expression: the use of the body for performance, the quotidian happenings , the poetics of landscape, and the indeterminacy of abandoned spaces.[8] From the high water mark of growing social and cultural unrest that was the May 1968 riots in Paris there

Museum of Modern Art, New York, USA.
Philip Goodwin and Edward Durell Stone
© MoMA

5   The original MoMA patrons were: Lillie P. Bliss, Cornelius J. Sullivan, John D. Rockefeller Jr., A. Conger Goodyear, Paul Sachs, Frank Crowninshield, and Josephine Boardman Crane.
See: GUILBAUT, Serge - How New York Stole the idea of Modern Art. Abstract Expressionism, Freedom, and the Cold War. Chicago: The University of Chicago Express, 1983. ISBN 13: 9780226310381

6   The project was given to the American architects Philip L. Goodwin and Edward Durell Stone.
See: GUILBAUT, Serge - How New York Stole the idea of Modern Art. Abstract Expressionism, Freedom, and the Cold War. Chicago: The University of Chicago Express, 1983. ISBN 13: 9780226310381

7   F. D. Roosevelt's speech given on the 10th of May 1939, a month after the invasion of Czechoslovakia by Nazi troops.
See: GUILBAUT, Serge - How New York Stole the idea of Modern Art. Abstract Expressionism, Freedom, and the Cold War. Chicago: The University of Chicago Press, 1983. ISBN 13: 9780226310381

8   See: O'DOHERTY, Brian - Inside the White Cube: The ideology of the Gallery Space. Berkeley and Los Angeles: University of California Press, 1999. ISBN-13: 978--0520220409

Guggenheim Museum, Bilbao, Spain. Frank Gehry
© FMGB Guggenheim Bilbao Museoa, Erika Ede.

Centre Georges Pompidou, Paris, France.
Richard Rogers and Renzo Piano.
© Georges Meguerditchian

9 Georges Pompidou was Prime Minister under Charles de Gaulle from 1962 to 1968. In 1969, he was elected President of the French Republic and died of illness in 1974. He did not live to see the completion of the cultural centre he began in 1970 in the Beaubourg district of Paris, later given his name and inaugurated in 1977.
See: SILVER, Nathan - *The Making of Beaubourg*, Cambridge: The MIT Press, 1994. ISBN 13: 9780262193481

10 See: BAUDRILLARD, Jean - *L'Effet Beaubourg: Implosion et dissuasion*. Paris: Editions Galilée, 1977. ISBN 13: 9782718600833

emerged an appeal for a culture that would stem from the action and self-determination of its citizens via the disintegration of the old boundaries between "high culture" and "popular culture".

France was witnessing a fundamental change to its cultural policies, which would take the country from the political paternalism of Gaullist minister André Malraux to the accommodating voluntarism of Georges Pompidou's new government.[9] Pompidou announced a public competition in 1970 for the construction of an unconventional museum to be a multidimensional and multidisciplinary cultural centre in the Parisian district of Beaubourg. The Georges Pompidou Centre, which was inaugurated precisely 40 years ago, designed by Renzo Piano and Richard Rogers, would become a late symbol of this *soixante-huitard* generation, which sought to change Western political systems through the unhindered interaction of culture and society.

In 1977, the year the building was inaugurated, philosopher Jean Baudrillard analysed the contradictory "Beaubourg effect,"[10] calling it a "black hole devouring cultural energy," leading to the total "implosion" of the idea of culture and to the total "dissolution" of the modern institutional space, albeit much to the delight of the endless stream of visitors who walk through the edifice to this date. Once again, it seems that there is no other building that better symbolises the domestication of the 1968 "counterculture" by the culture of late-capitalist political and economic power than the Georges Pompidou Centre.

The following decades were marked by a post--conceptualist and neo-conservative cultural shift, both in the reclaiming of traditional expressions in the artistic world (a formalistic return to sculptures on plinths and paintings on canvas), and in the historicist revival of typologies and classical languages in the architectural field. The architectures of culture were probably the most targeted programmes in this postmodern revival, as evident in the construction of numerous museums, archives and libraries in the 1980s and 1990s, particularly in the Anglo--Saxon and Germanic worlds, as in the challenging project for the Stuttgart Neue Staatsgalerie by James Stirling, probably the most ironic and iconic reinterpretation of Schinkel's Altes Museum typology, executed 150 years after the original.

The "post-modern museum"[11] required bringing together three crucial elements – the iconic, the mediatic,, and the "star architect" – particularly within a post-Berlin Wall (1989) geopolitical context in which the Cold War definitively surrendered to globalization, thus compelling nations, cities and their institutions to compete for a place on the international map of financial, touristic and cultural flows. It is in this context that a process of "cultural franchising" was launched in the 1990s by the director of the Solomon R. Guggenheim Foundation, Thomas Krens, whose intent it was to expand collections, exhibitions and institutional revenues.[12] The most significant success came with the inauguration of a new Guggenheim Museum in Bilbao in 1997, a deliberately iconic and newsworthy project designed by the renowned Frank Gehry, which sparked intense international interest in that northern Spanish city that was experiencing a severe post-industrial crisis at the time.

Neue Staatsgalerie in Stuttgart, Germany.
James Stirling. © Wikimedia Commons

A "Bilbao effect" fatally occurred over the following decade, several cities around the world sought to attract Guggenheim franchising projects, , inviting top architects to design them: Berlin (Richard Gluckman), Las Vegas (Rem Koolhaas), NY Soho (Arata Isozaky), NY Manhattan (Frank Gehry), Salzburg (Hans Hollein), Tokyo (Zaha Hadid) and Rio de Janeiro (Jean Nouvel).[13] Only the first three of these projects were actually implemented although they fell short of their anticipated cultural success. To a certain extent, these institutional failures marked the end of a euphoric decade of great investment in culture in the Western world, a moment which seemed to foretell the deep financial and social crisis that the USA and Europe would come to experience from 2008 onward. Recent history therefore points to the Bilbao Guggenheim Museum as the building that best reflects both the radiant and the dark sides of cultural mediatisation in the hands of global political and financial power.

In the West, we are presently experiencing the effects of this recent crisis, in contrast with the new euphoria of investment that is traversing the Middle East and Far East, two geopolitical worlds which have also begun to use museum culture as an instrument for affirming their new diplomatic and economic power. This "cultural franchising" has extended to the United Arab Emirates, where the Guggenheim Foundation and the Louvre Museum will soon open two "branch buildings," designed by Frank

11 See: CRIMP, Douglas - "The Postmodern Museum", in *On the Museum's Ruins*. Cambridge: The MIT Press, 1995. p. 302--305. ISBN 13: 9780262032094

12 See: GUASCH, Anna Maria; ZULAIKA, Joseba - *Aprendiendo del Guggenheim Bilbao*. Madrid: Akal, 2007. ISBN 13: 978-84--460-2278-7

13 Most recently, in 2014, the Solomon R. Guggenheim Foundation launched their first international public competition for the selection of a project for a new "museum-branch" in Helsinki, Finland, won by the Parisian Moreau-Kusunoki studio, from among an impressive number of 1715 competing proposals.
See: KOFLER, Andreas - "Le Guggenheim, Franchise Planétaire", *L'Architecture d'Aujourd'hui*, n° 415, Octobre 2016, pp.100-103. ISBN 13 : 978-2-918832-54-6

Gehry and Jean Nouvel, respectively. In China, between 2012 and 2015, more than 800 new museums[14] were inaugurated (an average of nearly one building per day), many of them designed in the West by the "stars" of global architecture. These were commissioned by the Chinese state, new economically emerging cities, or private investors wishing to showcase their new art collections. Aimed at an exponentially growing urban middle class, these spaces, just in 2015, housed 11,800 temporary exhibitions across the country, with an impressive number of 781 million visitors.[15]

The unstoppable globalization of events and cultural consumption – in which we should include the nearly 200 art biennales occurring regularly throughout the world[16] – have been generating criticism and debate amongst creative artists, curators and essayists, similar to that which took place amongst the avant-garde of the first decades of the twentieth century or during the counterculture movements of the 1960s and 1970s. As in past times, today's new voices claim their right to oppose dominant cultural policies in the globalised world as well as those based on "franchising" or other *top-down* impositions, thus returning decision-making power and cultural production to the various local communities in *bottom-up* actions. We are living in a time when new institutional experiences are emerging, one where events open themselves up to critical debate on the exercise of power, and more specifically, cultural power.

In this context, the exhibition that gives meaning to this text and this book - "Power Architecture" – constitutes an interesting perspective on the reality that we have described, documenting and comparing different architectures of culture in Latin America, Europe and the Far East, existing between the ephemeral and the majestic, between the imposition of a political vision and an investment in social and community participation.[17] It is, therefore, a current portrait of the longstanding power of culture represented in the consolidation of various cultures of power.

14 See: HUGRON, Jean-Philippe – "Musémania, La culture made in China", *L'Architecture d'Aujourd'hui*, n° 415, Octobre 2016, pp.58. ISBN 13 : 978-2-918832-54-6

15 *Idem*, p.59

16 See: Directory of Biennials, *Biennial Foundation*: http://www.biennialfoundation.org/home/biennial-map/

17 It is interesting to note that the selection of "Power Architecture" presents examples that result from political processes as distinct as: the sociocultural project of Arena do Morro by the architects Herzog & de Meuron (2014) and the Taipei Performing Arts Center by OMA / Rem Koolhaas (under construction); as well as the ephemeral pavilion "The form of form", designed by Johnston Marklee + Nuno Brandão Costa + Office KGDVS for the Lisbon Architecture Triennial (2016) and the telluric Porta Nova de Alhambra, in Granada, by Álvaro Siza (projected).

MEDIA POWER.
NOVELTY:
A DISPASSIONATE
STORY

Moisés Puente

"The oldest of social specialisations, the specialisation of power, is at the root of the spectacle".
Guy Debord

Of all the gods of the new pantheon of Enlightenment – Reason, Science, Technique, Economy, etc., it was the god of Progress who seemed to best represent the great universal enterprise of humanity in a single concept: the ceaseless creation of wealth. The new faith in Progress has been as blind and obtuse as the faith in God had ever been.

Curiously, the new god of Progress exercised full impact on ideology in its entirety, which in the early twentieth century would come to constitute the historical moment that we have come to call artistic avant-gardes. Yet, the avant-garde adopted a new name for the god of Progress: the New. As the creator of the past had to assimilate the values and criteria of Tradition, so was the modern creator obliged to submit to the New. The glorification of the New (understood not only as Progress, but as True) demanded that there be an unconditional rupture with the Old, whereas the New marked a new direction for time and precisely defined a new paradoxical, and yet necessary, relationship with its opposite, that is, with Tradition.

With a further twist, post-modernity took the value of the New to a point of no return. As the future lost its emancipatory capacity and realised it was unable to promote something new, the New was understood as a relentless repetition and set between infinite varieties of the past and present. The quest for the New as an end in itself , in reality led to a form of de-ideological absurd, as it annulled its own aspiration for a definitely New to appear after the New, and therefore, the hope for a new historical beginning[1]. Or, in the words of Walter Benjamin, we might say that the New lost its aura. In fact, the lifeless path which the New entered encouraged post-modernity to reflect on the meaning of the Old, assigning it the value of the New once again.

There seem to be no possible ways to create a rupture with the agenda of the New. If there were, the rupture in itself would inevitably mean opening a new path. Therefore, what is the purpose of this incessant search for the New? As Guy Debord said in *The Society of the Spectacle*, the demand for the new meets the economical requirements of the new society of the spectacle. The god of the New has become the god of Economy, thus returning to the long-standing idea of the god of Progress as the "ceaselass creation of wealth"[2].

Criticism and new media

Ever since its origin, as previously described by several authors, modern architecture has been associated to the priests and supreme inciters of the New: the media. Modern architecture cannot be understood without its direct association to this unbreakable desire for the New, manifested by the media, and its direct conversion of cultural value into economic value.

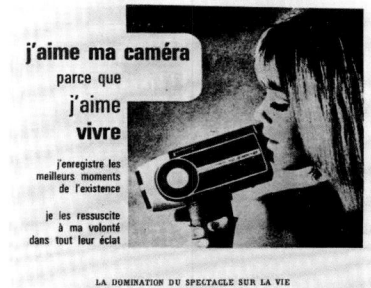

j'aime ma caméra
parce que
j'aime
vivre
j'enregistre les
meilleurs moments
de l'existence
je les ressuscite
à ma volonté
dans tout leur éclat

LA DOMINATION DU SPECTACLE SUR LA VIE

Eumig Camera advertisement.
Situationist International, October 1967. © SI

Throughout the history of the modern movement, criticism has been essential to explain the attitudes or trajectories of certain architects. Le Corbusier owes very much to Sigfried Giedion, as much as James Stirling owes to Colin Rowe or Aldo Rossi to Manfredo Tafuri. Yet, the days are over when critics could elevate or ruin a career, validate or condemn certain directions, or even dictate the future development of certain trajectories or inspire new paths.

During the modern movement, the most relevant architecture was accompanied by moments of critical lucidity, and often the critics encouraged certain practices, which were perhaps difficult to understand at the time, presenting these in a coherent and comprehensive form. However, for a few years now, criticism has fallen victim to a considerable level of atrophy, in quality as well as in extension. Criticism has gone from the elaboration of great treatises and masterpieces on modernity to critical studies of post-modernity, the witty articles of recent decades,

[1] In order to read further into the concept of "new", see: Groys, Boris, *Über der Neue. Versuch einer Kulturökonomie*, Munich: Carl Hanser Verlag, 1992 (English version: *On the New*, New York: Verso, 2014).

[2] See: Sánchez Ferlosio, Rafael, *Mientras no cambien los dioses, nada ha cambiado*, Madrid: Alianza Editorial, 1986.

and finally, in an accelerated decline, to the absurdity of the text format itself, limited to brief chronicles, blog posts and commentary – amongst the innumerable forms of disseminating contemporary architecture – including those few characters allowed by Twitter and to the even more succinct "likes" on Facebook. Opinion has come to replace criticism, and reasoned academic study has been replaced by occasional commentary. The contemporary critic only seems to be able to explain, comment and debate architecture, without addressing its substance directly.

Criticism has long disappeared from specialised magazines, which are now more preoccupied with publishing self-complacent texts for the promotion of case studies than in presenting a real critique about contemporary practices. On the other hand, architects have been constructing their own narrative. They have been pamphleteer critics of their own work – most notably, in the brilliant example of Rem Koolhaas – with self-absorbed and self-referential languages, which are increasingly insufferable. There is little space left for fostering incisive, intelligent and encouraging criticism, which i although it lacks the intention or ability to change the world, could nevertheless explain it.

If criticism yields to opinion, the former disappears, at best, in a lax work of content editing. These new characters, attempting to position themselves as "critics", the media narcissists, use all the tools within their reach via the Internet to fall into self-referential and self-complacent spirals, which reduce the information content to a complete absurd. Quantity of information is given priority over quality, memory disappears, hidden under a subtle and premeditated work of amnesia (as necessary as it is interested), which spreads a thick veil over the immediate happening in order to shift to the next character or event, and from there to another, and another, etc., and feed the thirst for New and for digestible information, replicated in infinite chains.

The new "junk criticism" – to use a simile of the title of a famous essay by Rem Koolhaas[3] – is absorbed in self--promotion and visibility in the media, increasingly disconnected from the true substance, of not only criticism, but also architecture. A great ally of opportunity and political correctness – a concept that has reached its maturity – "junk criticism" is dazzled by the present, by

3   Koolhaas, Rem, "Junkspace", *October*, n. 100, Cambridge (Mass.), June 2002 (Portuguese version: "Espaço-lixo", in *Três textos sobre a cidade*, Barcelona: Editorial Gustavo Gili, 2010).

the informational wind that barely leaves a trace. Subject to amnesia, unable to establish a relationship with what was previously stated, it is incapable of constructing trajectories and lines of thought that go beyond mere news, opinion or discovery of the endlessly New. Since the future no longer has any validity, the triumphant god of the New is now occupied uniquely and exclusively with the present.

A new visual culture

If architectural criticism seems to have been eclipsed, as observed, by these new critics described above, everything seems to indicate that we are facing a new cultural paradigm. In very little time, we went from an architectural culture that is almost exclusively literate and technical, to an eminently visual culture. In a world with a superabundance of images, these are no longer mere representations of things but images that are entirely meaningful; images are now much more powerful and more influential than words, and contrary to what people such as Peter Eisenman defended in the 1990s, architecture is no longer read as text, but as imagery. New generations of architects, of great capacity, culture and visual acuity, propose finding new ways of making criticism, which originate in the perception and analysis of our complex world of images. Yet, it seems that they only reiterate the same old values of the New. Literate discourse is abandoned to address other iconic discourses, visual, environmental or atmospheric, which when amalgamated transpose the traditional artistic disciplines. The new generations of creatives and architects, possessing a visual culture without precedent, could create a new interpretation of architecture, which without separating from the discipline, would seek to depend less on text to build from an image, as this was so denounced by previous generations. In this new way of understanding culture, where the historical background is added to other knowledge in a conscious search for environments and atmospheres that make use of new materials for architecture, the images from the history of architecture became part of a store of possible materials from which to establish a new operational criticism. History no longer has the same meaning that it could have had for Adolf Loos, Aldo Rossi or Rafael Moneo, for example, and now quotes techniques of pop *collage* or atmospheric constructions, as a mere reference within an autonomous visual discourse.

This is the visual culture that is best adapted and propagated by new media, and always eager for new images given that images do not need any mediation to be understood and that those produced in geographically distant places can be used immediately without the need for a "linguistic" translation required in other contexts. The visual or iconic image has come to constitute a new law that articulates ways of making architecture. It is the image, and not the word, that propagates in the globalised world, constructing the recent cultural paradigm of the New.

After all this, one might wonder whether all these new paradigms only reiterate something that is already known, something that has been rehearsed and has led us, over the years, time and again, to the same impasse: the seductive power of the New. Is it not time to leave aside the New to seek other values in architecture and in its diffusion, such as recovering something similar to the aura described by Benjamin, or proposing the Permanent as an antidote to the irrepressible speed of the media?

RITUAL POWER.
NOW I LAY ME
DOWN TO EAT

Joaquim Moreno

The power of ritual is the power to transform the forms that frame our coexistence, in a simultaneously absolute and accelerated manner. It is through ritual that new meanings are inscribed in ancient symbols, and new symbols are invented by manipulating symbols from the past. Persistent forms are transformed by these material and symbolic practices, in subtle or radical ways, gradually or abruptly. Inversely, architecture looks to safeguard itself from existential uncertainty through formal stability. The transformation of our contemporary ways of life exists in that interval, founded on and increasingly dependent from ritual mediations between solid and soft, intimate and public, visible and invisible. The duality with the greatest capacity to transform the common house, which we call city, exists between the sacred and the profane, between the secular and the religious, or between the rationality of public space of democratic representation and the symbolic and ritual order, introduced by religious freedom. These dualities presently establish new relationships, overlapping and distorting into new dynamics.

To consider the power of ritual offers an opportunity to think about the power of the scales that exist before and beyond form, inside and outside form, or overlapping beyond any linear dimension, intimate and public, in a web of culture, technology and politics, which effectively materially transforms the built environment, apparently without altering its contours. Thinking about the ritual invites consideration of the difficult formal representation of social differentiation in the same public space, which is generally accepted as the common space existing between these differences. This leads to the question of why the form of the minaret is particularly useful as a vertical element for urban orientation while contested as symbolic evidence of a public space that hosts religious freedom.

Or to question whether the problem of form would perhaps be irrelevant if a ritual or other symbolic order were associated with that form.

Religious rituals are in fact forms of shared intimacy, where individual construction is produced collectively, in community, appearing in public through rituals and in private yet collective ecstasies. Individual religious freedom only exists while it appears in public, and in order to be actually deemed freedom, this cannot be confined or domesticated. Freedom of worship is only truly free if the ritual which it symbolises has a place in the common house of the city. Yet, the intimacy of the ritual has a different nature to that of the secular public space of the city and should be sheltered in other spatial institutions and mediated by more complex portals and thresholds. But how to exactly describe these new thresholds where our symbolic rituals collide? Where exactly is birth, death, marriage or education mediated? Due to the fact that the majority of these rituals have left the house, many of us thought that these might have been transferred to the diffuse rationality of social organisation and techno- -scientific performance. Yet, we are now surprised by their return in all their symbolic and ritual capacity, demanding a new architecture and a new place in the city.

The table and the temple, the *locus* of communion and the *locus* of community, respectively, are perhaps the singular places, the *locus solus*, which display these spatial and performative confluences and the converging points of the debate about the ritual as constituent and transformative agent of our coexistence. The provocation made in the title of this article – borrowed from the title of a book for an exhibition of Bernard Rudofsky, a great modern who was acutely dissatisfied with the simplification and ritual loss of modernity – constitutes the absence of any confirmation of the centrality of the table as the technology of the founding ritual of communion and commensality. Rudofsky's critique refers to the ease with which we might imagine the past with imagery from the present, as in the Last Supper depicted without any vestige of the etiquette or ordinary customs of the New Testament era, almost as if the dinner guests were wearing a modern suit and tie and had just switched off their mobiles.

'Lay down to eat' has a humorous and transgressive connotation, despite the archaeological evidence that a reclining posture would have been the common etiquette at the time of Christ. Thinking about the Last Supper as a Roman *triclinium*, which is easier to imagine in the famous drunkenness of Plato's *symposium* (meaning to drink together), does not fit comfortably alongside the Renaissance image of a central Christ figure with a half--dozen Apostles seated to either side. Rudofsky confronts us with both our ignorance of the past and the facility with which we become accustomed to simple images of the past, ones with which we prefer to domesticate rituals.

The absent table described by Rudofsky is also the central theme of the ritualization of the impossibility of sharing, which establishes the community around the table, as proposed by Georg Simmel in his article, "The Sociology of the Meal." The ritual of the table and commensality offer the opportunity to socialise the most individual and universal impulse which humans enjoy, that is to eat, and thus impossible to share. We come together to eat although we realise that we cannot share food, as each one of us depends on our own sustenance to survive. Simmel presents the social structure that exists within this ritual of substitution, in which the most individual need is incorporated into our collective life. The mental *locus* of this contradiction in European society is the table. The symbolic meal that circumvents the contradiction in eating together is precisely the Last Supper. In this "each person eats in the totality of their mysterious indivisibility, which is attributed to all equally, thus transcending completely the egotistical and exclusive quality present in all meals." [1] The fiction or ritualization of equality as a form of social stabilisation of the most primitive necessity demands a form beyond ritual, and Simmel also describes these forms, particularly the equality of plates, their circular and regular shape associated with individual space and equity with others, transforming "the place at the table" into a regulator of what is eaten at the table: if it is food, there is an individual portion, if it is God, it is everything. A well set table immerses the community into a ritual obliteration of its most animal individuality. The etiquette of having one's own individual plate and glass makes the food vector clear and personal, allowing no feedback, prohibiting a licked spoon from dipping into the soup terrine or lapping up someone else's wine, and therefore avoiding yet another taboo, that of eating your neighbour at the table when we come together to eat.

More recently, Bernard Siegert proposes examining the Last Supper as a cultural technique, questioning what we actually eat when we come together to eat: "sharing

1 Georg Simmel, The Sociology of the Meal, 1905

food with the purpose of creating a community is rarely a peaceful event. Inevitably, something will have to be killed and suppressed, substituted or transfigured in sacrifice. It is not surprising that shared meals are characterised by semiotic complexities and endless confusion." [2] As means of provocation, he starts by analysing the founding ritual of Catholicism as a strategy for differentiation and absorption of other rituals, noting how the concept of transubstantiation transforms the wine (a taboo in itself as alcohol is prohibited in some religions) into blood (also a general taboo in certain religions), which is offered as a sacrificial gift as the blood of Christ, or wine, as in a Dionysian ritual. Siegert's scrutiny extends to the most precarious point in this relationship with language. "No other text expresses the double aspect of language, caught between speech and food, good and bad, poison and sweet, eroticism and religion, more clearly than the Epistle of St James."[3] The sensorial mechanism of flavour and taste coincide in the mechanism of speech, which makes this ritual simultaneously a means of communion and communication. The Last Supper is, in this way, continuously transformed by its interpretations, images and materialising rituals.

Last Supper, Milan, Italy. Leonardo da Vinci.
© Wikimedia Commons.

The other singular *locus* of this ritual transformation, which alters form without modifying its contour, is the temple, the sacred architecture, which has always had a difficult relationship with the essential secularity of public space. The ritual is perhaps the point of convergence between these two parallel places and the moment that transports the temple to an absolute form, parallel to modernity and to a normative relationship to use and function. Adolf Behne described this modern paradox in 1926 in the introduction of *The Modern Functional Building*,[4] where he addresses architecture, especially the house, as oscillating between the relative character of tool and the absolute character of a toy or game. Behne noted that: "The primitive man is not strictly utilitarian. He demonstrates his instinct for games and play in the way he crafts his tools, which are more polished and beautiful than strictly necessary, painting or decorating these with ornaments." This formal excess made architecture absolute, a game or play in itself, or a strictly rational construction of form, a recognition reflected in the inclusion of a passage from Behne's book in the anthology of "rationalist" texts, organised to accompany the catalogue of the Milan Triennial of 1973, to which Aldo Rossi gave the title,

2 Bernhard Siegert, "Eating Animals – Eating God – Eating Man", in *Cultural Techniques: Grids, Filters, Doors and other Articulations of the Real*.

3 Ibid. p. 40

4 Adolf Behne, Der moderne Zweckbau, Munich, Drei Masken Verlag, 1926

"Rational Architecture."[5] Form would therefore be absolute because it was a rational construction in itself, and not determined by purpose. The excess of the ritual of game, pleasure or gesture without a purpose – which organised form, opening a field of formal exploration in which the temple, the use without a function, and the merely symbolic use despite its material reality – could be pondered once again. This is because the purpose of the temple is to produce a community and to circumscribe shared intimacies. However, in order to produce a community, the temple's space cannot be immediately determined by eventual subjects, and therefore it needs to be absolute, determined by its own internal reasons.

To say absolute architecture is, in fact, to say total architecture, or complete, or perfect, or unconditional, or pure, or real, or limitless, or certain, or infallible, or incomparable, or refined, or exquisite, or simply independent. Here we come increasingly closer to the famous manifesto written in 1962 by Walter Pichler and Hans Hollein, Absolute Architecture.[6] The brief introduction by Conrads states clearly that:

Absolute architecture – "human beings are merely tolerated in their domain."
This affirmation of Walter Pichler (b. 1936 in Ponte Nova) is the most absolute thesis of architectonic manifestos of our century. Because absolute means separated. It means here: separated from history, separated from acts, separated from thought. Absolute architecture means here: architecture liberated from its objective, men: the non-objective architecture. The chain of adventures, experienced in this century by those who purposed to learn a new architecture, ends in this totally independent or uncompromised phenomena of an "Absolute Architecture". It is, adds Hans Hollein (b. 1934 in Vienna), useless, without a purpose.

The house for all, or the community house, cannot be the house of any singular person; this is the paradox that allows for the sharing of intimacy which organises community. As the architecture of the temple in this case does not have an objective and is absolute, it becomes capable of being the space where the ritual engenders a community in the widest interior of society. Conrads points out that this absolute architecture exists outside history, or at least outside history understood as progress, as a justification of form given its technical viability. Pichler and Hollein clarify that in a world where "all is possible," being possible is no longer a viable reason. This proposal is

5   Aldo Rossi, ed. Architettura Razionale, Milano, Franco Angeli, 1973

6   Walter Pichler, Hans Hollein, "Absolute Architecture", in Ulrich Conrads, *Programs and manifestoes on 20th century architecture*, Cambridge Mass. MIT Press, 1971.

radical because it is outside purpose and outside possibility. Also, it is clearly ritual: "Architecture is a spiritual order realised through building. All construction is religious. Architecture is elemental, sensual, primitive, brutal, terrible, powerful, dominating."[7]

A few years later Hollein apparently contradicted this manifesto, proposing that absolute architecture or ritual materialises in its communication, not in its form or materiality. All is Architecture, we are all Architects, said Hollein in the magazine BAU in 1968.[8] Yet, the contradiction is only apparent, because for everyone to be an architect, we must move from the anonymous and uniform modern being to return to living in tribes, this time through technology, the same technology that according to Marshall McLuhan expands the tribal scale of the village to the global space of the satellite. The ritual communicates and the acceleration of communication organises communities, which makes the temple a little more absolute and a little more immaterial, more intersected with other networks and other circulations.

To think about ritual as the means for the absolute and accelerated transformation of the environment of our coexistence without altering its contours is to think beyond form, or to consider how the procession justifies the longest path taken to arrive at the chapel, as Souto de Moura evokes in his Maia project. The path only gains materiality in the procession, in the symbolic walking in ritual, with the *Via Crucis* to arrive at the chapel organised along the succession of each different station in which the traditional Way of the Cross is overlapped onto the simplest path to reach the chapel. The ritual inscribes one onto the other without any need for great material alteration, turning one possible path into the best path, simply put. The communion with the sacred, which awaits in the interior of the temple, in the case of Souto Moura's project, is achieved through the simple golden inscription on the smooth surface of the rock, otherwise left as the architect had found it. To inscribe the gold as an icon of sacred light is, in fact, a demonstration of the ritual's power to alter matter without altering its form.

To think about ritual is to think of the framing of a circle, as in some church in Rennes or some mosque in Dhaka. The symbolic operation of inscribing a circle onto a square, one pure form over another, allows for positioning the temple with respect to the Prophet's homeland, aligning the faithful appropriately for worship. In these cases,

Bait Ur Rouf Mosque, Dhaka, Bangladesh.
Marina Tabassum © Hassan Saiffuddin Chandan / MTA

Baitul Mukarram Mosque, Lisbon, Portugal.
Inês Lobo. Photomontage: Inês Lobo

7   Ibid. p. 181

8   "Alles ist Architektur," in *BAU 1/2*, 1968, p.2

Anastasis Church, St-Jacques-de-la-Lande,
Rennes, France. Álvaro Siza © Nicolò Galeazzi

the ritual inflects the symbolic value of absolute forms, independently of the particular style of worship practiced in each temple. Or it may be to think about the new mosque in the Mouraria designed by Inês Lobo as being simultaneously a public square and a house, that is, a space simultaneously intimate and public where the passage from the public space to the sacred space of prayer is made through the intimate ritual of ablution and the construction of the sacred ground for prayer. The ritual permits overlapping the intimate construction with the new public space, which makes a block that is rather long more permeable and renders the most sacred practices more compatible with the secular necessities of the community.

It is also through the concept of ritual that we can conceive of the entrance way of the Lisbon synagogue by Ricardo Back Gordon not just as the doorway to the temple but as a way to bring the temple onto the street. When Ventura Terra built the synagogue, the practice of the Jewish faith was foreign and thus absent from the public space, denied a façade on the public thoroughfare and any place at the common table of the city. The new entrance way is an effort to make the intimacy of worship more public, but also to articulate nearness and distance, overlapping paths and the symbolic directions of worship with urban mechanics. This ritual architecture is a portal since it allows for a change in dimensions, enabling entry into places where humans, as Pichler and Hollein would say, are simply tolerated.

COLLECTIVE POWER

Several imbalances undermine the sense
of well-being in the *Westernized* world
(an expression that globalization has made
vague), albeit under an aura of privilege
and *development* (another vague term).
 The chaotic growth of cities, the precariousness
of infrastructures or transport networks
used to be major difficulties; today there
are other problems, associated with a way
of life based on consumption and waste.
As collective power, we aim to think the
common purpose in the defence of collective
well-being, both socially and ecologically.
In this regard, some questions arise:
Can public or private architecture be sensitive
to energy consumption and climate change?
Can architecture contribute to biodiversity?
Can architecture promote processes of
participation and social mixing?

Galkadawala Forest Lodge, Habarana, Sri Lanka (2007)
Vijitha Basnayaka

Before renting a room or house at the Galkadawala Forest Lodge, a guest will come across this caveat: "If you are looking for a place with cable or internet, you should look elsewhere". Vijitha Basnayaka, the architect of this property in Sri Lanka, offers us an experience, a "return to nature", where we can sleep under the stars and hear the rustling of wildlife around us. This small 4-hectar paradise was once a land devastated by cultivation and burning. Vijitha Basnayaka began by reforesting the property, which today has more than 300 trees and 80 species of medicinal plants. The presence of a water line guided the main design options: the extraction site of the clay for the bricks and the creation of a brook that feeds a small lake and supports the development of a small ecosystem of plants and animals. The awareness for the water paths and their retention was also one of the undertaking's causes of success. More than 100 species of birds and 45 species of butterflies can be spotted here.

From an architectural point of view, the intervention tried to make use of traditional constructive methods (brick and clay) and recycled timbers, and frames of old demolished houses. Everything is recycled and reused, implying the architect's creativity. The architectural language may at first seem rustic, but it reveals itself as sophisticated in the careful selection and *assemblage* of *objets trouvées*. In a way, it makes use of one of erudite architecture's traditions, that of reusing materials from other constructions – a practice which dates back at least as far as the Romans.

The Galkadawala Forest Lodge is the expression of ecologically and culturally responsible housing tourism, which seeks harmony with nature and local customs as well.

The terrain before Vijitha Basnayaka's intervention

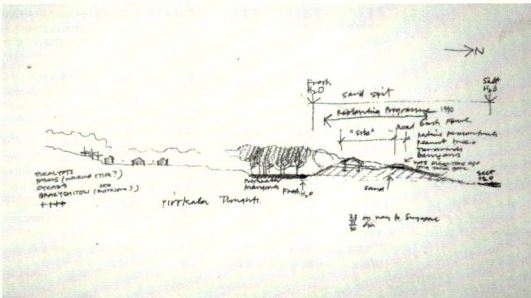

1 SLA: Hans Tavsens Park and Korsgade, Copenhagen
2 Hans Tavsens Park section detail
3 Glenn Murcutt: Marika-Alderton House, Australia.
   Section with topography and natural elements
4 Patrick Geddes: Valley Section

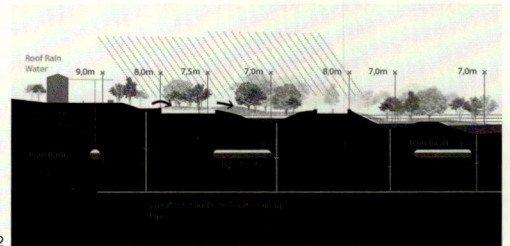

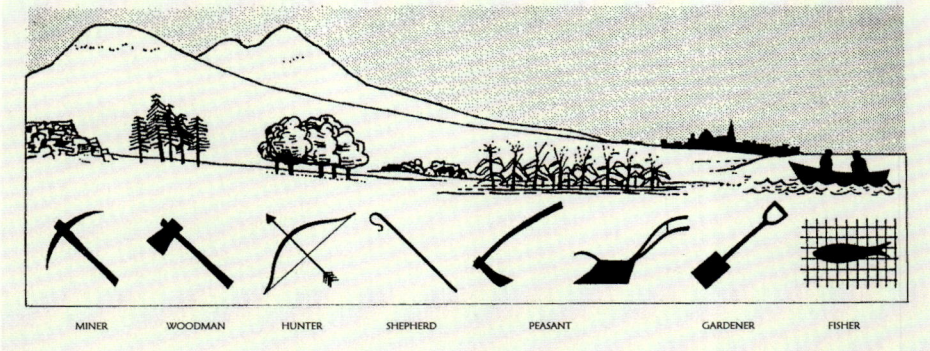

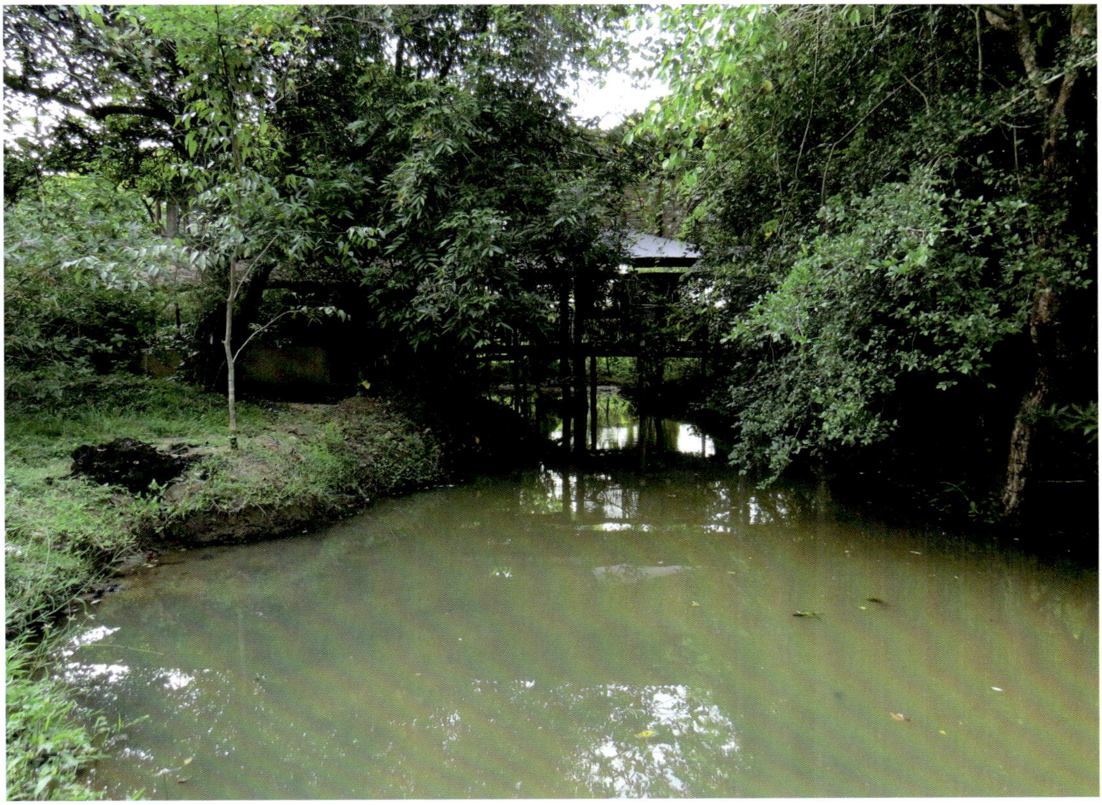

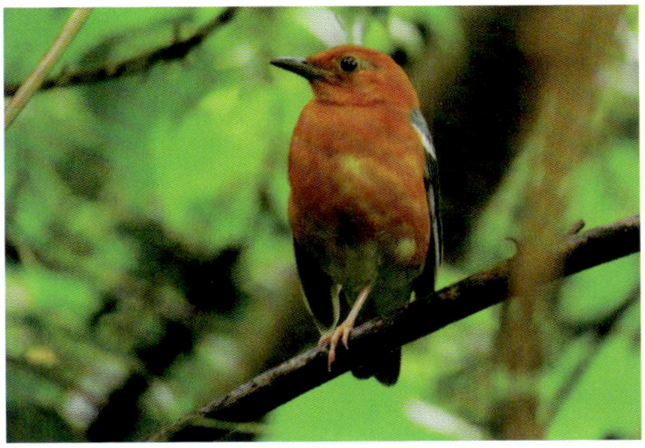

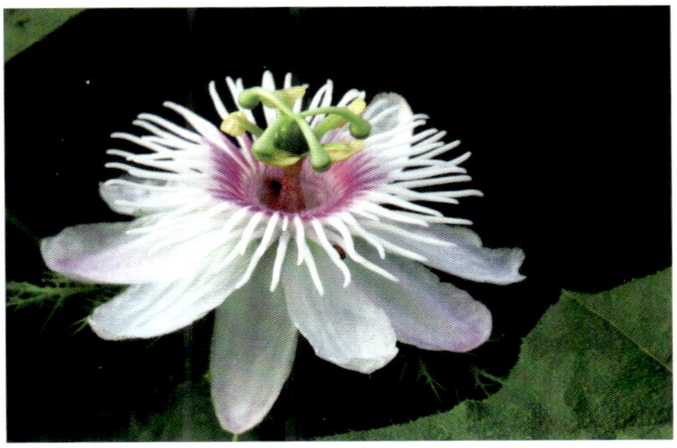

1   Chena farmers' hut, Sri Lanka.
2   Tree house, by Vijitha Basnayaka
3   A. and P. Smithson: Hexenhaus, Bad Karlshafen
4   IBUKU: The Green Village, Bali
5   Jaime Lerner: Free Environmental University, Curitiba

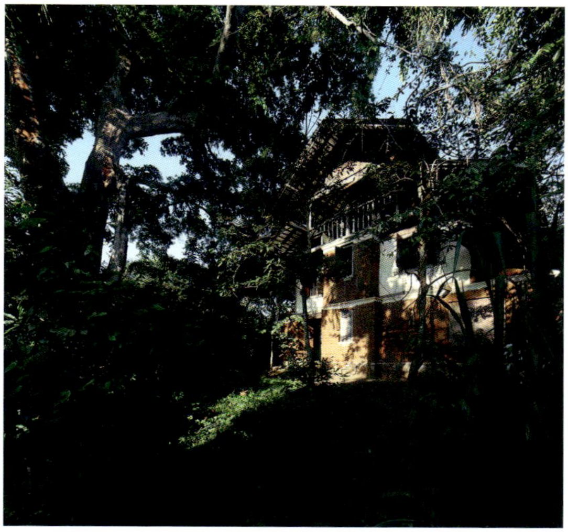

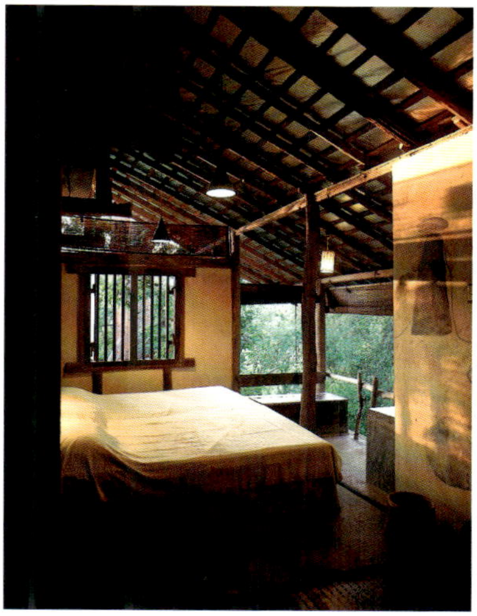

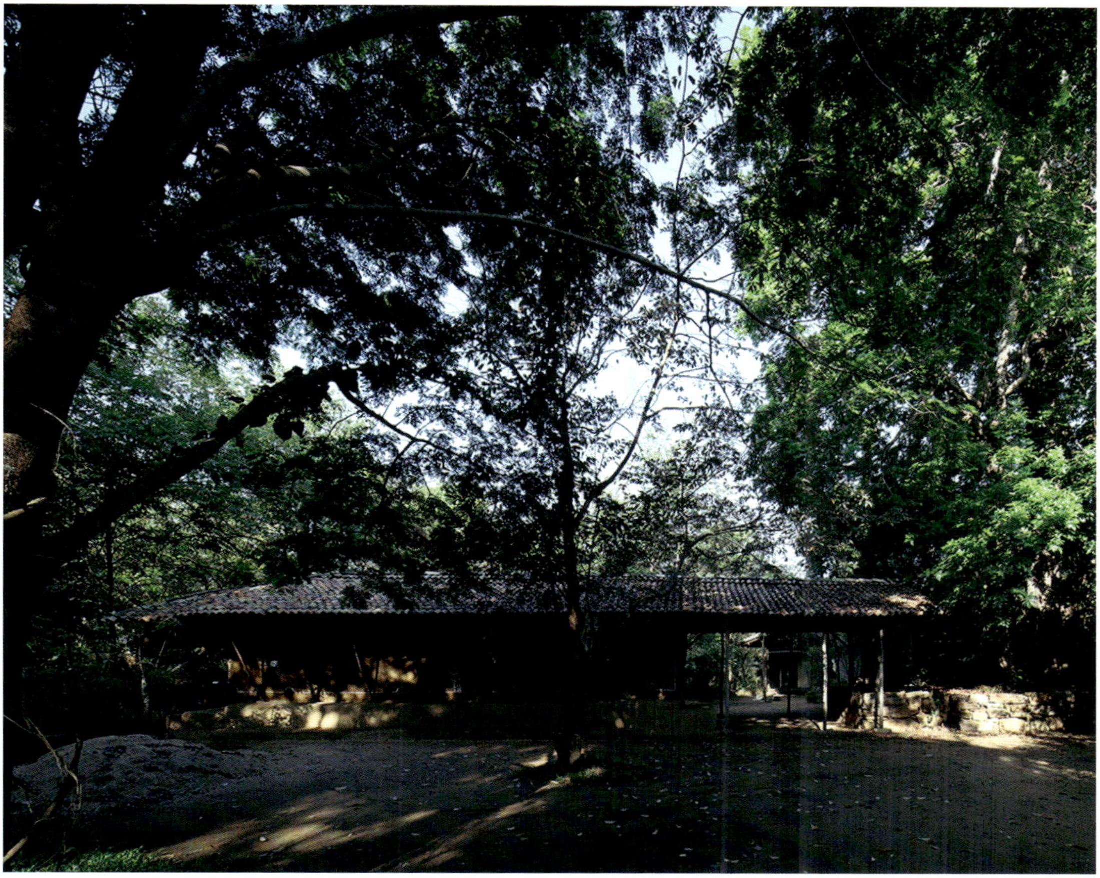

Granby Four Streets, Liverpool, United Kingdom (2011- ongoing)
Assemble

"Granby Street was once a lively high street at the centre of Liverpool's most racially and ethnically diverse community. The demolition of all but four of Granby's streets of Victorian terraces during decades of 'regeneration' initiatives saw a once thriving community scattered, and left the remaining "Granby Four Streets" sparsely populated and filled with tinned up houses. The resourceful, creative actions of a group of residents were fundamental to finally bringing these streets out of dereliction and back into use. Over two decades they cleared, planted, painted, and campaigned in order to reclaim their streets.
In 2011 they entered into an innovative form of community land ownership, the Granby Four Streets Community Land Trust (CLT) with the intention of bringing empty homes back into use as affordable housing. Assemble worked with the Granby Four Streets CLT and Steinbeck Studios to present a sustainable and incremental vision for the area that builds on the hard work already done by local residents and translates it to the refurbishment of housing, public space and the provision of new work and enterprise opportunities.
The approach is characterised by celebrating the value of the area's architectural and cultural heritage, supporting public involvement and partnership working, offering local training and employment opportunities and nurturing the resourcefulness and DIY spirit that defines the four streets." (Assemble)

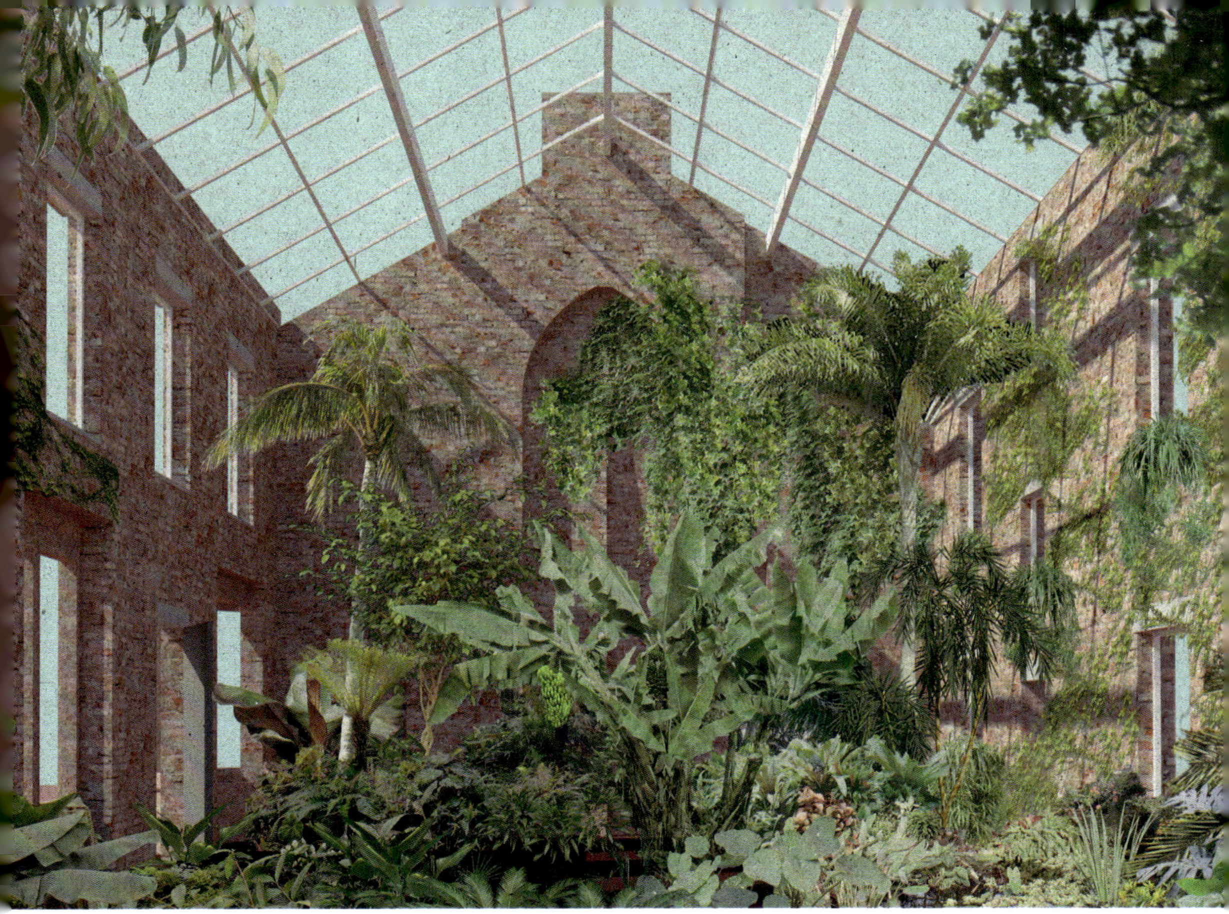

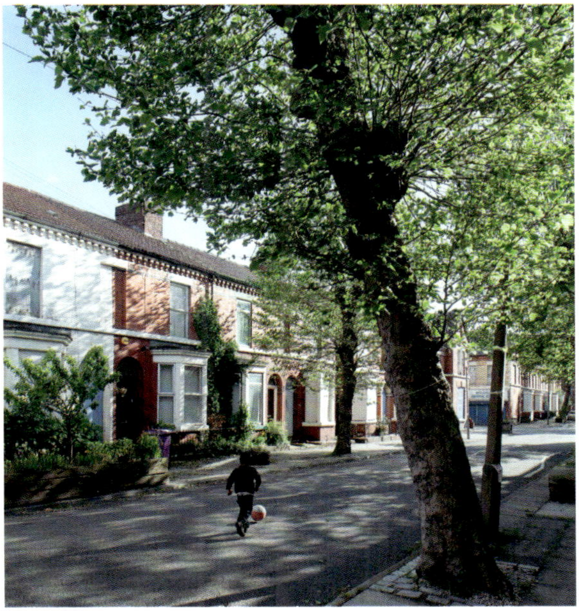

ARTIST-IN-RESIDENCE'S BEDROOM
CHAMBRE DE L'ARTISTE EN RÉSIDENCE
BATHROOM
SALLE DE BAIN
MEETING ROOM FOR CONTRACTORS
SALLE DE RÉUNION POUR LES ENTREPRENEURS

Assemble: Granby Workshop showroom at Tramway, Glasgow

1 Street market
2 Assemble: Granby Workshop's set of products
3 Assemble: Granby Workshop Tiles
4 Assemble: Granby Workshop
5 Granby Workshop team
6 J. Mendes Ribeiro: public discussion of the project
   for the reconstruction of Sala Roxy, Guadalajara
7 João Figueira e Associados: public discussion
   of the project for the Nova Aldeia da Luz
8 "City: Political Action and Participation", Coimbra

Warwick Junction, Durban, South Africa
designworkshop:sa

It is a place in the city of Durban marked by the presence of the African and Indian communities, with little connection to the white city and its economic system. The project aims to link two antagonistic urban realities with a shared past of segregation by using an unfinished viaduct. The bridge, an archetype of the transformative action of architecture, is an infra-structural artefact and a political action. A bridge over an expressway that runs counter to the divide between the centre and the margins, between comfort and exclusion. An architecture of connection, that beckons Arte Povera and acts as a social catalyst.

This is the summation of designworkshop:sa's Warwick Junction project. "A prefabricated steel and timber, bridge and tree / A mechanical insect, mobile, permanent, temporary, static / Noah's Arc, Jonah the Whale A Jackson Hlongwane sculpture, a found object / Connecting two divided shores, market places on each / Up the stairs, under the shade, to safely cross a deadly river of vehicles / Bent and welded in an open-sided shed, on the edge of the City / One crane, a team of riggers, installed over a few weekends / MassiveSmall, to quote Kelvin Campbell / Like a heart bypass, a stent, a single action to enable vibrant life / An immense return on infrastructural investment / An action in the heart of the thriving beast".

1 30 year vision of transportation, Durban, 1965
2 De Leuw Cather: Durban area transportation study, 1968

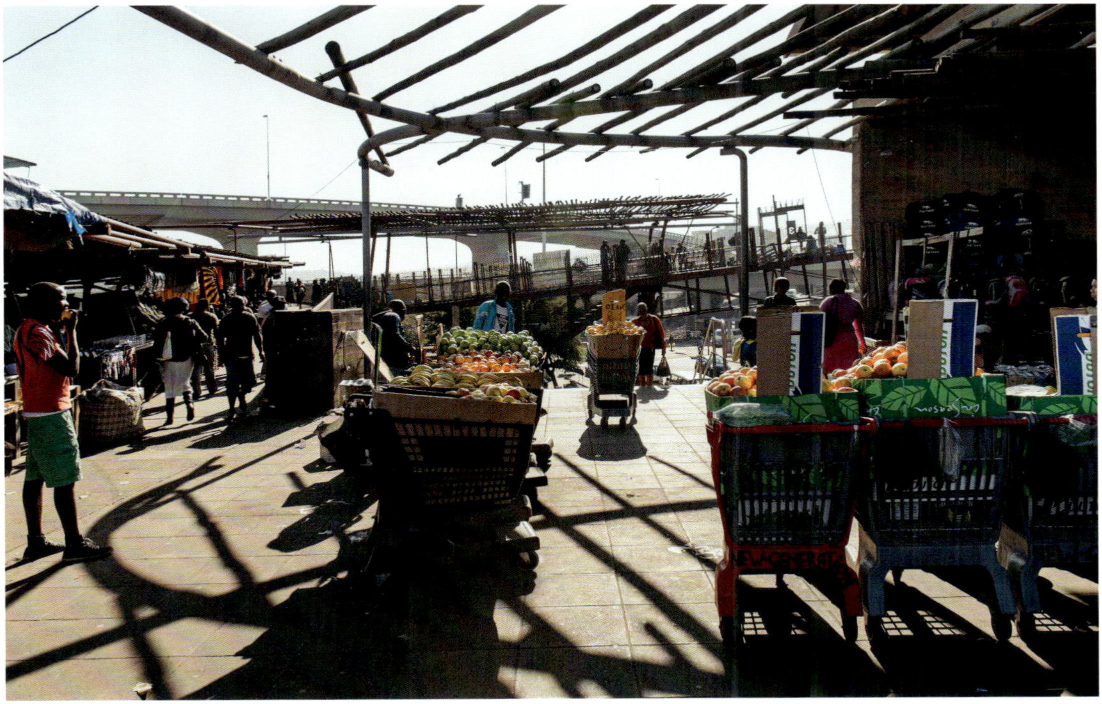

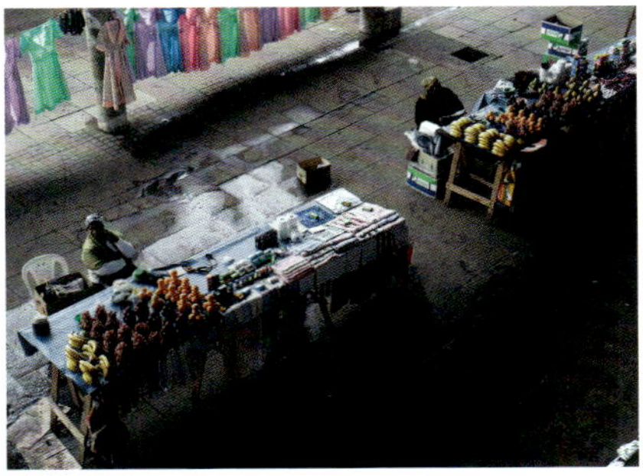

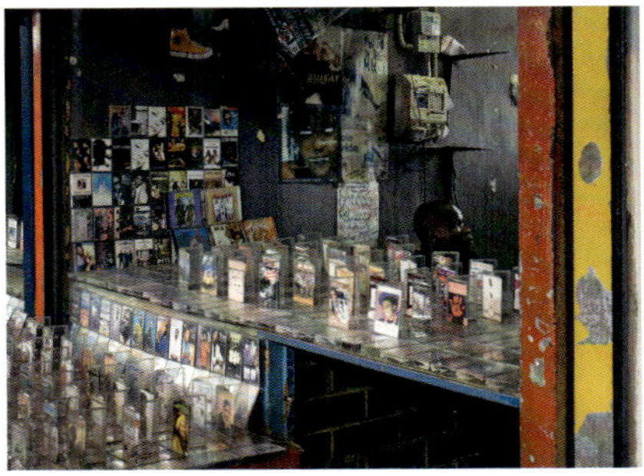

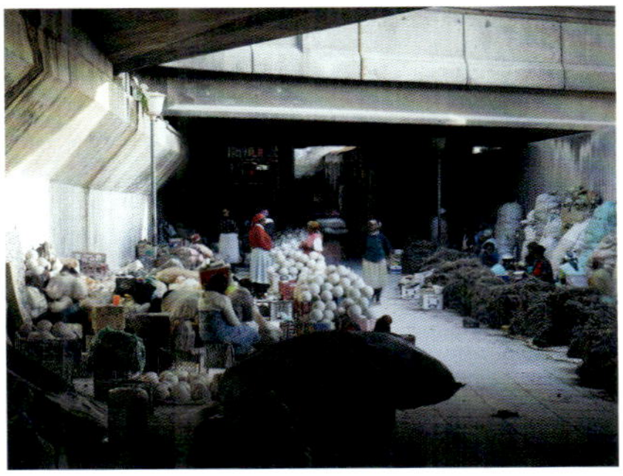

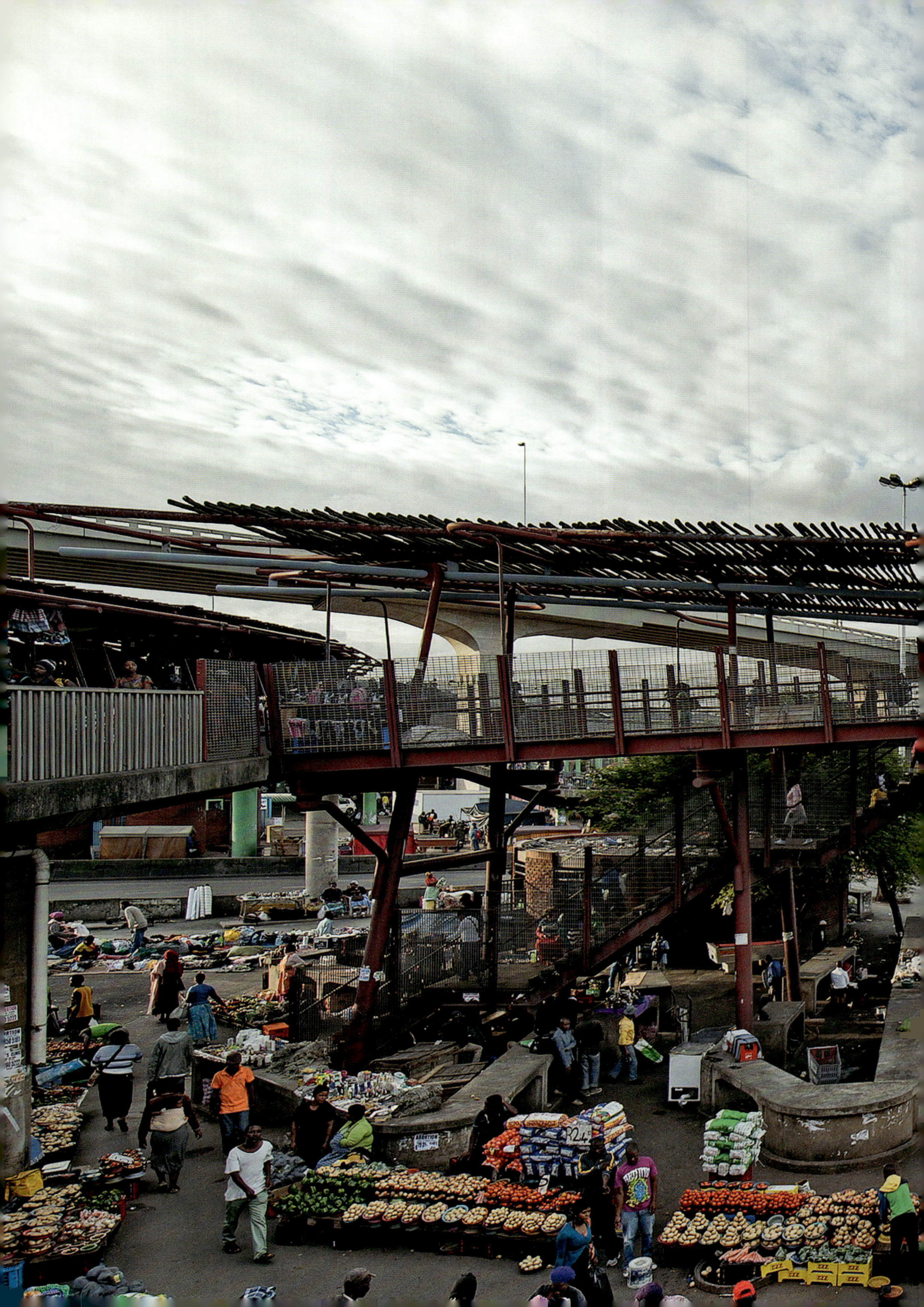

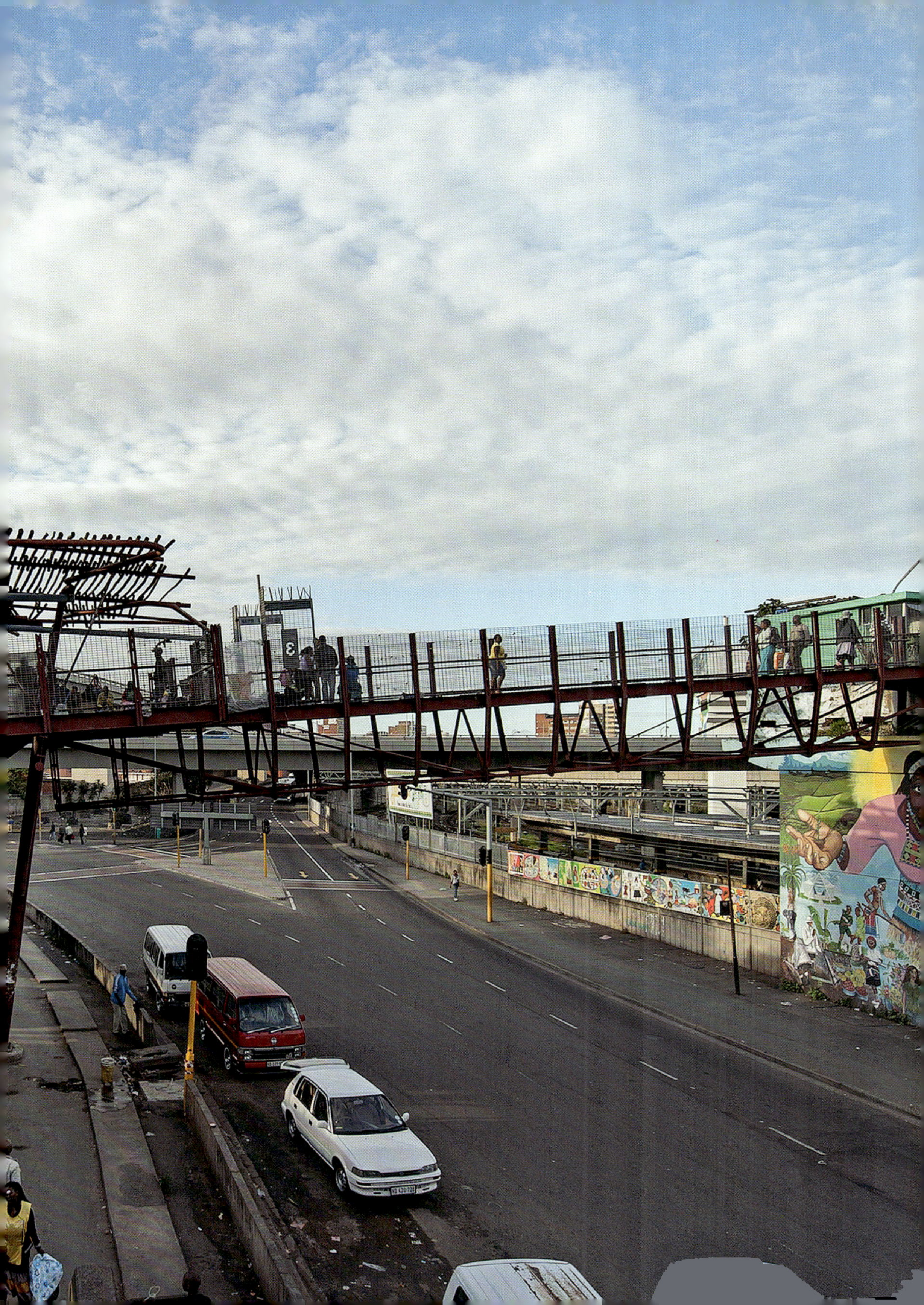

1 Ponte Vecchio, Florence
2 Glass Age Development Committee: Crystal Span Bridge, Londres
3 J. Álvaro Rocha: Parque da Maia's Metro Station / Bridge, Porto
4 Diller Scofidio + Renfro: High Line, New York
5 Territoires: Serge Gainsbourg Garden, Paris

Arena do Morro, Natal, Brazil (2014)
Herzog & De Meuron

While not exactly a *favela*, Mãe Luiza is a somewhat ostracized neighbourhood with few connections to the city of Natal in north-eastern Brazil.
The Herzog & de Meuron Arena gymnasium is the first building built as part of an urban intervention aiming to better integrate this community into the city's structure. Herzog & de Meuron propose a new axis of connection perpendicular to the oceanic waterfront, a set of new buildings and spaces that will provide a wide range of public activities.
Developed and financed by the Swiss foundation Ameropa (a philanthropic entity) with the support of the Centro Sócio Pastoral Nossa Senhora de Conceição, Arena do Morro is a community building where various sportsand cultural events are held. Built with practically only two types of materials (industrial aluminium panels in ventilated roofing, and locally manufactured concrete bricks on curvilinear walls), it does not fail to exhibit a formal complexity, simultaneously capable of articulating the scale of the gym itself with the scale of its more informal context.
Contrary to the idea that large architectural offices are only interested in large budget works, Herzog & de Meuron demonstrate the willingness to do a lot with very little, warning us that the success of the building will always depend on the continuity of the "vision for Mãe Luiza ". For now, we can say that, coincidentally or not, since the opening of the Arena do Morro, crime rates in Mãe Luiza have dropped dramatically.

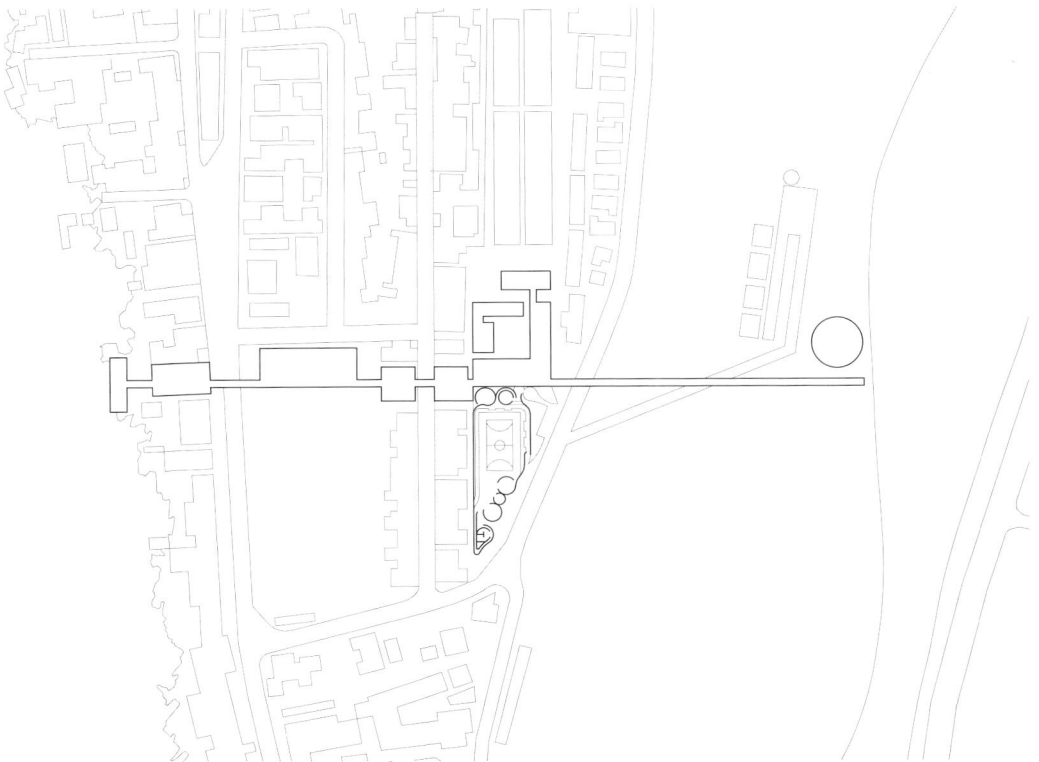

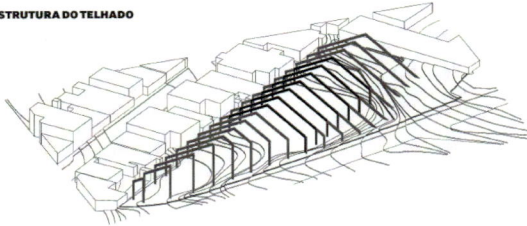

Herzog & de Meuron: Plan for Mãe Luiza, connection to the waterfront

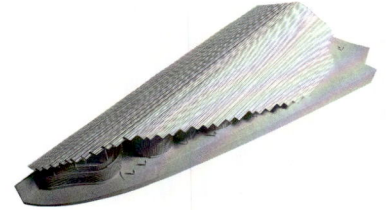

ESQUEMA DA ESTRUTURA DO TELHADO
■ Existente
■ Nova

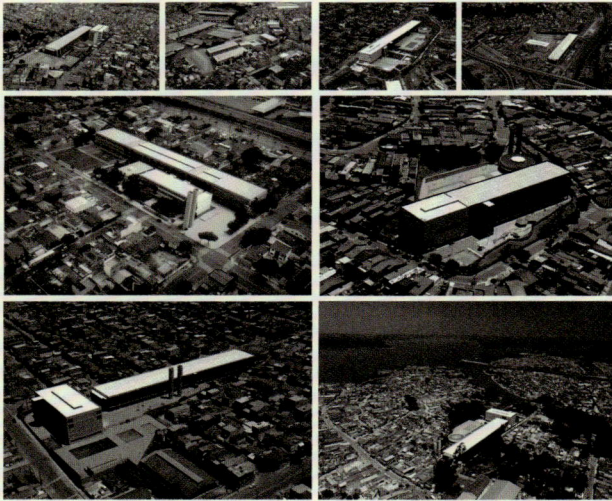

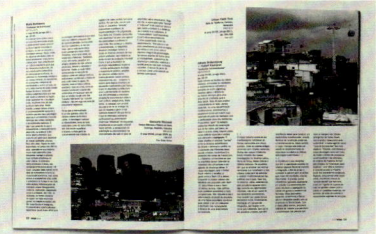

1 "Arena do Morro Gym sends
violence in Mãe Luiza crashing
down"
2 Project CEU (Unified
Educational Center),
investment in education
in São Paulo's peripheries
3 Una Arquitectos: Telêmaco
Melges School, São Paulo
4 Urban Think Tank:
Cable car network, Caracas
5 Torre David, Caracas:
Informal Vertical Communities

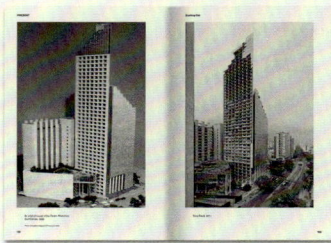

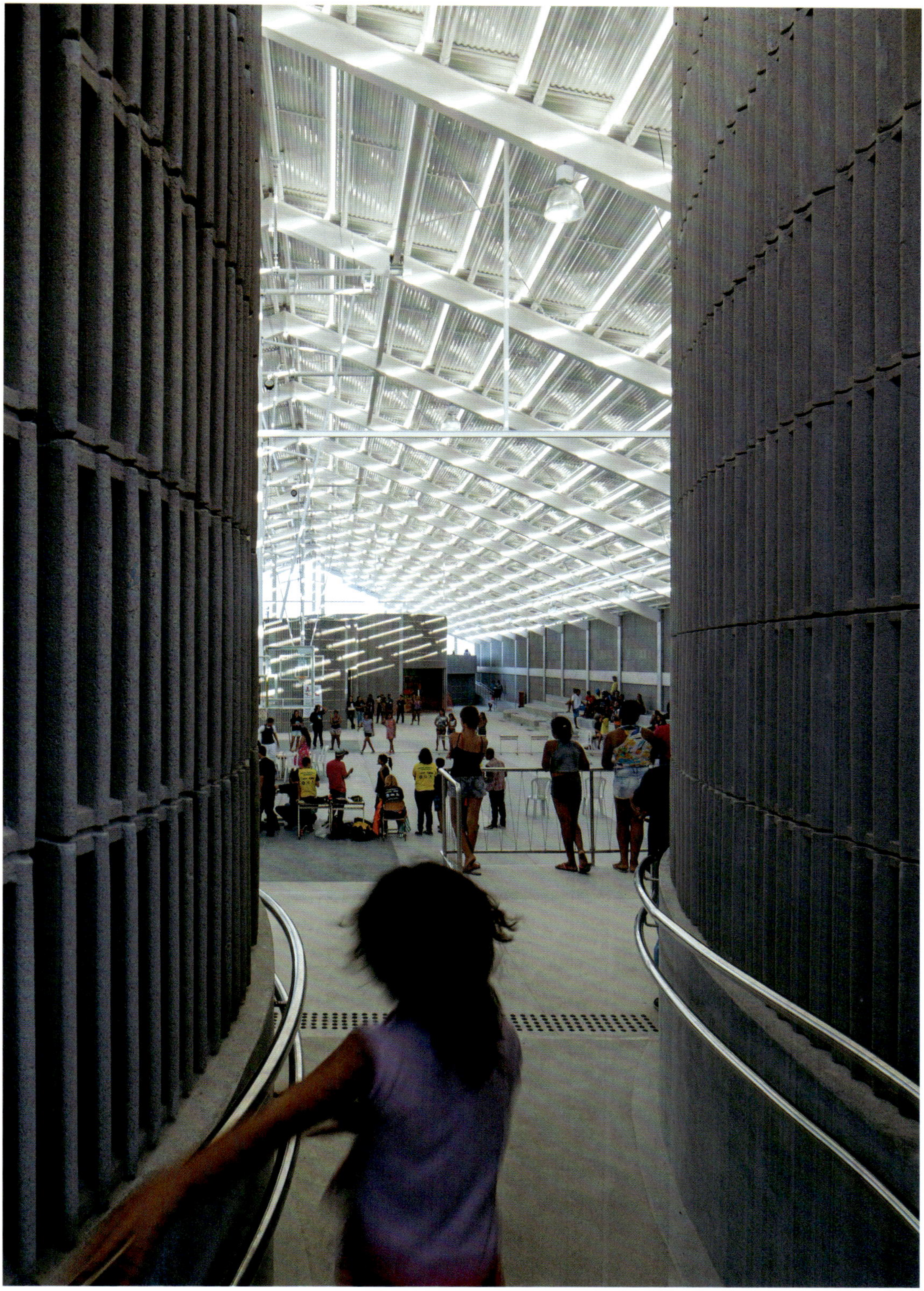

SESC 24 de Maio, São Paulo, Brazil (2017)
Paulo Mendes da Rocha + MMBB

A building in S. Paulo, inaugurated in 2017, which vertically aggregates programs that are usually not found together. The new SESC 24 de Maio has a theatre in the basement, and it stacks restaurants, a dental clinic, a library, a climbing wall, as well as a rooftop swimming pool, which overlooks the immense expanse of the city of S. Paulo. It is a form of civic centre that, in Brazil's context, took the form of the SESC in the private sector.

The SESC (Serviço Social do Comércio – Social Service of Commerce) is a non-profit institution, maintained by entrepreneurs of commerce, services, and tourism, with a view to giving its members a collective way of life (in the areas of Education, Health, Leisure, Culture and Medical Assistance), but it is open to the community as well. The SESC has a high point in the history of Brazil in the form of Lina Bo Bardi's project for the Pompéia neighbourhood of São Paulo, where the architect rehabilitates an old factory and adds new buildings to it. In the SESC of Paulo Mendes da Rocha and MMBB, the project transforms a mixed-use building in the centre of the city by inserting a new structure made up of four large concrete pillars that reinvent the basement spaces and allow for the pool on the roof.

With its free corners and urban views, the serial stacking of different programs and the vertical circulation through ramps offer an ever-changing relationship with the city, which culminates in discovering the top of the building. This project could be described as a set of covered piazzas that foster public life, and intensify meeting and sharing.

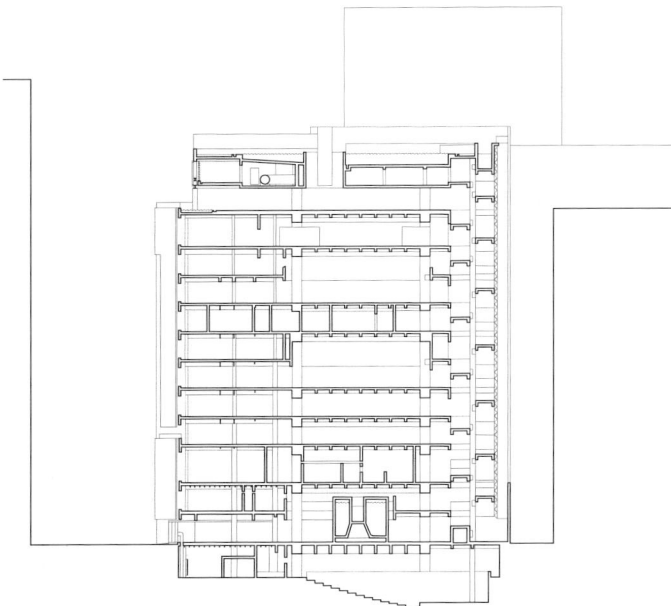

1 Lina Bo Bardi: SESC Pompeia, São Paulo
2 Herzog & de Meuron: 111 Lincoln Road, Miami
3 Urdi Arquitetura: São Luís College Sports Hall,
   São Paulo
4 G. Mattè Trucco:The Fiat Lingotto factory, Turin

REGULATORY POWER

The practice of democracy is still associated with an idea of control and social regulation. A fair balance between individual freedoms and collective interests has never been easy. There are also added interests that find in the absence or in excess of regulation an opportunity to exercise their power. So often does political discourse contradict statistical values and blackmail by fear to validate its excessive control. In the name of order and security, architectural firms specialized in the design of barriers, shielding, video surveillance systems, etc. began to emerge. We ask: Can architecture lessen or reverse an oppressive idea of regulatory power? Is there an emotional security in architecture? Can ports of entry offer a sense of hospitality and warmth?

1

2

3

4

American Institute of Architects (AIA): Prohibit the
design of spaces for killing, torture, and cruel,
inhuman or degrading treatment

Architects/Designers/Planners for Social Responsibility

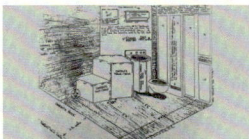

In 2011, United Nations bodies determined that long-term solitary
isolation is a form of torture or cruel, inhuman, and degrading
treatment prohibited by international law, and made special
reference to the United States use of supermax prisons and
juvenile solitary confinement as violations. All international
human rights bodies have also long included abolition of the

5

1 Ilona Gaynor: Objection!!! "A contemporary court of law is a literal demonstration
of legal-theatre"
2 Weinmiller Architekten: Justizzentrum, Aachen
3 Hohensinn Architektur: Leoben Judicial Complex

Mariposa Land Port of Entry, Nogales, Arizona, USA (2014)
Jones Studio

When social and economic asymmetries are extreme between neighbouring countries, the border becomes the focus of tension. Transposing this line does not only mean moving from one territory to another, but also ensuring a livelihood and aspiring to a widely-publicised way of life and exported as a veritable dream-come-true. Donald Trump's promise to complete the existing wall on the US-Mexico border is the most visible recent expression of this issue, but it is not an isolated and distant affair. We need only think of the recently completed walls between Turkey and Syria, in Bulgaria, on the border of Calais, in Ceuta, between Greece and Macedonia, between Israel and Palestine, etc. This control point of the border crossing between Mexico and the United States, established in the 1970s, was the object of important improvement works, in order to ease the experience of crossing the border. Renovated by the architect Eddie Jones (Jones Studio), the border post is surrounded by green spaces, has canopies that allow rainwater collection, large glass surfaces and artistic interventions evoking migratory movements. It is through this door that about 40% of the trade between the two countries passes by truck, as well as a huge amount of workers coming in by car, on foot or by bicycle. At a time when walls are erected, this piece of architecture focuses on the door – in what unites the two sides of the border, rather than on what separates them.

The General Services Administration of the United States of America denied permission for graphic material concerning this project to be published, citing security issues.

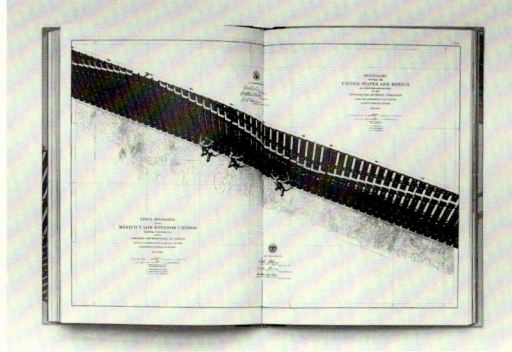

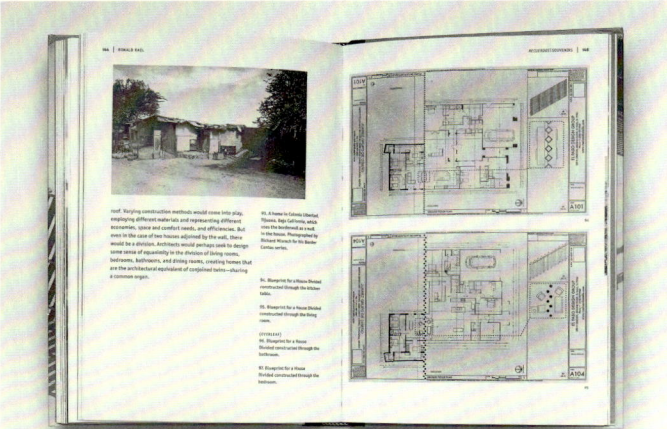

PASSAGE

Passage is a large, sculptural shade structure designed for the Mariposa Land Port of Entry in Nogales, on the border of Arizona and Mexico. It depicts the abstracted topography of an inverted mountain range, its craggy peaks pointing down. The piece was inspired by my deep connection to the Arizona landscape, as well as the dramatic mountain passages that frame the otherwise flat terrain of the Southwest. Passage takes its shape from the nearby Baboquivari Mountains, which run north-south across the border. For millennia, mountain ranges have served as important navigational landmarks for both people and animals. They surround and direct the flow of human population throughout this seemingly perilous environment. To evoke this sense of migration, I affixed a pathway of colored acrylic markers across the artwork's metallic landscape. These markers also reference the daily passage of travelers through the port facility. The dynamic play of shadows cast by the artwork and the light filtering through and bouncing off its aluminum surface create ever-changing experiences for those

1

2

3

4

3   R. Rael, V. San Fratello: Borderland Dreams
5   Ronald Rael: House Divided

5

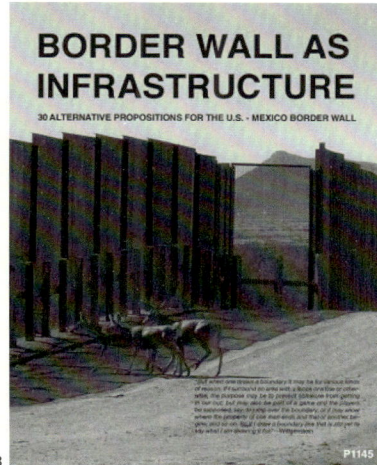

BORDER WALL AS INFRASTRUCTURE

30 ALTERNATIVE PROPOSITIONS FOR THE U.S. - MEXICO BORDER WALL

P1145

In silence, pope remembers those who cross Mexican-U.S. border

Posted on February 17, 2016 by Administrator1

Pope Francis prays at a cross on the border with El Paso, Texas, before celebrating Mass at the fairgrounds in Ciudad Juarez, Mexico, Feb. 17. (CNS/Paul Haring)

1 Surfing the U.S. – Mexico Border Fence
4 Melilla Border (Morocco-Spain)
5 Office KGDVS: Border Crossing, Anapra

Cologne–Bonn Airport Terminal 2, Germany (2000)
Helmut Jahn

Traveling by plane usually goes hand in hand with stress: the anxiety of arriving in time, the fear of flying, or the fatigue of commuters in a world where business is increasingly independent of geography. Safety rules for travellers are becoming more restrictive and, in an airport that receives around 10 million passengers per year, passenger control occupies a significant part of the time and space at an airport. There is a contradiction between the contemporary informality of airplane travel and the control and time involved.

Cologne-Bonn is one of these transitional places, a huge warehouse between fast trains, road transit and air transport. In this vacant territory between cities, the new terminal designed by Helmut Jahn is generous in its large areas with natural lighting and ventilation.

If, for each trip, a passenger spends about 2 hours confined in an airport, the design of the space can contribute to decrease tension and sense of claustrophobia. The project model thus seeks to replicate the qualities of the public space by using sophisticated constructive devices, with an aim to minimise visual impact, almost to disappear: slender metallic support elements, large spans, glass walls and roofs.

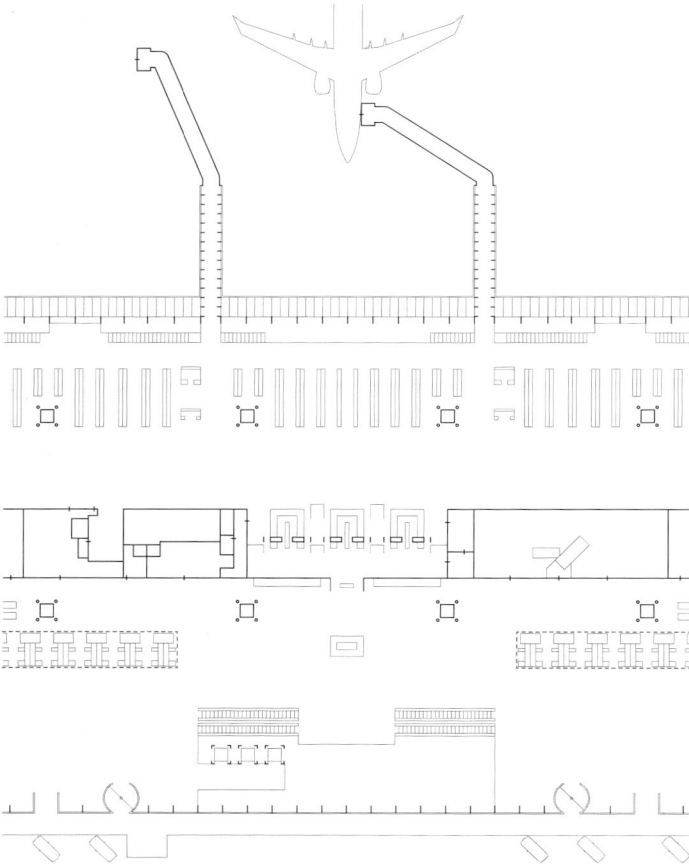

2   Defense and Airport Architecture
3   Milimiter wave scanner. Security utopia /distopia

PLAN

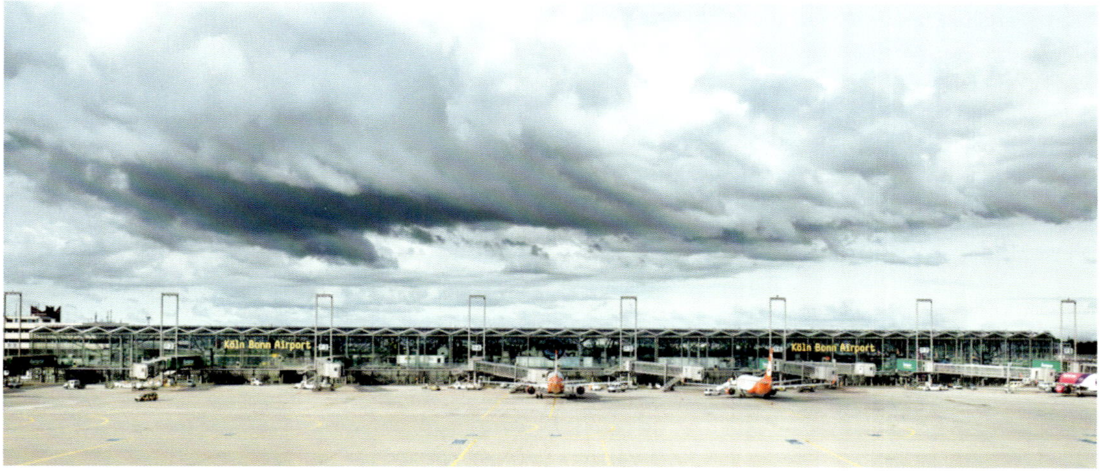
Köln Bonn Airport
Köln Bonn Airport

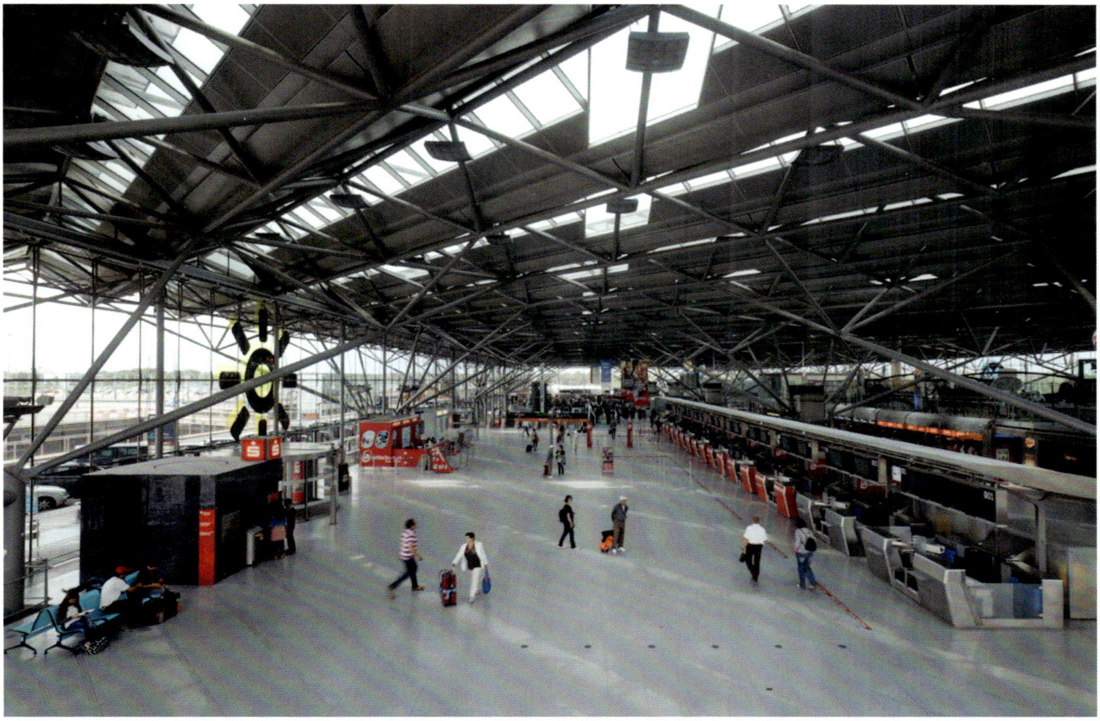

Cruise Terminal, Lisbon, Portugal (2010- ongoing)
João Luís Carrilho da Graça

Despite the increasing and more accessible international transit of people, we have also witnessed, since September 11, a sort of civilizational backwardness regarding the inspection of the points of entry and exit of countries that once thought themselves at peace. In the city of Lisbon, where urban transformations are fuelled by the growing influx of tourists, the presence of colossal cruise ships on the riverfront is clearly changing the city's image. Lisbon has always been a port city, but it lives between the contradiction of favouring cargo and passenger transport and the improvement of the public spaces connecting the city to the river. The future Cruise Terminal has thus a dual function: a powerful control device, but also a new and elegant port of the city, boosting the improvement of the gardens and public spaces in its surroundings. The building's layout, with exterior access ramps, stairs with views to the gardens and an exterior terrace facing the hill, immediately puts the visitor in touch with the city. With regard to this building, it is important to reflect on the possibility of architecture being able to respond simultaneously to global impositions and local needs; of the possibility of favouring a function like tourism, not just a form of consumption and misrepresentation of the culture and the urban landscape – the so-called *Disneyfication* –, but being able to reciprocate, improving the quality of life of permanent city-dwellers.

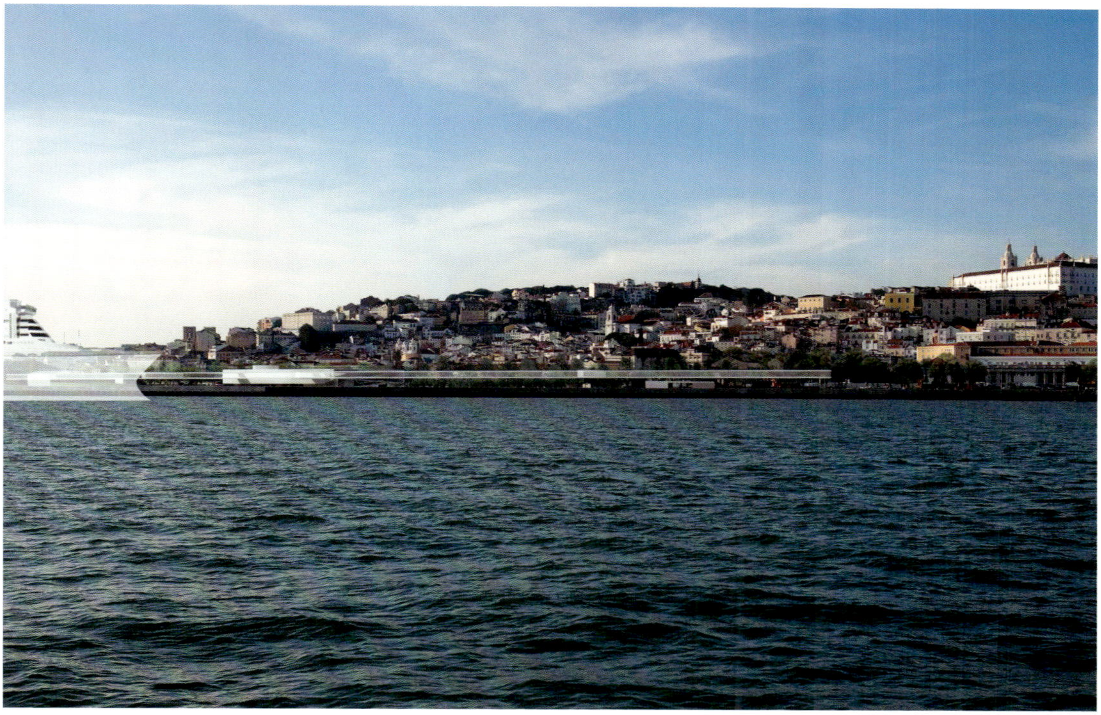

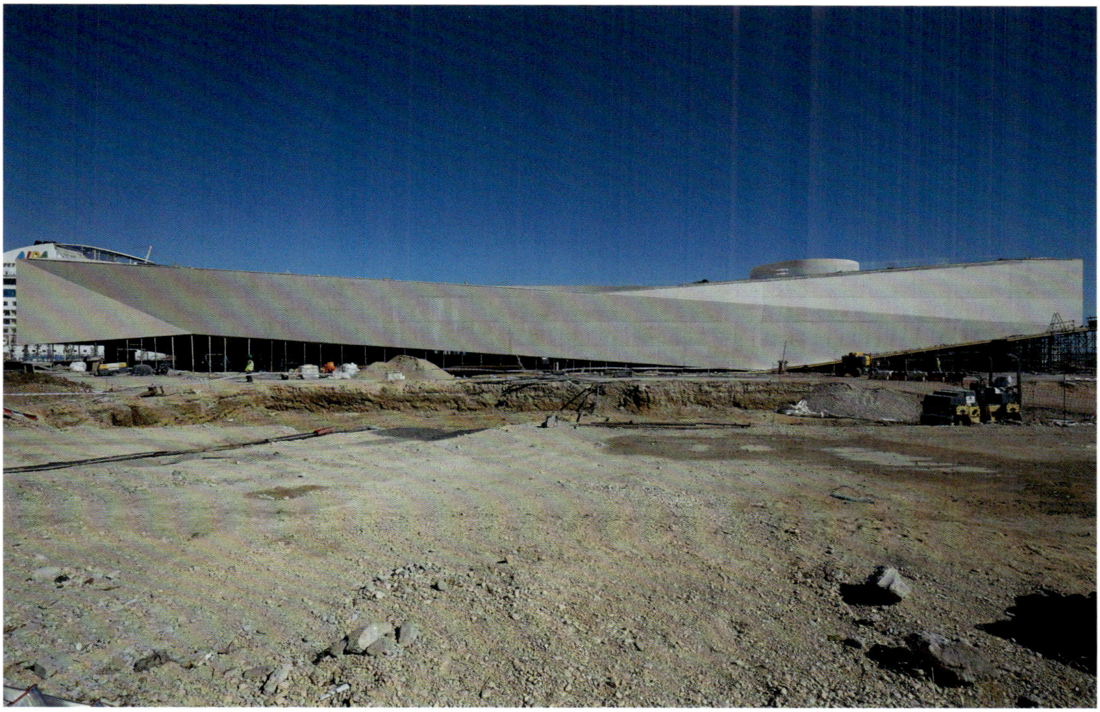

1

Lifestyle

SEP 29, 2016 @ 07:05 PM 98,475 ●

Venice Is Fed Up With Cruise Ships And Angry Protesters Are Blocking Them

● ❶ ◉ ⓘ ⑧

Cecília Rodriguez, CONTRIBUTOR
FULL BIO ∨

Opinions expressed by Forbes Contributors are their own.

TWEET THIS

🐦 UNESCO, in fact, warned the Italian government in July that if the country fails to resolution urging the city to implement the "prohibition of the largest ships and tankers" from Venice's lagoon by 2017, the organization will place it on the list of endangered heritage sites, along with 38 other locations mainly in Africa and Asia.

🐦 According to local officials and observers, the relations between tourists and locals have reached a new low.

Venice, which this year logged a new low of fewer than 55,000 inhabitants—down from 164,000 in 1931 - registers up to 30,000 cruise ship passengers tramping through the small, ancient city *per day* during peak season.

A massive cruise ship dwarfs Venice as it pulls into town. Photo: World Monument Fund

2

The total of visitors per year is calculated to be almost 22 million, an overwhelming number considering the size of the fragile, salt-corroded city, which has long required constant attention to keep it from sinking, literally.

City breaks
On the radar

First Venice and Barcelona: now anti-tourism marches spread across Europe

Demos in San Sebastián and crackdowns in Rome and Dubrovnik as locals vent frustration at city-breakers and cruise ships

● ❶ ✉ ●●●

≺
33k 1,001

Will Coldwell

🐦 @will_coldwell

Thursday 10 August 2017
06.30 BST

ⓘ Cruise ship visitors on the streets of Dubrovnik, where cameras now monitor the numbers of people in the old town. Photograph: muckylucky/Guardian Witness

3

PIRES DE LIMA | Ministro da Economia

Três ministros na inauguração de estrutura do Porto de Leixões

TELEJORNAL
20:20

4

1 J. L. Carrilho da Graça: "I'm not afraid of the Cruise
   Terminal becoming the symbol of the Lisbon of tourists."
4 L. P. Silva: Cruise Terminal, Matosinhos
5 OMA Office: Hamburg Science Center

5

Svalbard Global Seed Vault (2008)
Peter W. Søderman / Statsbygg

Hidden within a 130-foot-high mountain, in a location permanently covered with ice, the Seed Bank's presence is made known only by a door, in a volume of reinforced concrete and glass – the rest of the structure unfolds in three large underground vaults, more than 100m inside the earth. The site's natural conditions – permanent very low temperatures, protection from seismic activity and possible military attacks – guarantee the usefulness of what has since 2008 been one of the largest reserves of plant species in the world. The value of this reserve could be decisive in securing the planet's biodiversity, as well as the replenishing and planting of areas critical to humanity's survival that have been devastated by war or natural causes.

This is a facility for an extreme, post-apocalyptic scenario, but the need to resort to seed reserves during the conflict in Syria suggests that its usefulness may become more commonplace.

The architectural expression of the building is barely evident. We are talking about a bunker meant to be impregnable and with an absolutely controlled environment, capable of operating autonomously (thanks to the cold climate of the region) for several decades or, with additional cooling, for hundreds or thousands of years, depending on the resistance of different species. Only the door with its ornate stained glass window, which becomes a bright lantern during the region's long winter nights, seems to have been worthy of careful design, a piece of art by Dyveke Sanne entitled *Perpetual Repercussion*. As if the last survivor of Earth could be guided by its light to find the last stronghold of civilization.

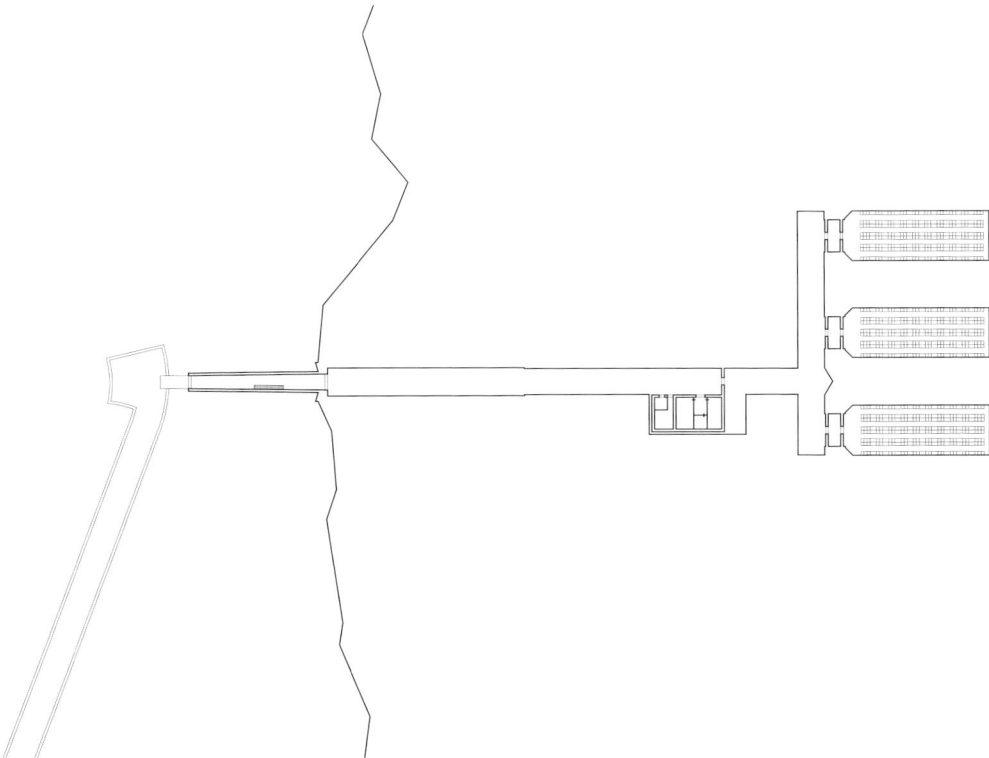

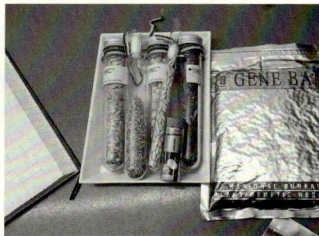

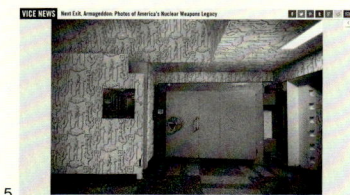

2   Seed bag for deposit at the Svalbard Global Seed Vault
3   A.H. Williams: Turrets, Cockley Cley
4   Underground Radioactive Waste Warning on Plot M, Chicago
5   Greenbrier Bunker. Houses the U.S.A. Congress in the aftermath of a nuclear holocaust.

What's Inside the Swiss Secret, Underground Data Center Bunkers?

Oh, God... what's in there?

1

2

3

2   Albert France-Lanord Architects: Pionen, Stockholm
3   Facebook Data Center, Oregon

TECHNOLOGICAL POWER

With the vague promise of making work easier, technology is transforming our daily lives: the relationships between people, between people and their activities, and between people and objects. Technology has become ubiquitous. In architecture, technology is radically transforming the methodologies of conception and representation of the project, but also construction itself, and the experience of the building. In projects, the increase of technological specialties mirrors this new reality, and seems to push Architecture into merely aesthetic issues, as if these were not ultimately achieved through a general coordination of the project. Expressions such as "smart home" or "home automation" have become commonplace and familiar, but, beyond any mercantile opportunism, how do the connections of power between architecture and technology reveal themselves? What are the relations between technology and form? What does Architecture require of robotization? Is there still room for low technology?

Tua Dam Building, Portugal (2012- ongoing)
Eduardo Souto de Moura

Architecture is often seen as being on the opposite side of nature, transforming it irreversibly. The Douro Vinhateiro, a world heritage site, is hailed as if it were another natural phenomenon when, in reality, it is a highly altered landscape, extensively marked by the successive technologies of cultivation. Dams like the Tua Dam, undeniably a factor of tension in the landscape and ecosystems, are at the centre of the contemporary debate between seemingly antagonistic values: concrete and green, culture and progress, etc. A more controversial topic, since its operation can already be done remotely, thus failing to promote the creation of small communities of technicians as it had happened since the mid-twentieth century. As a way to mediate this discussion, between technological and cultural powers, architects and artists were called to intervene in these dichotomous environments, as a way of rethinking their visual identity.

The design of the support building of the Tua Dam, designed by Eduardo Souto de Moura, can be seen as a project of complicity between architecture and engineering where the technical elements – the equipment of energy transformation and transport, spillways and floodgates, ventilation shafts, pathways, water storage and the Observation and Control Point – appear as a strict composition carefully laid out on the landscape.

1   P. Cabrita Reis: Bemposta Dam
2   E. Mini + C. Metz: Cloud Foundation
3   Serôdio, Furtado: Douro 41 Hotel (photomontage)
4/5 C. Rebelo +T. Pimentel: Côa Museum

1   Serôdio, Furtado: Douro 41 Hotel
2/3 Fránek Architects: Dolní Morava tower
4   Close to Bone: Vlooyberg Tower
5   E. Souto de Moura: Robinson Space auditorium
6/7 People's Architecture Office: Tubular Living

125

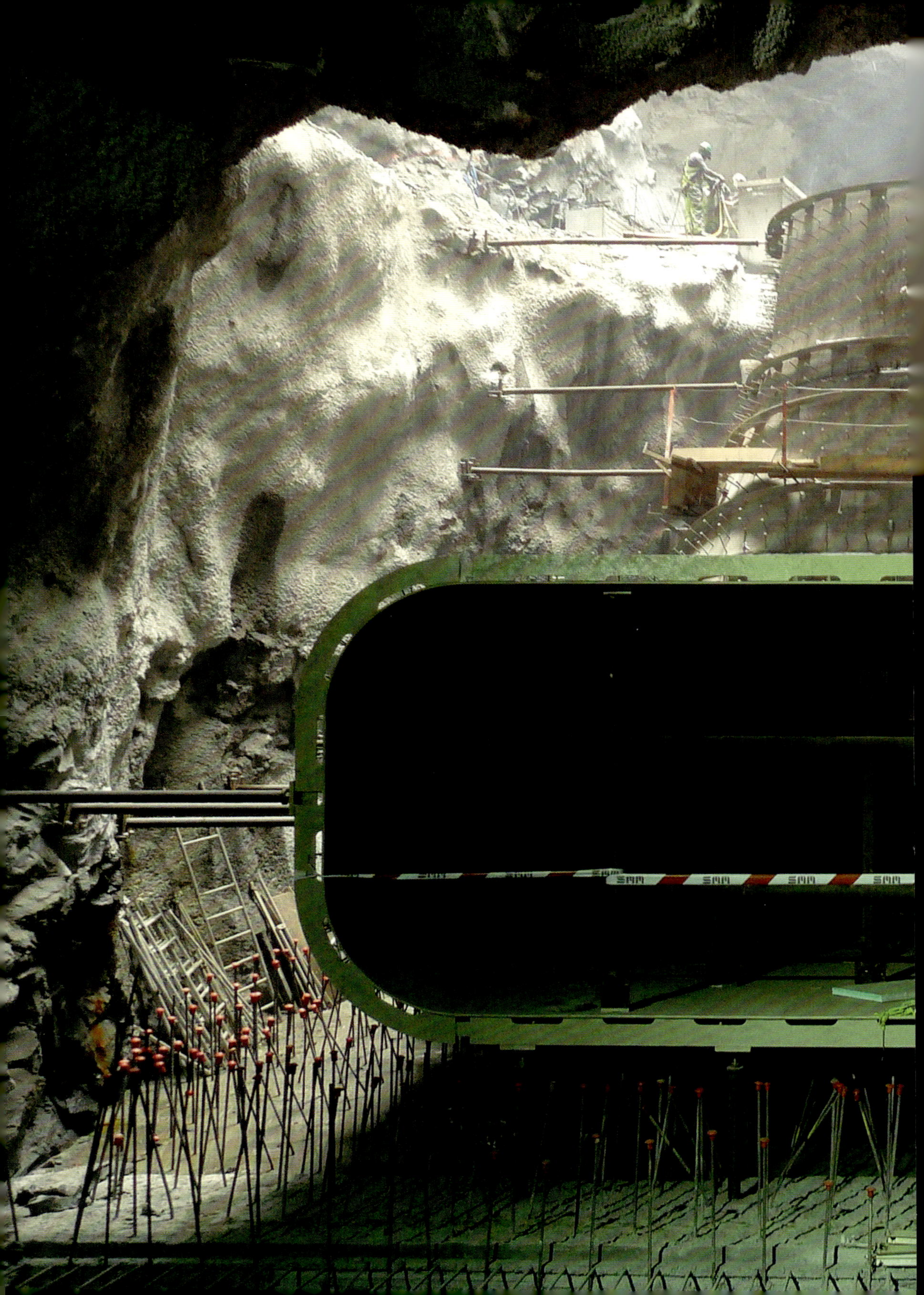
SMM

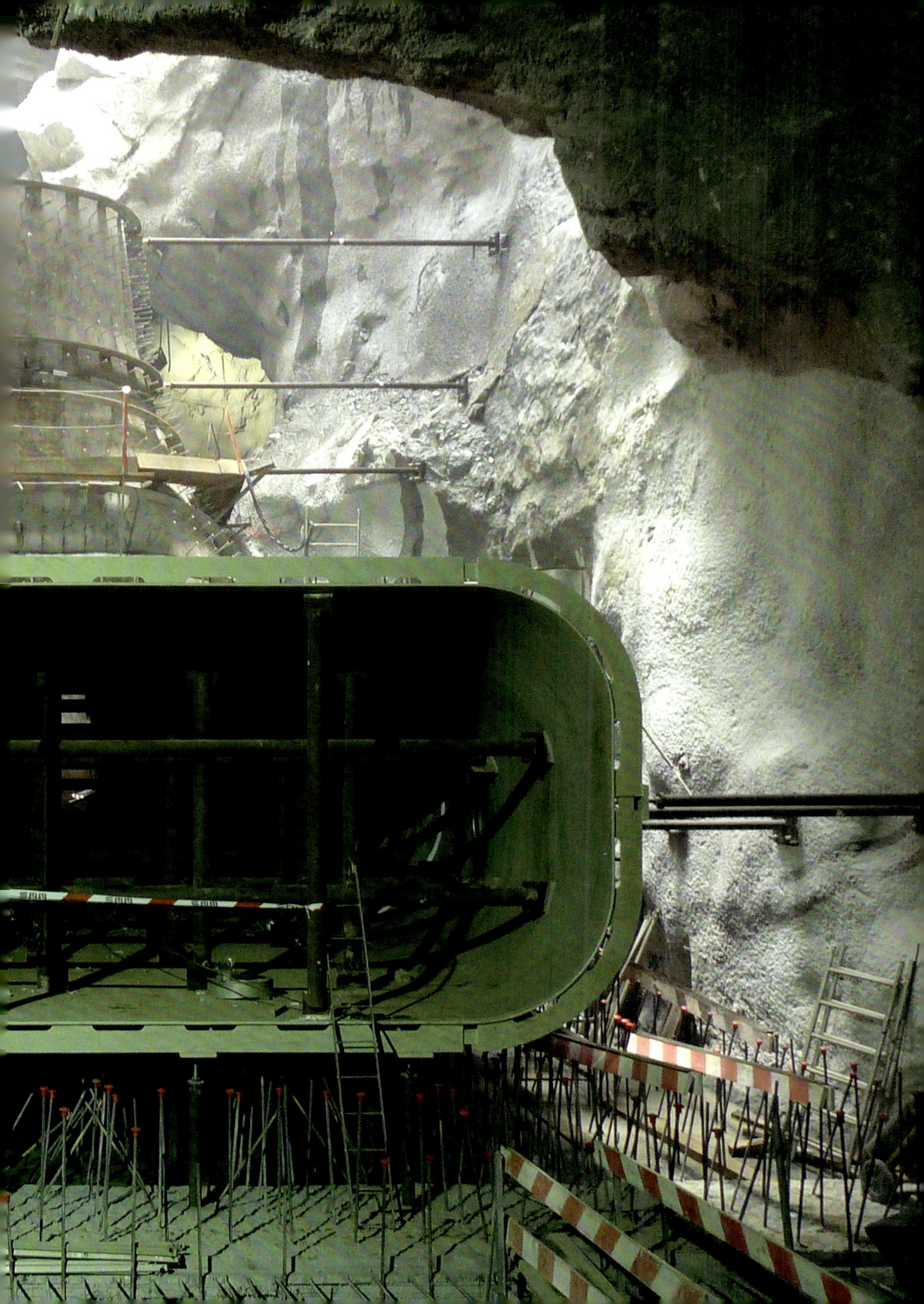

Fovam Ter Subway Station, Budapest, Hungary (2014)
Sporaarchitects

The Budapest metro line is the oldest in continental Europe, but not the largest. To better serve the territory, a new extension has recently been inaugurated, linking the south of Buda to the centre of Pest. Sporaarchitects was commissioned to think about the design of two twin stations on the M4 line on the Danube river bank. Buried at a depth of about eight floors, it was necessary to construct an enclosed concrete box intersected by cross beams to overcome the load's horizontal pressure. Its functional logic notwithstanding, the design of this shoring structure does not lack a poetic form. The network metaphor emerges as a hidden, coded order because the beams appear to be placed at random, intersecting this shaft at different angles and heights. The spatial experience of traversing this entanglement on a mechanical stairs is unique. It is an image of the future that contrasts with the historic 19th century city above. Investing in the spatial quality of the stations, penetrated in depth by natural light, is meant to draw more people to public transportation, but also to foster an "alternative city" with its own qualities, not just a place of passage.

In these types of brief, engineering often controls the operations, to the point where it defines the space's final characteristics, appearing at the end of the architectural design as remedial. In this case, we are clearly faced with an example of a balance between the two disciplines from the outset – allowing the aesthetic sense that constructive tech can offer to emerge from the depth of the subsoil.

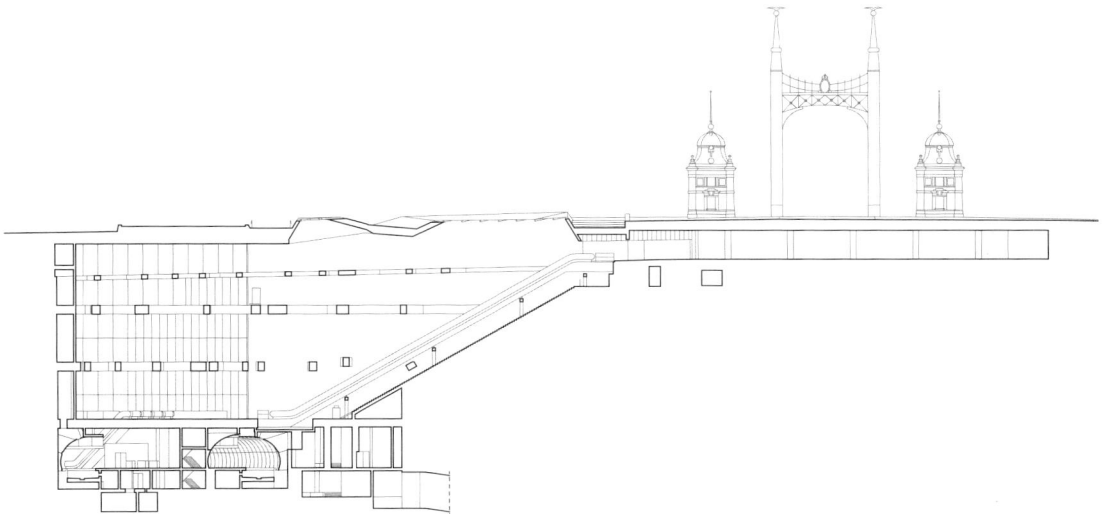

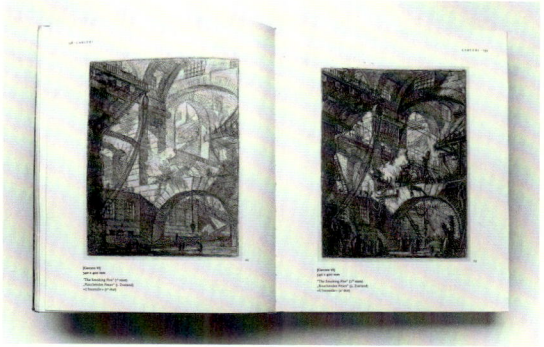

1

2

3

1   Yona Frieman: The "umbrella" of Les Halles
2   G. B. Piranesi: Prison
3   Digging Fovam Ter Underground Station
4   Bone Interior Structure

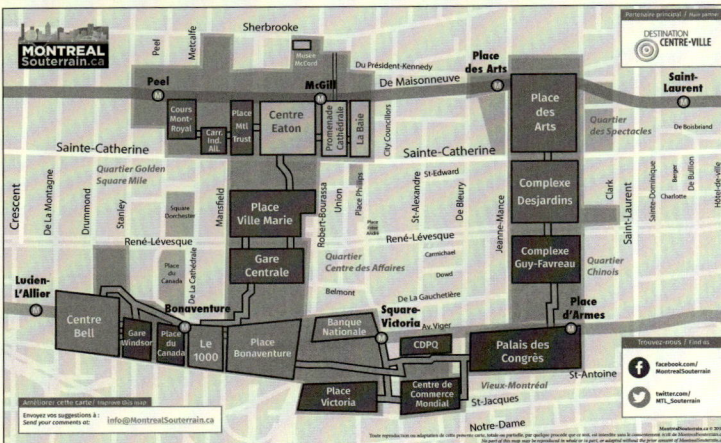

1 OMA: Souterrain Tram Tunnel, Haia
2 Montreal Souterrain
3 M. Figueira, P. F. Vieira, C. Azevedo: Inverted Tower, Dubai
4 M. Figueira, P. F. Vieira, C. Azevedo: Samarra Minaret, Iraq
  (Iraque)

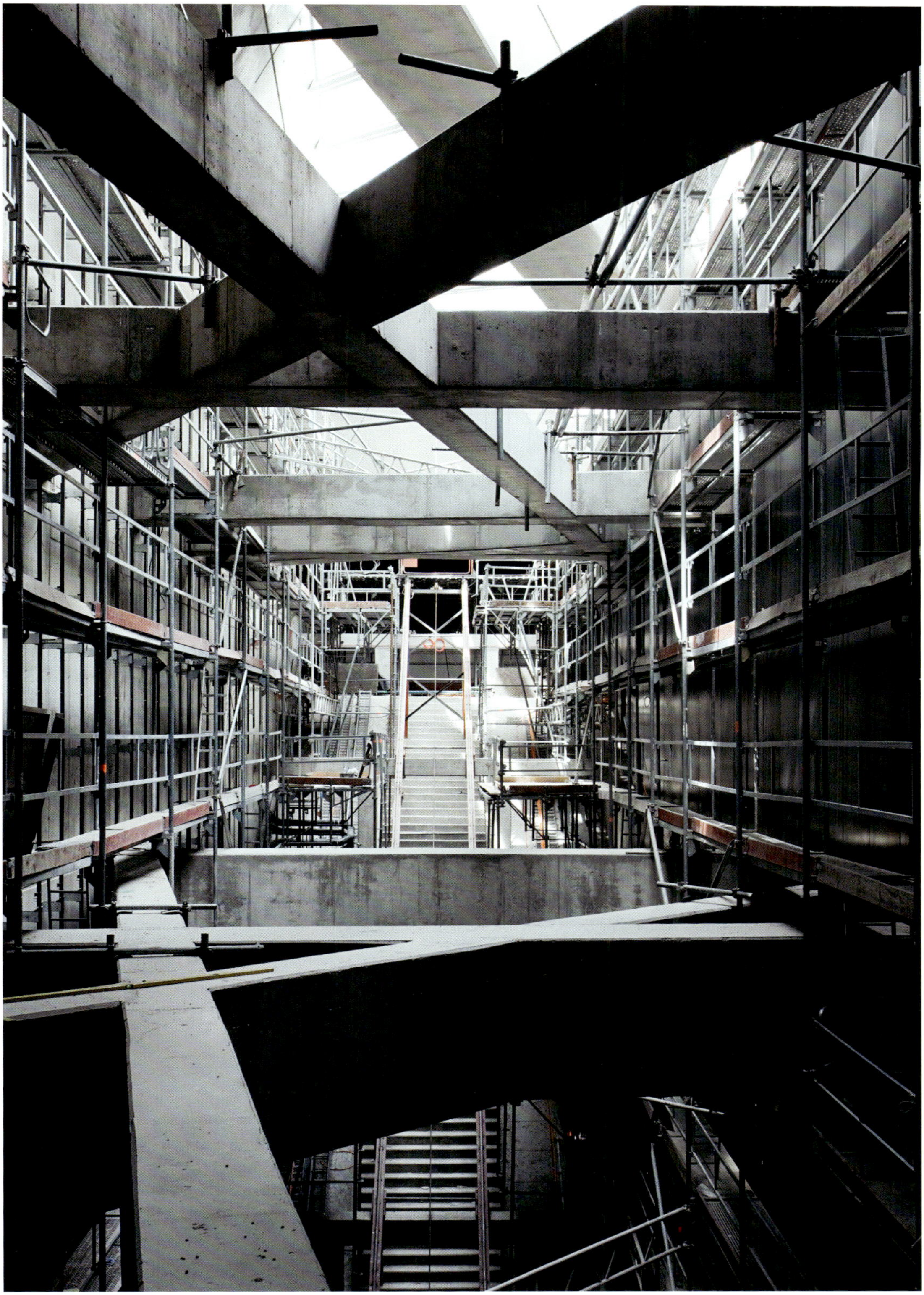

Winery Gantenbein, Flash, Switzerland (2008)
Gramazio & Kohler + Bearth & Deplazes

Wine production is an age-old practice. It is not always easy to remember that it is a highly technological process which causes profound transformations in the landscape and requires a quasi-laboratory level of control, from the selection and refinement of grape varieties to their transformation into precious nectar. It is therefore not inappropriate that the building of this wine cellar has been built with sophisticated methods of robotic manufacturing, which allow it to breathe a new life and meaning to the ancestral material that is ceramic brick. Leading technologies are usually developed in laboratory environments. In this case, the robotic brick laying process, which defies the artisanal dimension to which this material is associated, was conceived at the ETH in Zurich. The architects were entrusted with the job of giving expression and taking advantage of this technology. On the one hand, the brick draws a three-dimensional decorative pattern with a rigor and economy of means that would have been impossible to obtain manually. On the other hand, the interval between each of the multiple pieces produces a massive and impermeable effect when viewed from the outside, but it allows for a surprising, although controlled, amount of light and air into the interior, suitable for the production of wine. The success of digital construction processes, heralded as the future of construction, depends on both technological innovation and the inventiveness of architects.

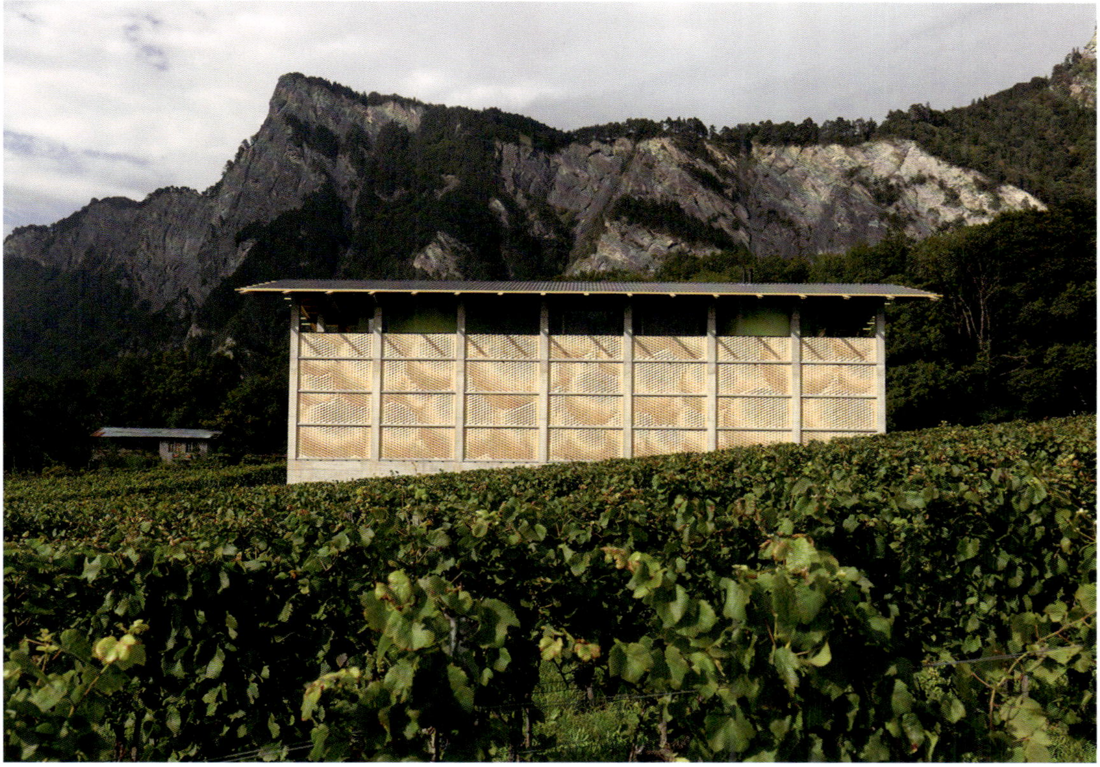

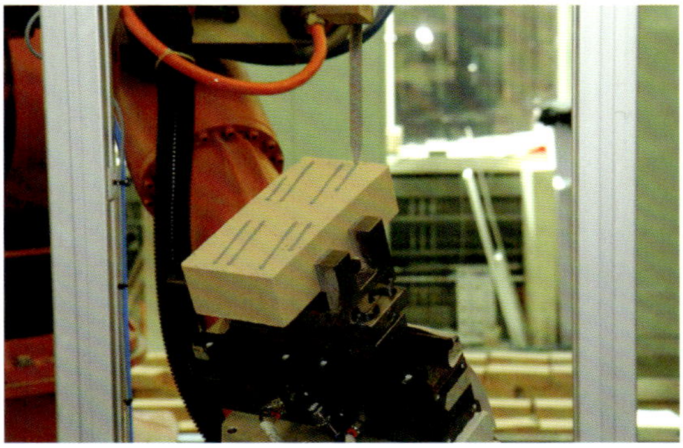

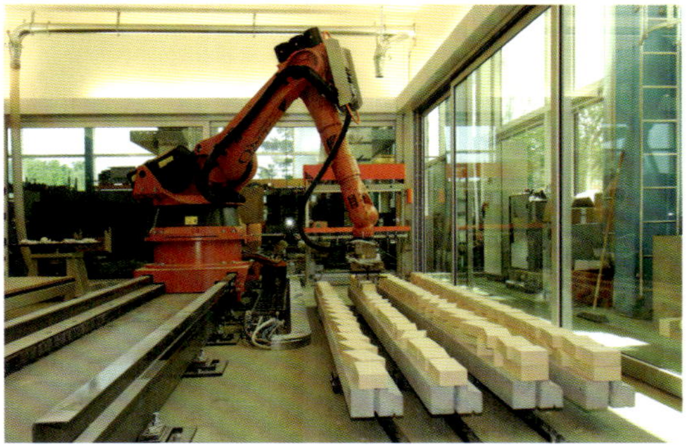

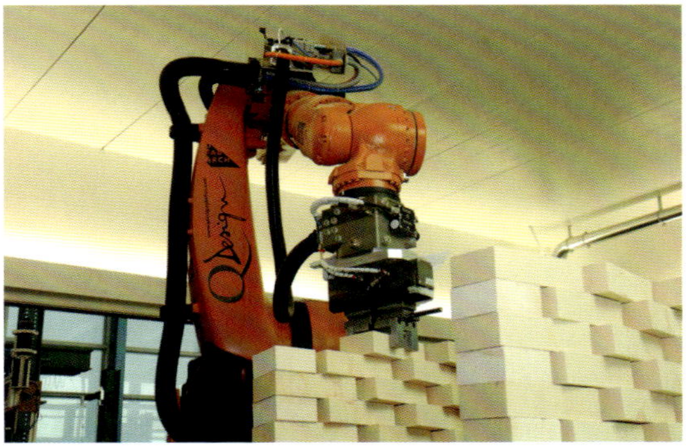

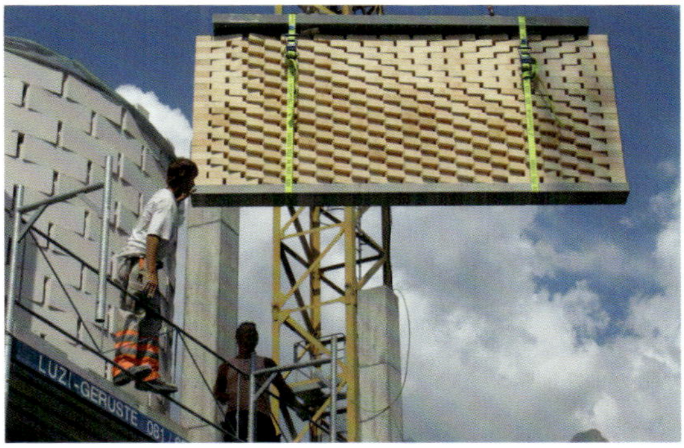
LUZI-GERUSTE 081

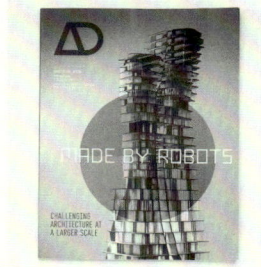

1 W.J. Mitchell: Computer-Aided Architectural Design
2 Three-dimensional CAD model and corresponding
   NC-milled foam model.
4/5 Mediated Matter Group: Silk Pavillion
6 Gramazio & Kohler Group: Aerial Construction
7 Chuck Hoberman: Expanding Sphere and Iris Dome
8 Shoei Yoh: Municipal Sports Complex, Odawara, Japan

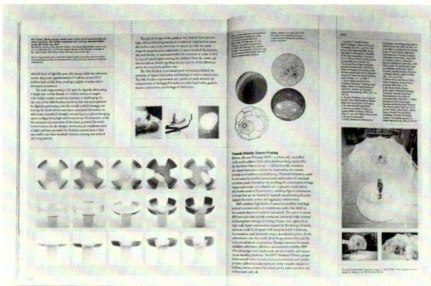

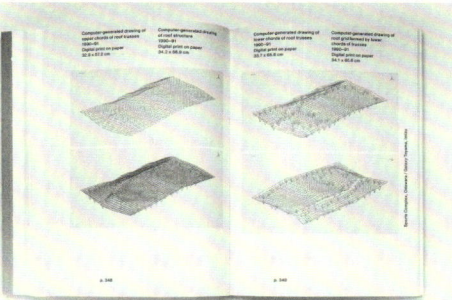

Data-Center, Covilhã, Portugal (2013)
João Luís Carrilho da Graça

Hidden but omnipresent, the information that runs on fibre-optic cables or the air on radio signals is absolutely fundamental to our daily lives. PT's Data-Center is one of the few visible faces on the web. It is an architectural artefact of high technical performance and, simultaneously, a possible image of an immaterial reality. If, formally, the construction has a symbolic dimension – an abstract cube reflected in a mirror of water, punctually immersed in the mist –, the literal representation of the "cloud"; materially, it responds to its enormous energetic and security demands in an effective maner. The data stored in buildings of this type are considered a precious asset in our society: the technological system

of surveillance and access control, barbed wire, the lake and the moat are ways to bar access to unwanted intruders. But the factor that most threatens data storage is the computer equipment overheating and the continuous supply of electricity. What appears to be a massive, windowless, impassable cube is actually an air-permeable volume, hiding in the apparent elementality of its form a series of redundant systems of energy generation and system cooling. This building is, therefore, a double contribution from Architecture: simultaneously being able to give visual expression to an immaterial entity, and contributing to improve the operation of highly demanding technologies.

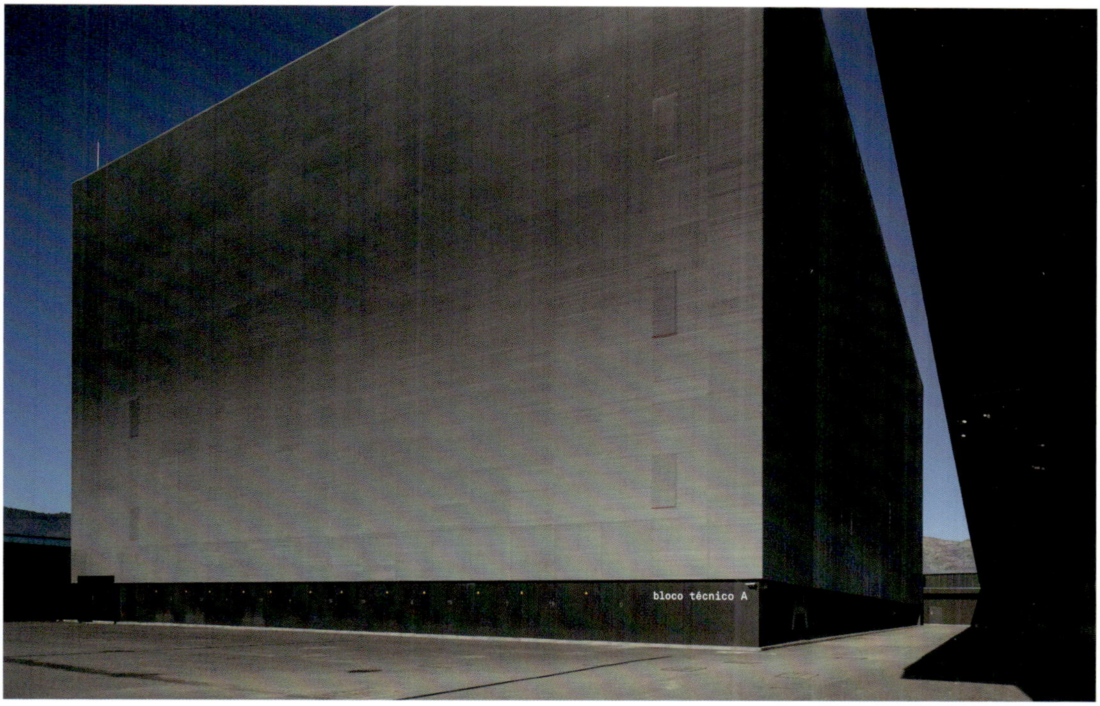
bloco técnico A

Smithsonian.com

ART   BOOKS   DESIGN   FOOD   MUSIC & FILM   VIDEO   NEWSLETTER

Decoding The City: The Road Graffiti Placed by Utility Workers

These infrastructural lines mark the pathways of pipes and wires beneath the paved surface — but what does each color mean?

By Jimmy Stamp
SMITHSONIAN.COM
APRIL 26, 2013

Infrastructural graffiti in the streets of New Haven, CT (original photo)

1 FFBK Architekten, Jauslin, Stebler AG:
   Datacube, Münchenstein
2 Diller and Scofidio+Renfro: Blur Building,
   Yverdon-les-Bains
3 Blur Building, Detail

4 Ralph Walker: Western Union Building, New York
5 One Wilshire Data Center & Telecom Center, Los Angeles
7 Worldwide network of submarine fiber optic cables

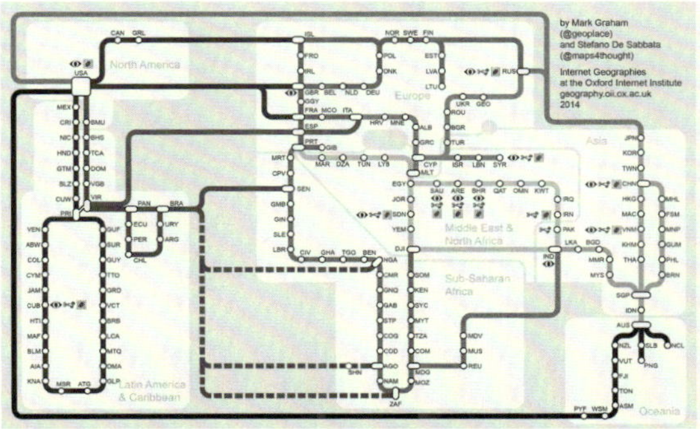

Mauli de Seram House, Colombo, Sri Lanka (2000)
Vijitha Basnayaka

It is in the details that the value of this house makes itself known, based on an economic and structured commitment to the idea of reusing constructive elements, revisiting a common practice of Buddhist culture and current construction in Sri Lanka. The use of natural pigments, aged wood, the roughness of the different bricks, the iron grating, the earth floor, or even the corrugated zinc plate (all materials that could be extracted from a slum) acquire an unexpected dignity here. In this context, the formal execution project gives rise to a careful selection process of materials to be reused and of detail in construction (with a great degree of rigour), in intense dialogue with the builders and clients.

This option implies a clear, though formally open, project structure. The elements are organized in an apparent free form, under the zinc cover which guarantees the unity of the whole.

The sense of comfort in this house stems from its relationship with the garden, worked topographically so as to elevate the living space. This relationship between interior and exterior is effectively organic, with no room for boundaries or limits. Even the street elevation, the more complex one in the house, is still open. With dirt pavements entering the building, with the zinc cover running through the garden or with protruding stones to serve as a foundation, the Sri Lankan architect Vijitha Basnayaka has achieved, with this "windowless house", a sophisticated and complex spatiality, based on simple and accessible technologies, which support local work and are environmentally friendly.

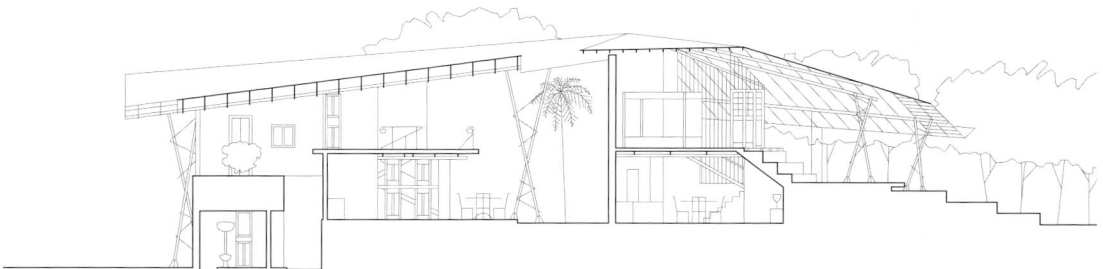

1   Trade in reused building materials, Sri Lanka
2   Re-using wooden railway sleepers, Sri Lanka
3   Habit of St. Francis of Assisi, Church of St. Francis, Arezzo. Material reduction culture
4   Buddhist *kesa* robe. Material reuse culture

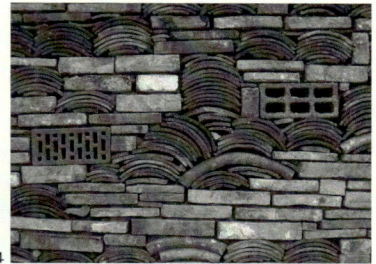

1 Aldo Andreani: La Roccheta, Bosisio
2 Glass House, Freetown Christiania, Copenhagen
3 F. Cheval: Palais Idéal, Hauterives
4 Wang Shu: Ningbo History Museum, Jinzhou
5 Statue-menhir, 2nd millenium BC, Ponte da Barca
6 P. Moreira: House at the Rua dos Caldeireiros, Porto

ECONOMIC POWER

The economy and financial markets seem to have taken over the political space, calling into question the sovereignty of States. Complex cash flow systems shy away from tax and other fiscal responsibilities. But there seems to be no room for prosperity without credit or investment. The financial system made the words "debt" and "crisis" become part of our daily lives and made the economy extremely volatile. The real estate sector is symptomatic of mood swings in economic games, although it operates on the steady ownership and registration regimes provided by the States. How does Architecture participate in various aspects of the economy? What architectural specificities arise in the so-called *emerging* economies? How does Architecture respond to market dynamics? How does it currently shape workspaces? Can Architecture bring about other models of consumption, counteracting the uncritical repetition of corporate models and values?

Lubango Centre, Lubango, Angola (2014)
Promontório Arquitectos

The economic growth of "emerging" countries (as defined by the IMF) reveals, among other characteristics, the existence of a process of rural exodus and a consequent demographic pressure on urban centres. Lubango, in Angola, like many other African cities, has grown informally and outside any planning rule. The Lubango Centre project of the Promontório Arquitectos atelier is integrated in an urban strategy of densification of the city centre, an attempt to halt the peripheral growth of the city in the post-colonial period. The building stands out from its surrounding context through its height and invests, in addition, in a wide range of uses (trade, services and housing). On the ground floor it offers a pathway for public enjoyment, functioning as a covered commercial gallery, naturally ventilated, adapted to the Angolan climate.

With the growth of a middle class, it is also important "the idea of finally being able to build a simple building with a direct and civic relationship with the street, in latitudes that have accustomed us only to extremes; between private enclaves of great luxury, on the one hand, and the scarcity of humanitarian operations, on the other".

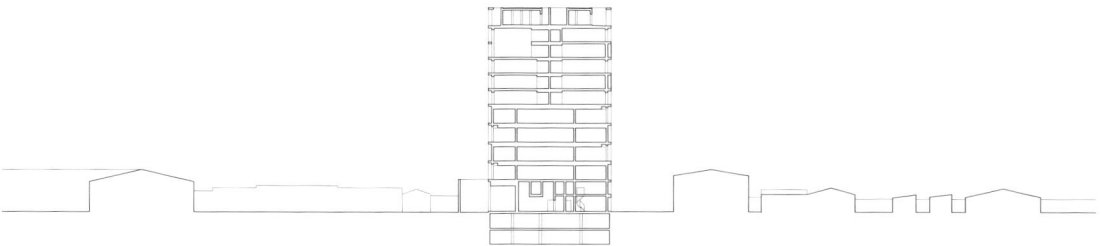

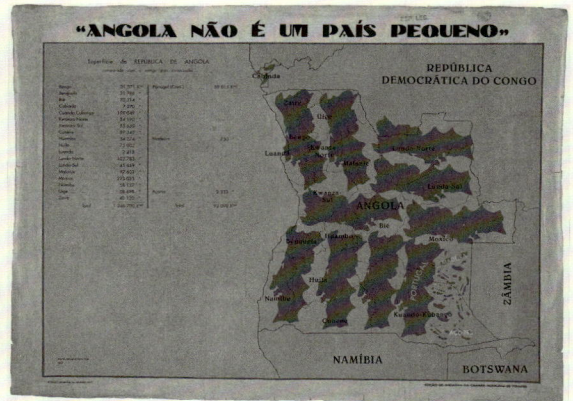

1 Lubango's Periphery Growth
2 Paulo Moreira: "Angola is not a small country"
3 Promontório: Latitude Building, Pemba

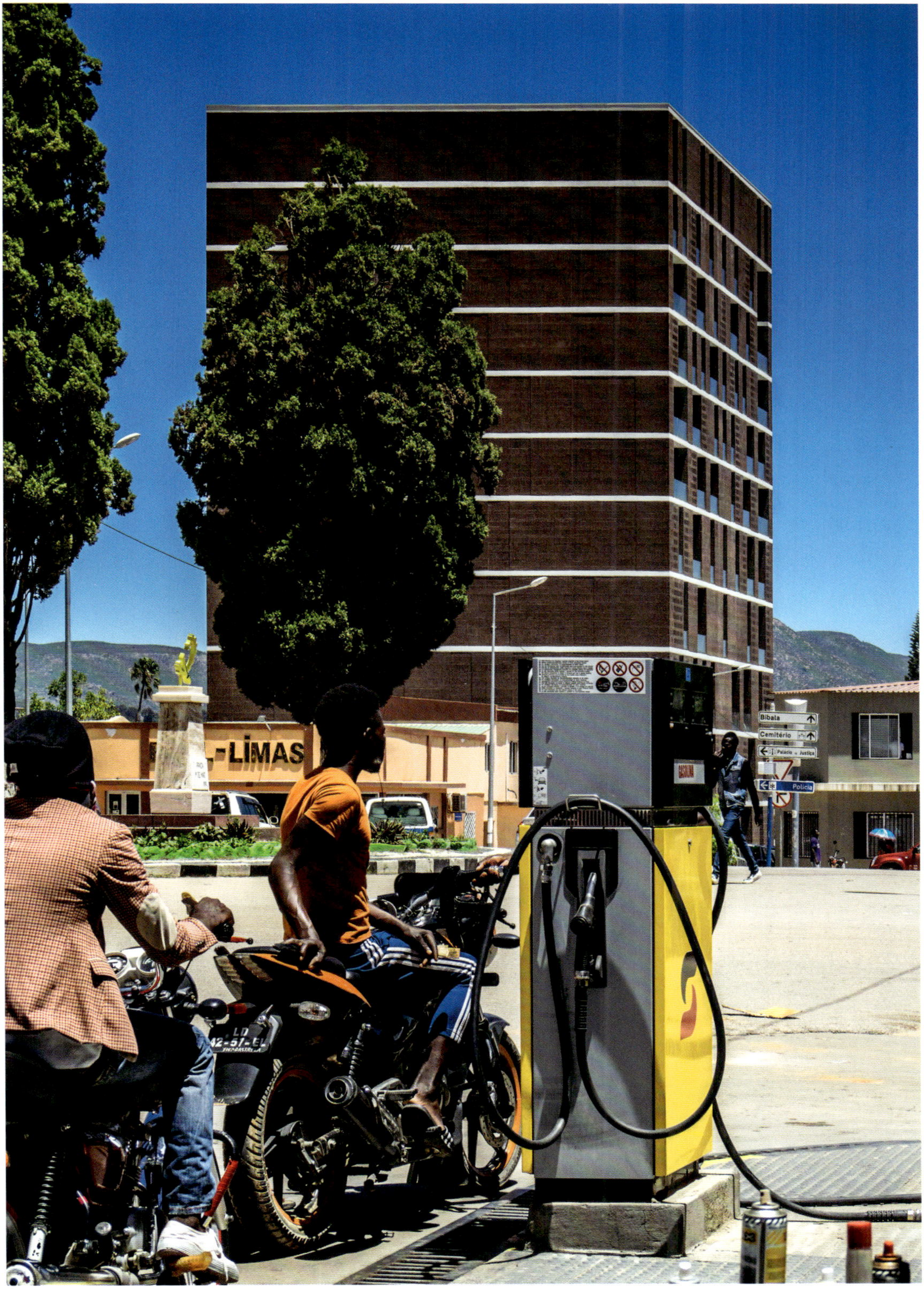
-LIMAS
Bibala
Cemitério
Polícia

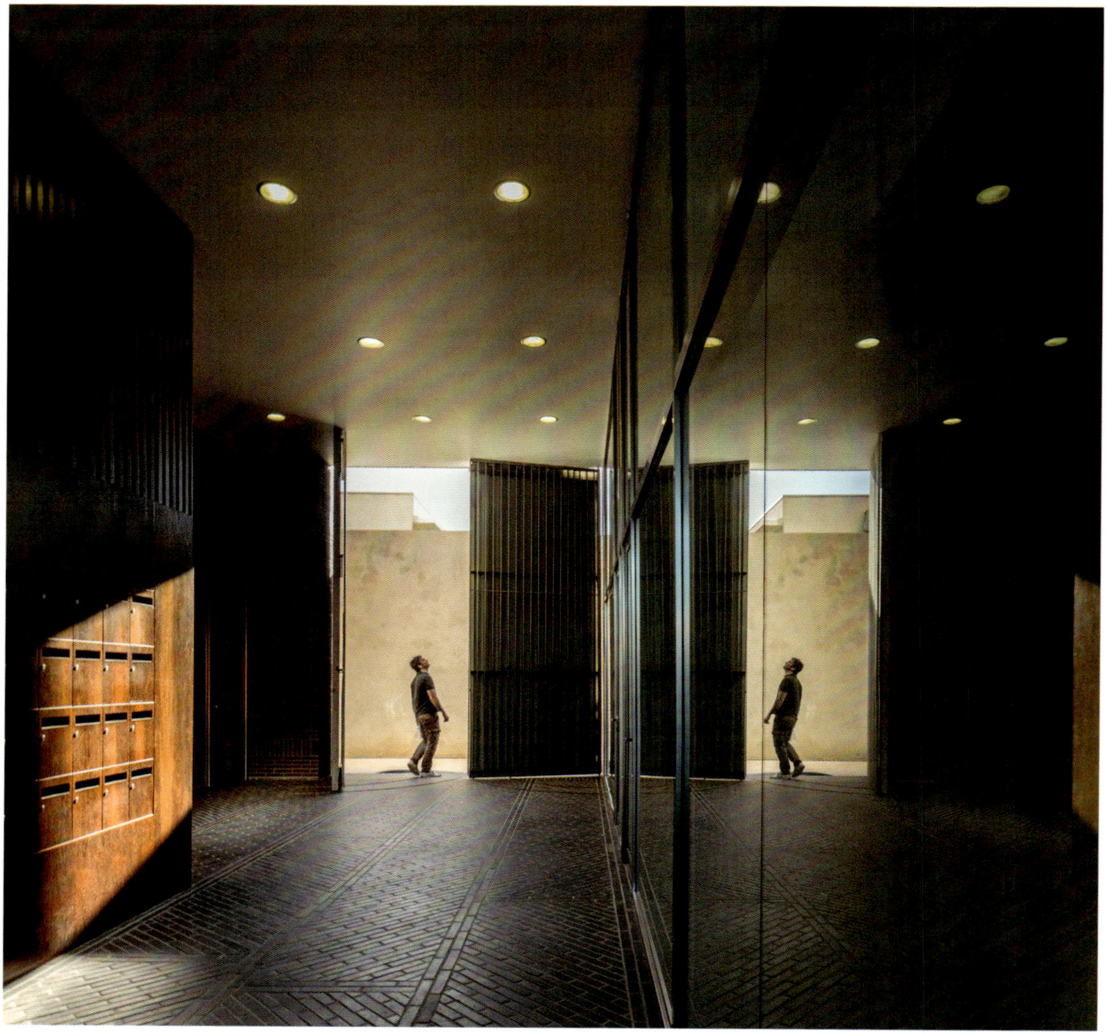

1/2/3 E. Souto de Moura: Zhengzhou towers (render)
4 Promontório: Kempinski Rafal Tower, Riyadh
5 Barbas Lopes Arquitectos: Av. Fontes Pereira de Melo
Tower, Lisbon (render)
6 A. Siza, Gabellini Sheppard: 56th Street Condominium,
New York (render)
7 M. G. Dias, E. J. Vieira: Lisbon "Manhattan"

De Rotterdam, Rotterdam, Netherlands (2013)
OMA

The De Rotterdam building, designed by Rem Koolhaas' OMA, remained on the drawing board for about 12 years. During this time, its composition was adapted to the fluctuations and expectations of the market. In the end, it resulted in a building with three 150 metres-high towers, with a total of 162,000m2 and with a mixed use of offices, apartments, shops, restaurants, cafes and a hotel. This "vertical city" and the set of towers around it is part of a 1992 plan by Norman Foster that aimed to give an urban sense to the old port. The place where, in the past, thousands of immigrants left for New York, finally gets its own small Manhattan. Density and diversity are given form in the brief and shape of De Rotterdam, where gaps, strides and setbacks and volume stacking add visual complexity to the city's new skyline.

The interior design of the De Rotterdam Town Hall office was designed by Studio Makkink & Bey with Group A and Roukens. The metaphor of the "vertical city" was also the pretext for the search for a diversity of environments codified by chromatic variations. It occupies 33 floors of the central tower, providing collective spaces of socialization and informal work meeting.

Practically without ever giving up the view of the city or the river, the elements that separate the workspace are almost always transparent or translucent. The space is relaxed, with nooks tucked away for a little escaping. The carpet lends the space the comfort of home. Work is taken home, home is brought to work.

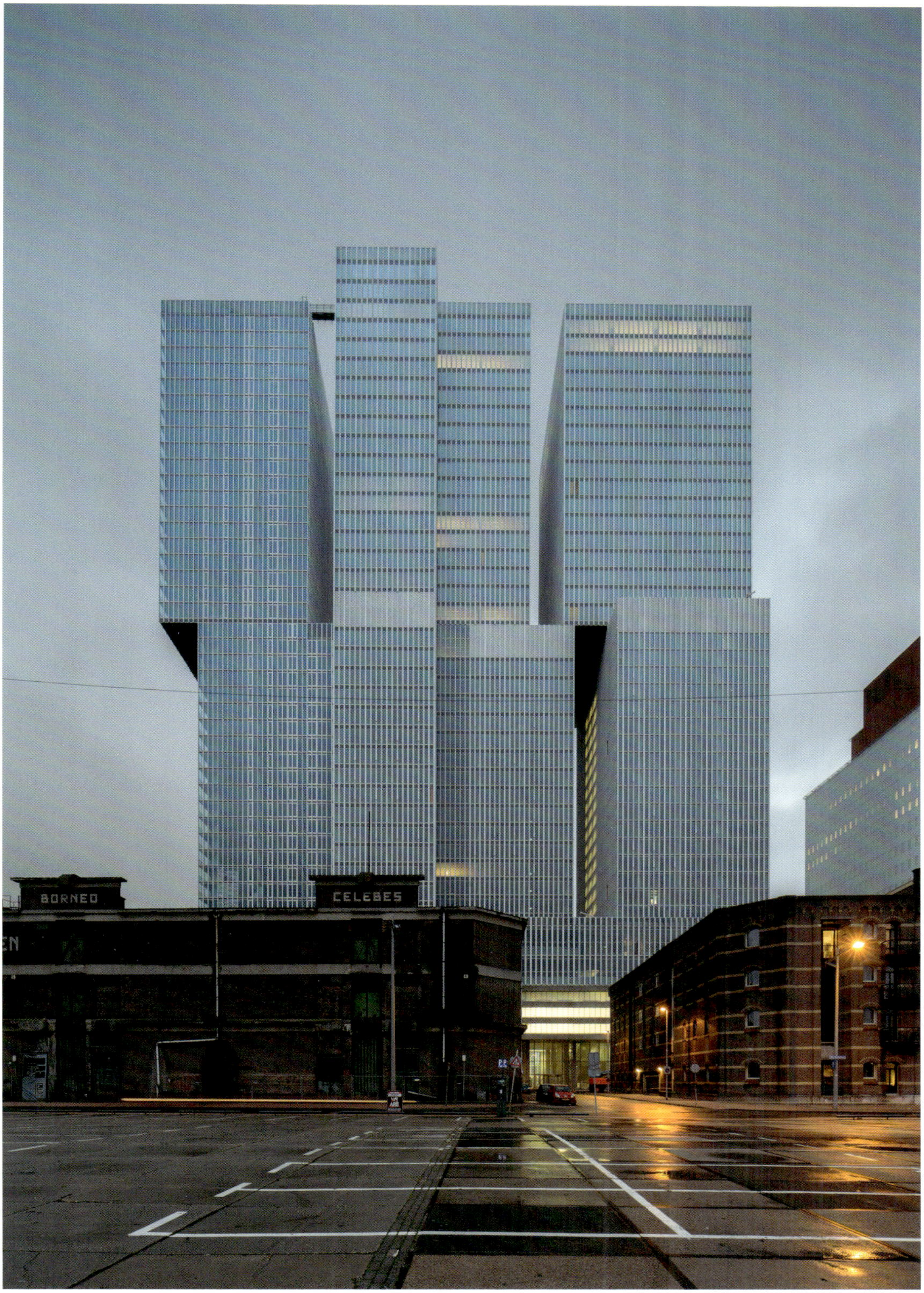
BORNEO
CELEBES

1

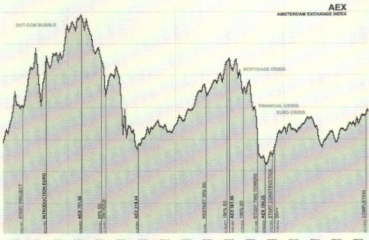

2

1 "Throughout history the control of land has been the basis of power. Cadastral maps, records of property ownership, played an important role in the rise of modern Europe as tools for the consolidation and extension of land-based national power"

2 E.R Graham: Equitable Life Insurance Building, New York. The visual codes and codes of action of the capitalist metropolis subject to the Marxist critique by Manfredo Tafuri.

3 Amsterdam Exchange Index and De Rotterdam's several lives 1997-2013.

3

4

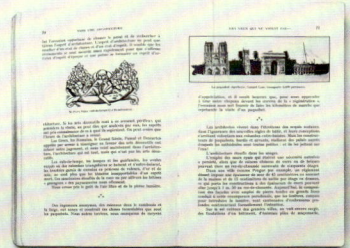

5

6

4 Tsunehisa Kimura
6 Scale ratio between boats and buildings

7

1   Starrett & Van Vieck: Downtown Athletic Club, New York
2   E. Otis: Demonstration of the elevator's safety system, New York, 1854
3   Manhattan's architects perform "the Skyline of New York"
4   Harrison and Abramovitz: Alcoa Building, Pittsburgh. The curtain wall
      described by Charles Jencks as the universal symbol of the corporate look
5/6   Larisa Bulibasa: A critical vision of the City, London.

Studio Makkink & Bey in collaboration with Group A and Roukens + Van Gils:
Interior design of the Municipality Offices, De Rotterdam, Rotterdam

1   Eberhard and W. Schnelle: BP Benzin und Petroleum office space
    organisation, Hamburg.
2   Eberhard and W. Schnelle: Buch+Ton Gütersloh office space
    organisation
3   K. Roche J. Dinkeloo and Associates: Ford Foundation, New York
5   Clive Wilkinson Architects: TBWA /Chiat /Day, Los Angeles

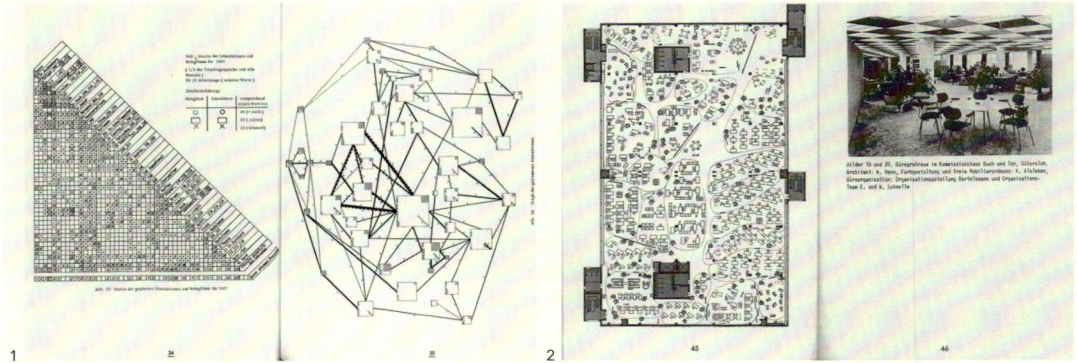

Fish Market, Besiktas, Turkey (2009)
GAD Architecture

The Fish Market in the Besiktas district in Istanbul, designed by Gokhan Avcloglu, aims to restore the dignity of the traditional street market with its simple and elegant design. A contrasting piece to the informality of adjacent buildings, it also seeks to compete with the hegemony of large shopping malls or shopping centres, which are comparatively more hygienic, comfortable and safe. An ambiguous border was consciously created between the physical continuity of the public space and the responsibility of its management, which depends essentially on private traders. In a culture where the public space is heavily and extensively used, experiences such as the Besiktas Fish Market have become veritable laboratories in terms of regulation and maintenance. The latest painting of the Market with decorative flowers expresses an important sense of appropriation. But there is another level of public awareness in relation to the street market: by presenting itself as an alternative to larger markets, it gives the small seller an opportunity to personalize the service, create relationships by reducing the distance between production and consumption. Looking at the seller and the fish in the eye, consumers will know more about the origin and the freshness of what they take home.

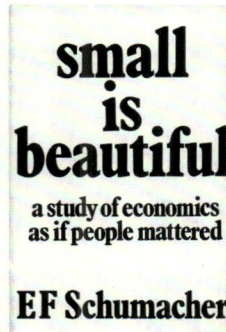

1   Besiktas Market before construction of the roof
2/3/4 The Decorators: Ridley's Temporary Restaurant

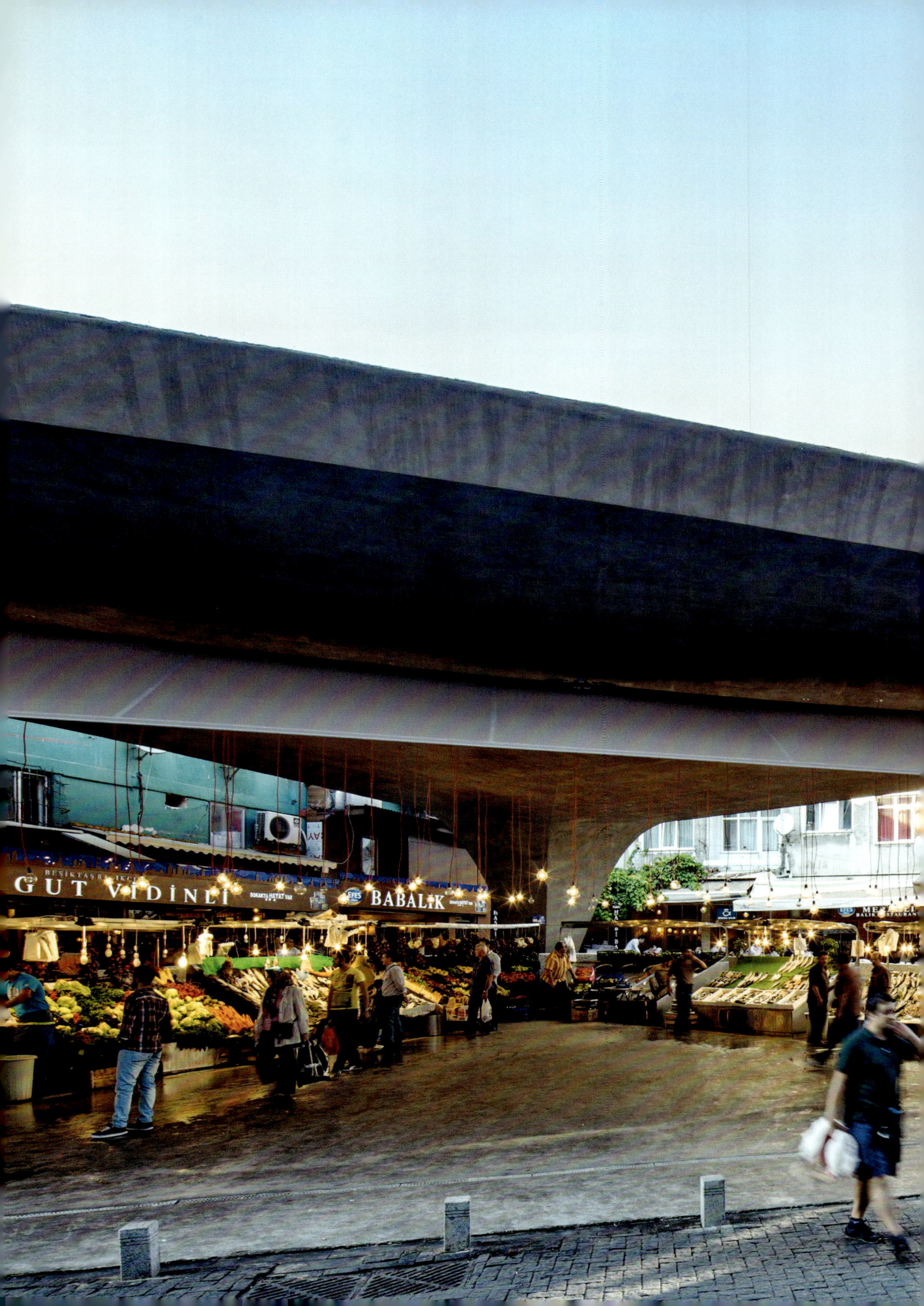
GUT VİDİNLİ
SOKAKTA HAYAT VAR
EFES
BABALIK

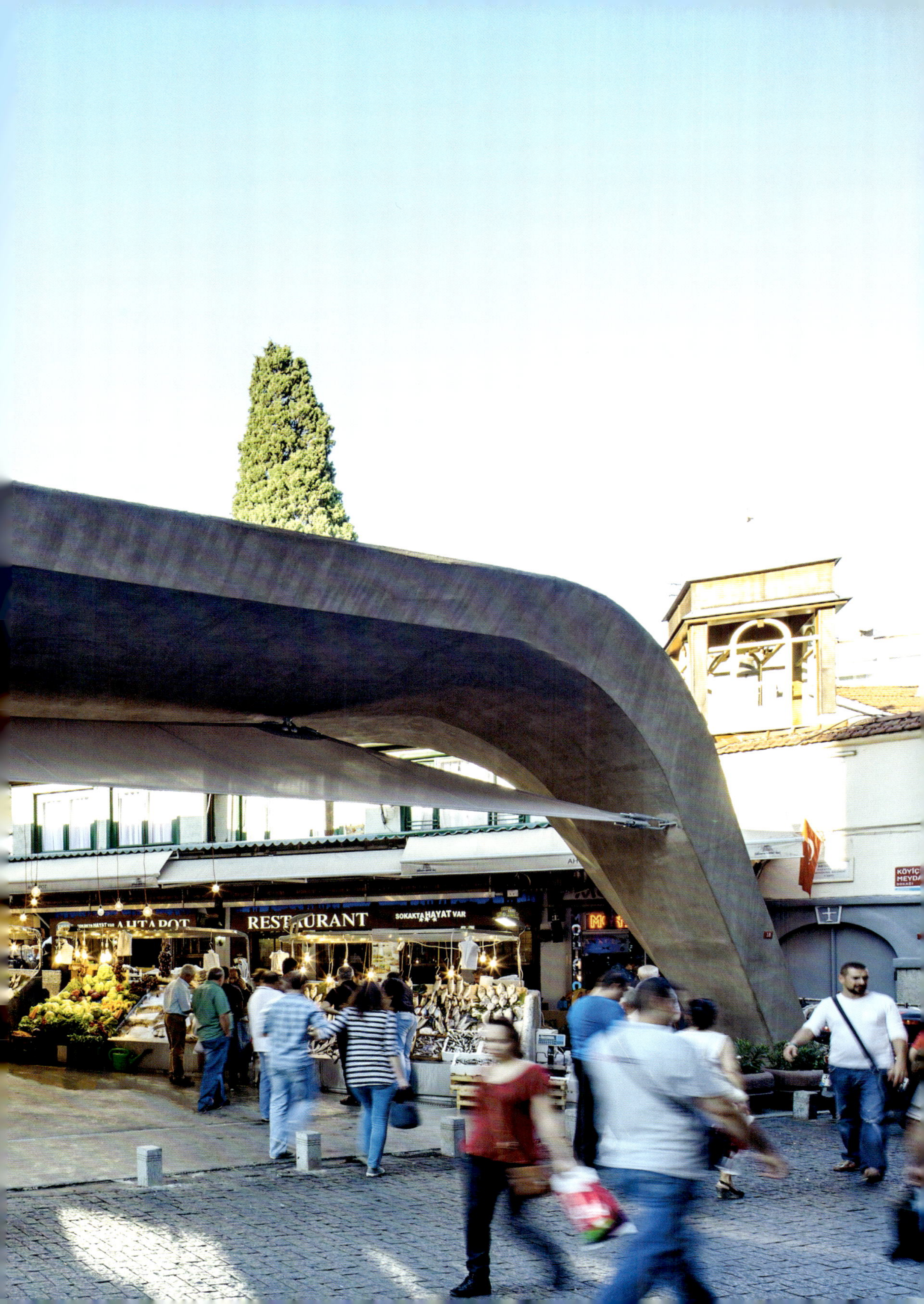
AHTAPOT
RESTAURANT
SOKAKTA HAYAT VAR

1

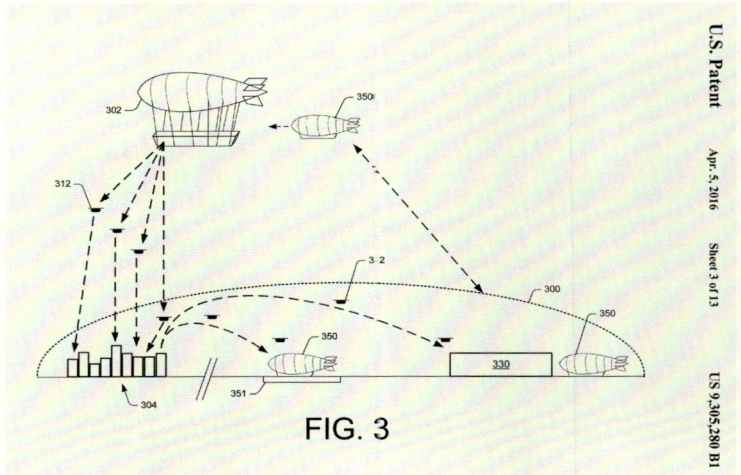

U.S. Patent   Apr. 5, 2016   Sheet 3 of 13   US 9,305,280 B1

FIG. 3

2

3

1   Amazon UK Fulfilment Centre, Cambridgeshire
2   Amazon: Drone delivery system patent.
3   Assemble: Granby Workshop products

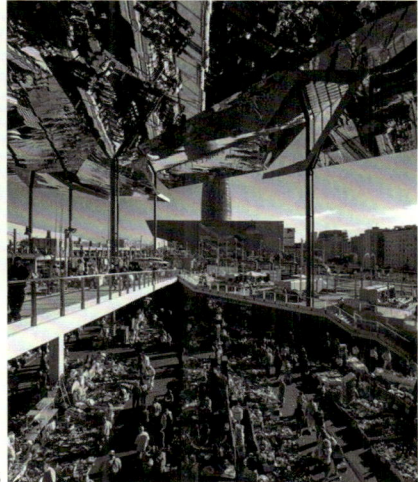

The glimmer of consumption:
1 PPAG Architects: Steirereck Restaurant, Vienna
2 REX architecture:Vakko Fashion Center, Istanbul
3 David Adjaye: Aïshti Foundation, Beirut
4 Hiroshi Nakamura: Tokyu Plaza Omotesando
   Harajuku, Tokyo
5 B720 Fermín Vázquez: Mercat dels Encants,
   Barcelona

DOMESTIC POWER

Owning or renting a house is to delimit a tiny part of the world, expressing the need for intimacy and security and a specific idea of comfort. Domestic power is idealized as inviolable. There is a primitive essence of the house that seems timeless to us, even when the ancient place for fire is replaced by the television and the television taken over by Wi-Fi. But flexibility of work, changes in family structure, or simply purchasing power, alter the sense of permanence of the houses we inhabit. A house is no longer for life. What kinds of housing arise in the face of social mobility? What solutions allow us to think of collective housing as an accessible and shared space? How can we promote flexibility of use in housing? Does the house continue to represent shelter in the ever paradoxical relationship between humans and nature?

Star Apartments, Los Angeles, USA (2014)
Michael Maltzan

Star Apartments is a mixed-use residential project run by the Skid Row Housing Trust – a Los Angeles organization that supports homeless people with health problems, disabilities or some form of dependency. With 102 apartments, the project of the architect Michael Maltzan also offers a set of community spaces – clinic, canteen, social areas, gardens and vegetable gardens – all arranged in six levels laid over a pre-existing garage and shop. The intervention model focuses on multifunctionality, but also on density, as a strategy to counteract the sprawl of Los Angeles.

In spite of its somewhat exuberant formal appearance, far from the monotonous and repetitive image we have of social housing, the Star Apartments were built in very little time and a very limited budget, opting for prefabricated modules on the raised floors of residential units. The resulting volumetric fragmentation lends the building an urban and exceptional character, a characteristic that contributes to the dignity of this collective residence and simultaneously gives visibility to the social project behind it. Combining shared spaces with the intimacy of the residential modules, the Star Apartments are, as their residents well testify, a success story to watch closely.

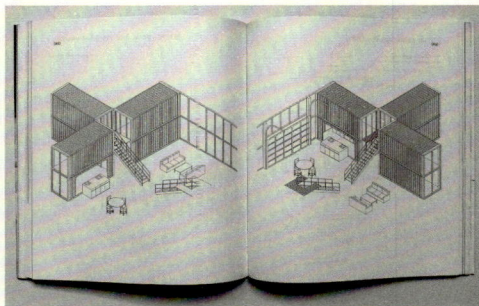

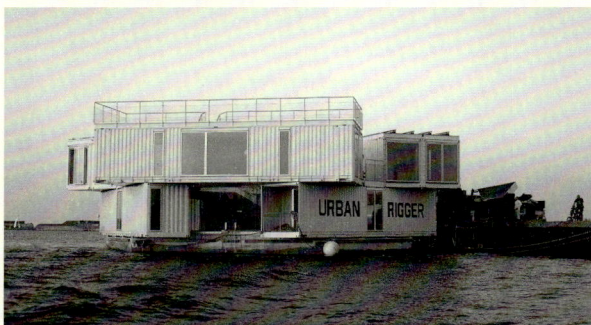

1/2   BIG: Urban Rigger Student House, Copenhagen
3   Adam Kalkin: House for Matt and Anne

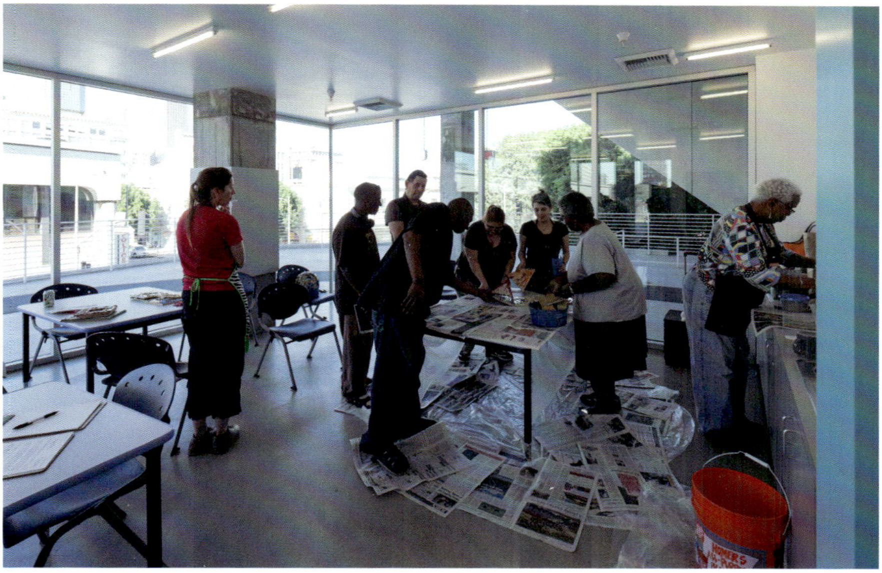

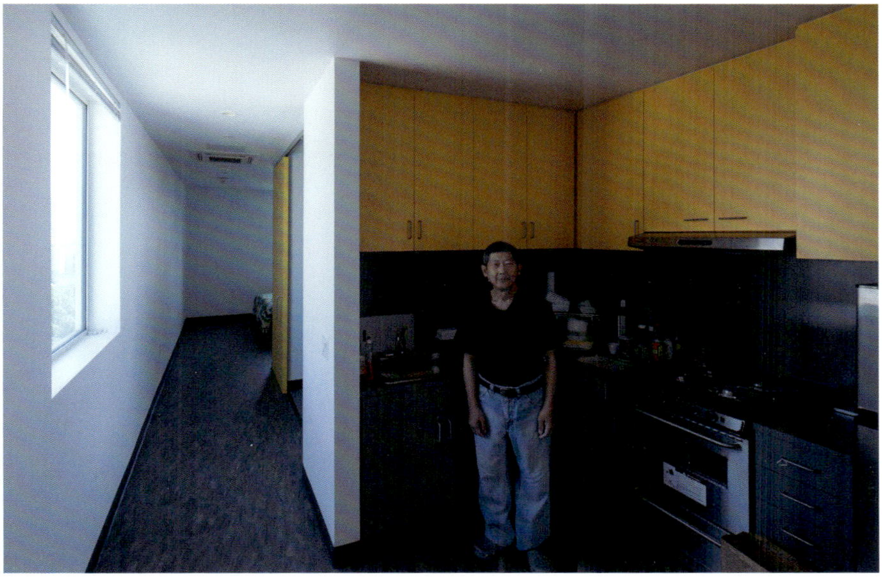

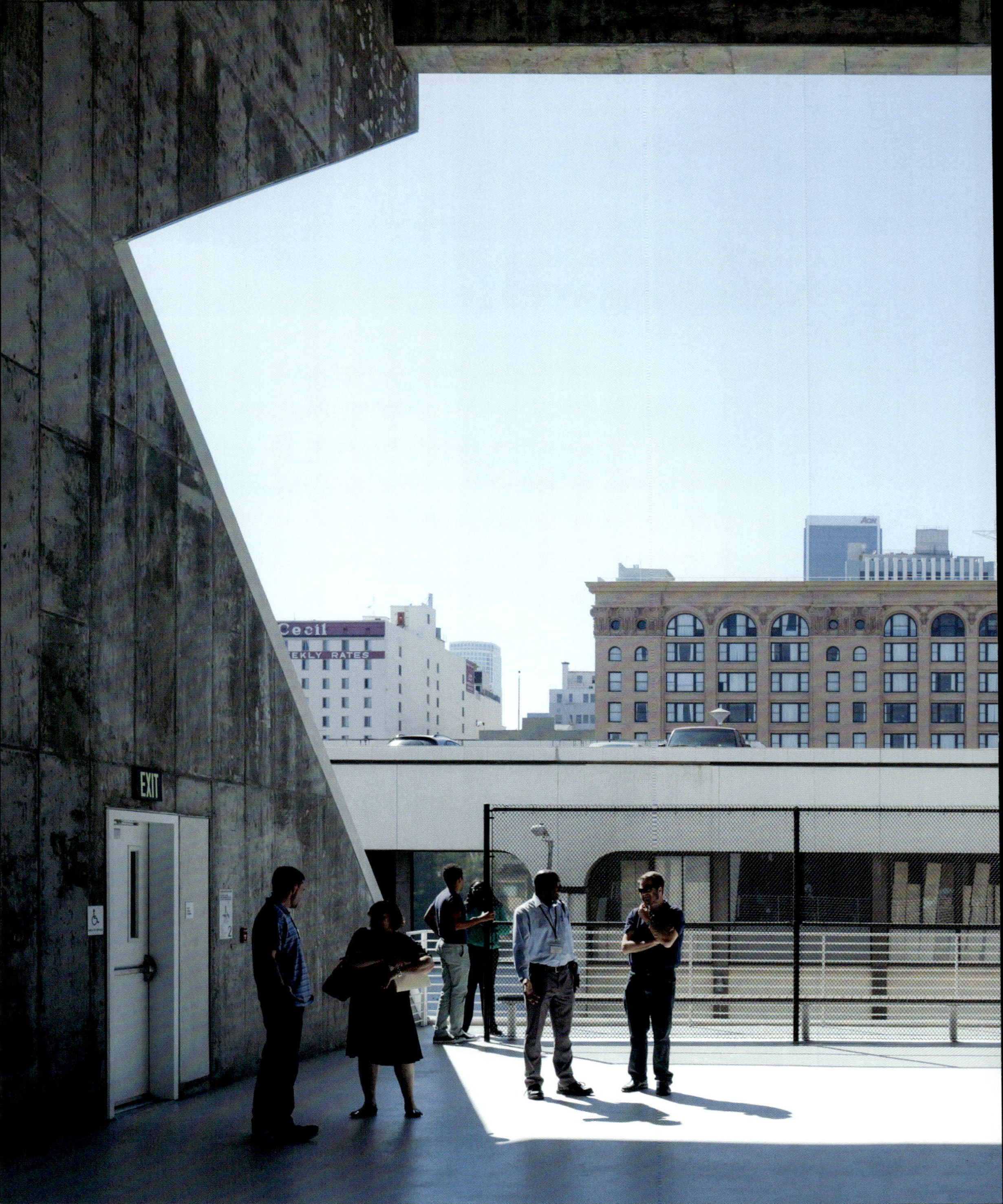
Cecil
EKLY RATES
EXIT

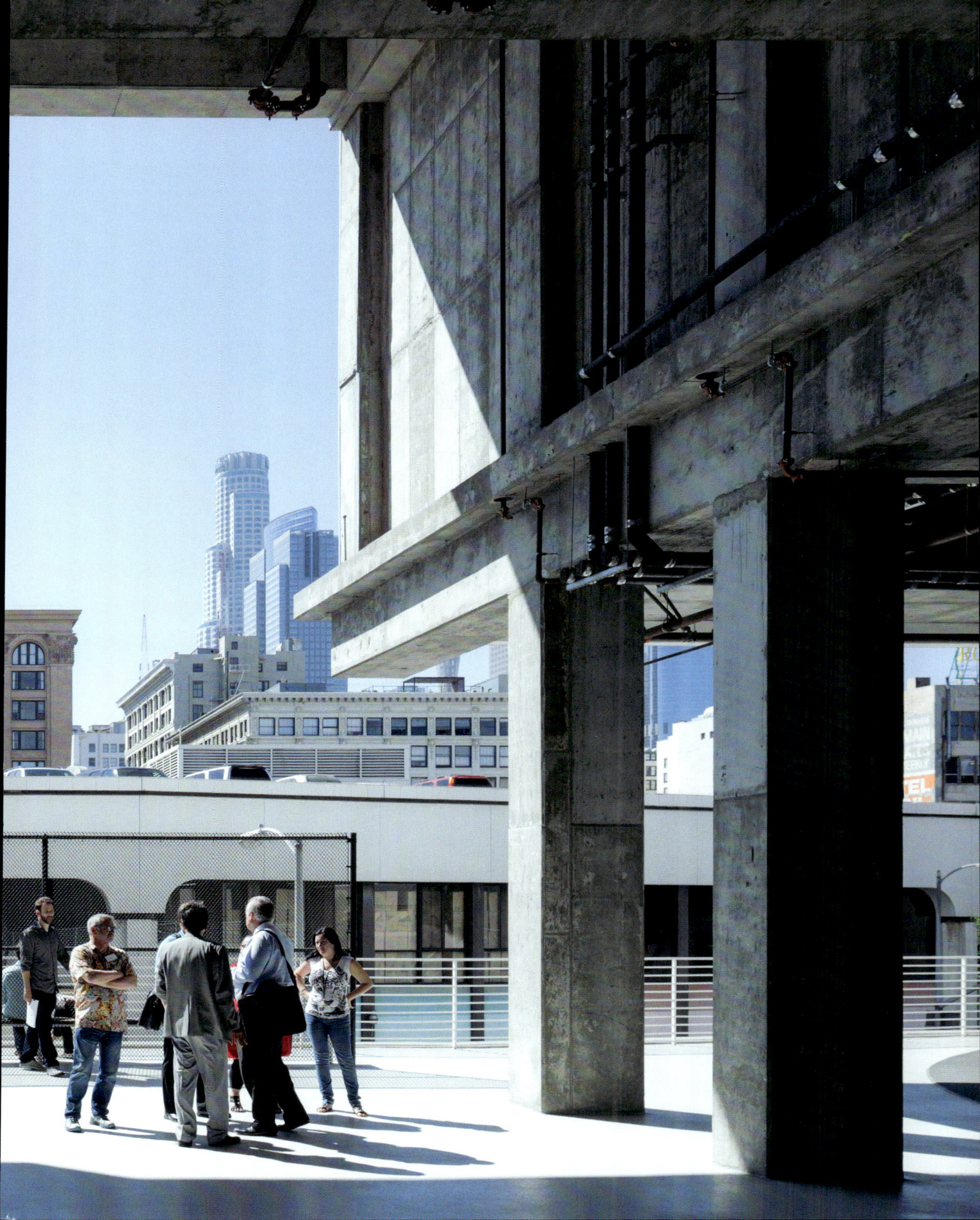

Mulhouse Neppert, France (2015)
Lacaton & Vassal

The workshop Atelier Lacaton & Vassal started by developing in 2005 in the city of Mulhouse a first experience of social housing as part of the plan *Cité Manifeste* (coordinated by Jean Nouvel). This French studio's proposal stood out by offering more housing with the same budget initially stipulated, as a result of the use of prefabricated industrial systems and the hierarchy of zones of thermal comfort. This has resulted in a generously-sized "greenhouse", which lends itself to various uses and activities, for at least 8 to 9 months a year. The same client of *Cité Manifeste* (Department of Social Housing in Mulhouse-Sonco) once again invited the Lacaton & Vassal studio to develop a new project

aimed at low-income families. Like the first time, the client accepted the risk of trying new typologies that would attract other tenants as well, thus promoting a desired and desirable social mix. These typologies are larger in area than the first kind, but the same principle remains, offering an intermediate space between the interior and the exterior. If at first glance the space may appear somewhat cold or informal (exposed concrete, aluminium roof panels and steel stairs), the fact is that the images of the inhabited houses reveal an enormous potential for full and diversified ownership, showing that more *is* more.

1 E. Muller: Cité ouvrière, Mulhouse
2 Cités ouvrières de Mulhouse
3 T. Garnier: Cité Industrialle
4 Cités ouvrières de Mulhouse

1 Druot, Lacaton & Vassal: Les grands
  ensembles de logements – Territoires
  d'exception
2/3 Atelier Tho A: FA House, Vietnam
4/5 Adam Kalkin: Collector's House

1

2

3

4

5

Building A, Mehr Als Wohnen, Zurich, Switzerland (2014)
Duplex Architekten

Mehr Als Wohnen is a housing cooperative in Zurich that seeks new ways of living within a strategy of urban densification but is simultaneously generous in terms of public space. With around 370 flats, nursery, offices or restaurants, this small city designed by the Duplex Architecten includes 13 buildings of different typologies, the result of the plan involving the participation of five different architecture offices. This plan's building A stands out by the way in which it combines private units of flats with the sharing of common spaces of rooms and kitchens in each floor, as part of a logic of cohabitation. The social space is complex, avoiding the rigidity and orthogonality in plan design and allowing a hierarchy of uses with some informality. Providing the autonomy of the most intimate spaces along with community-sharing activities was a concern of the architects: all private units have their own sanitary facilities and sometimes a small *kitchenette*. The distance between units contributes to the sound insulation. Cohabitation, with the sharing of common spaces like the kitchen, begins to breathe a new breath in urban centres. While not necessarily an original way of living, it is worth noting that this is choice is not always, as in this case, motivated by the low rents, but by the voluntary search of the possibility of socialization inherent to it.

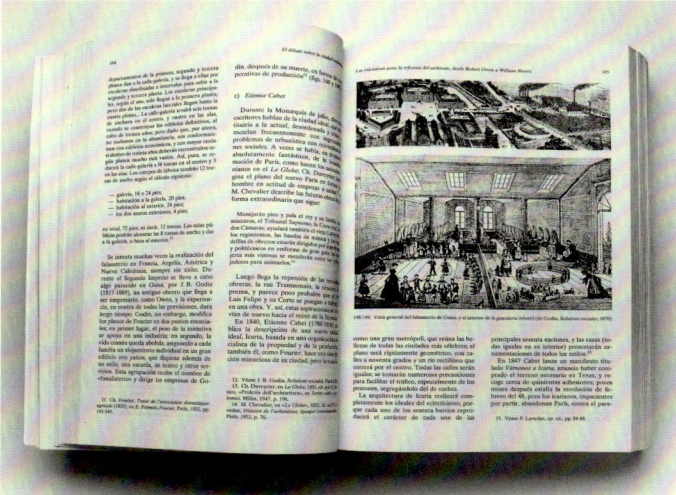

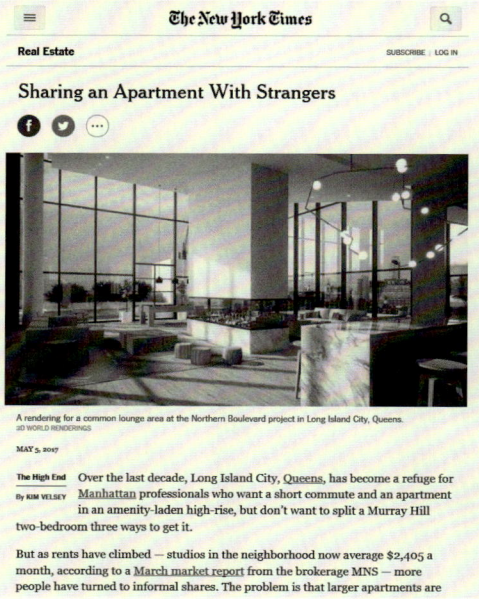

The New York Times

Real Estate

SUBSCRIBE / LOG IN

Sharing an Apartment With Strangers

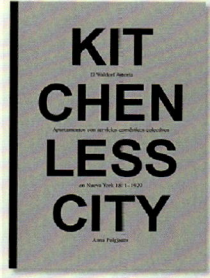

A rendering for a common lounge area at the Northern Boulevard project in Long Island City, Queens.
3D WORLD RENDERINGS

MAY 5, 2017

The High End

By KIM VELSEY

Over the last decade, Long Island City, Queens, has become a refuge for Manhattan professionals who want a short commute and an apartment in an amenity-laden high-rise, but don't want to split a Murray Hill two-bedroom three ways to get it.

But as rents have climbed — studios in the neighborhood now average $2,405 a month, according to a March market report from the brokerage MNS — more people have turned to informal shares. The problem is that larger apartments are

1 Duplex Architekten: Mehr als Wohnen, Haus M
2 Jean-Baptiste Godin: Familistère of Guise
5 Sharing an apartment with strangers
6 Kitchenless city, shared kitchen, alternative housing models

De Lork Assisted Living Residences, Brussels, Belgium (2014)
51N4E

De Lork is an assisted living building designed by
the Belgian studio 51N4E in the district of Sint-Gillis
in Brussels.
"Permanent home to 30 people, De Lork is organized
in small communities. Between the privacy of one's own
room and the communal living& dining, inhabitants are
provided with additional spaces for casual socializing:
a small garden, a terrace, and the circulation spaces,
designed to be perceived and function as proper
rooms. The organization of every floor places all private
rooms on the front side to give cues of street life to all
inhabitants. The street façade, alternating convex and
concave parts, maximizes window surface and viewing
angles for the rooms as well as integrating the mass
of the building to the small & dense terraced houses
adjacent to the plot.
The back of the building bears a peculiarity: it is the
fourth (and missing) wing of a cloister garden.
A continuous, monumental, largely translucent brick
façade covers the back and side of the building. It
offers the necessary privacy for the cloister as well
as generous light for the circulation and living spaces:
Modest but rich in experiences, the building inverts
expectations on all levels" (51N4E)

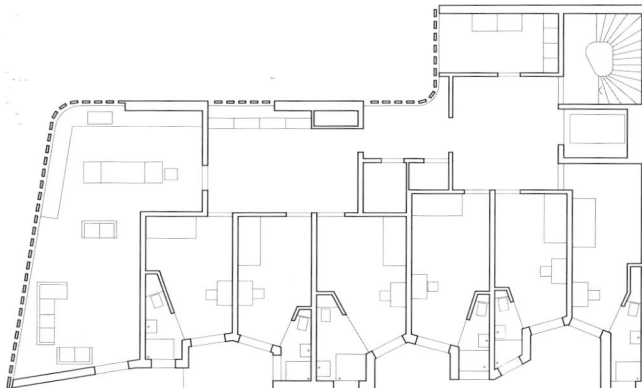

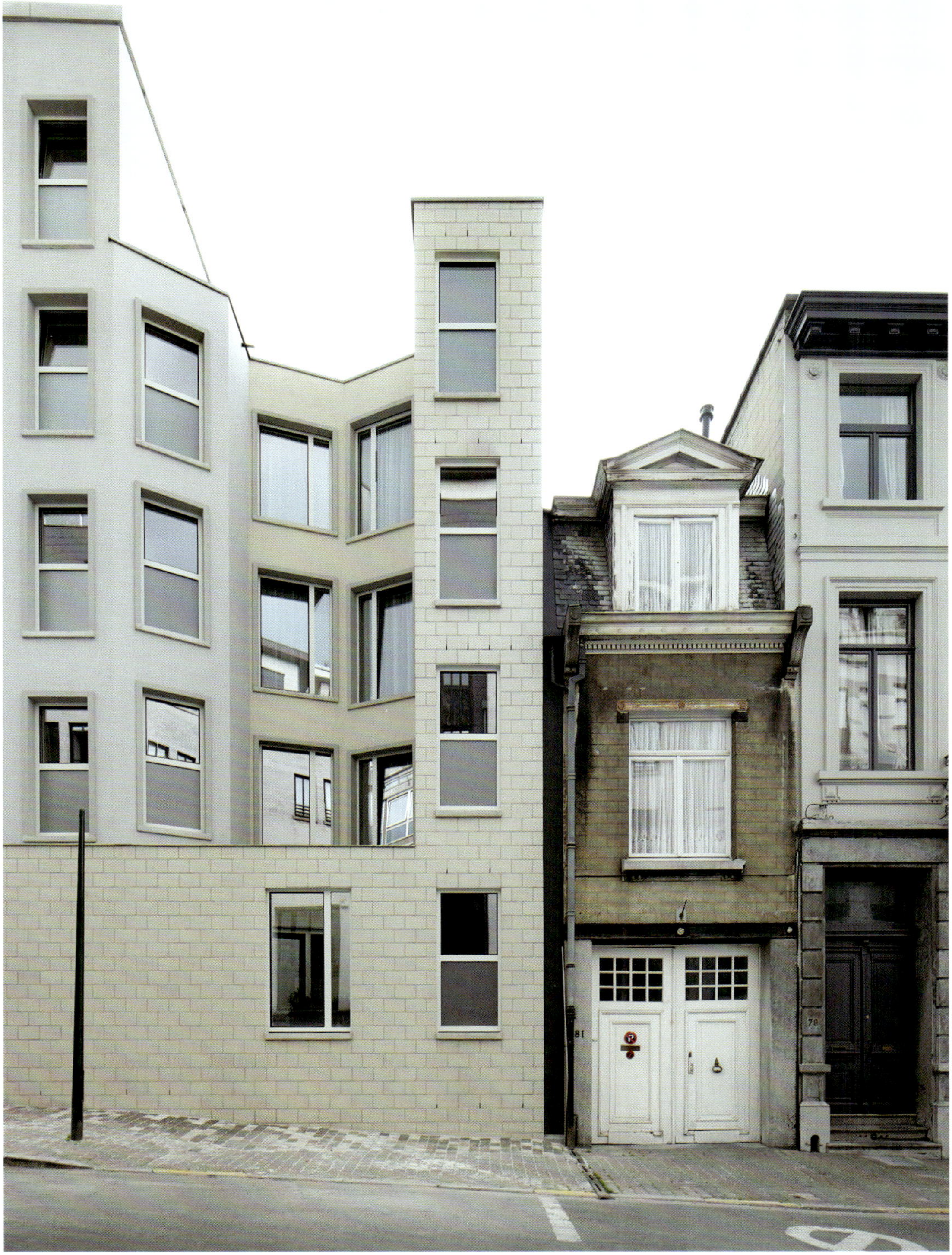
81

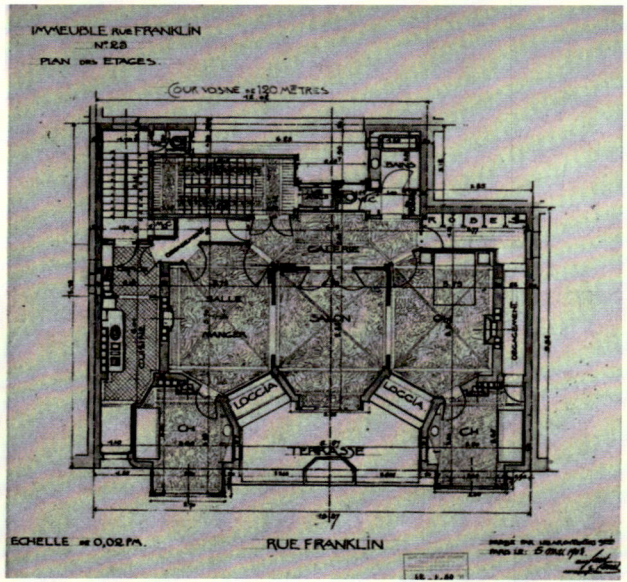

1 Auguste Perret: Building on the Rue Franklin, Paris
2 J. A. Coderch: Girasol Building, Madrid
3 Auguste Perret: Building on the Rue Franklin, Paris
4 J. A. Coderch: Girasol Building, Madrid

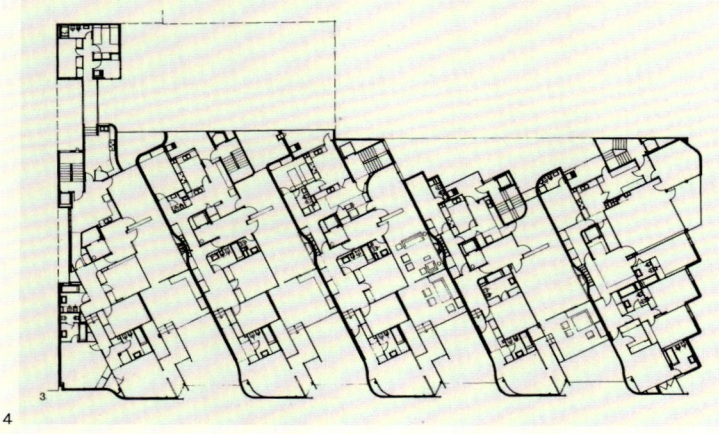

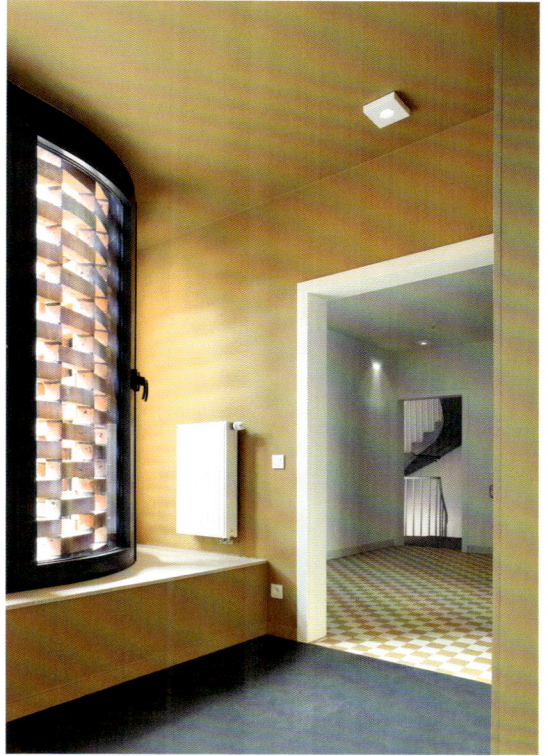

Bern Heim Beuk House, Belgium (2011)
Architecten de Vylder Vinck Taillieu

Tree house or tree turned home. With just 99m2, this wooden house, designed by the Belgian studio De Vylder Vinck Taillieu, develops around a central column in reinforced concrete. This openly intrusive structural element assumes the shape of a tree with projecting beams, as if they were its branches. Nature has always been generous in its supply of structural metaphors. Outside, another tree is embraced by a false extension of the house, creating a small transitional garden between the interior and the exterior. This will be the pretext to fuse the "natural" with the "artificial" (as if the natural did not today make part of the artificial). But domestic power is still based on this dichotomy, or distance, that protects us from the elements. This distance is symbolically cancelled out in this house, as it tries to strike a balance and a harmonious form that opens to let nature in or let itself be consumed by it. In the end, we are faced with two archetypes of the image of home and the image of nature. Both are validated, both are nullified.

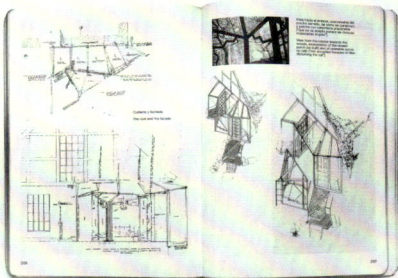

1   René Heyvaert
2   A. and P. Smithson: Garden Building, Oxford
3/4 A. and P. Smithson: Hexenhaus, Bad Karlshafen
5   Camilo Rebelo: Promise House

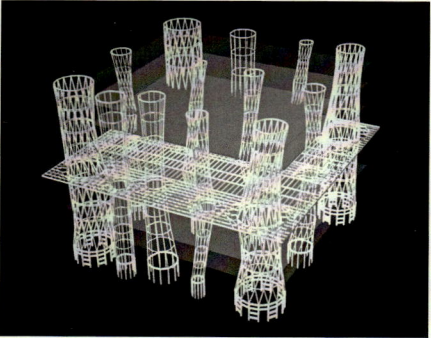

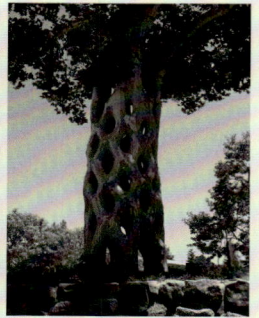

1 Toyo Ito: Sendai Mediatheque
2 Axel Erlandson: The Wet Tree
3 H. Oliveira: Baitogogo, Palais de Tokyo

Quinta da Tília, Ponta Delgada, Portugal (2015)
P. Maurício Borges e J. André Simões

Tília (linden tree) House, as its name indicates, was built around a pre-existing large tree that provides a generous shade. The house's social zone, the centre of a linear program that starts in the garage, establishes and prolongs the relationship with the tree's yard. The boundary between interior and exterior is complex: the glazed elevation detaches itself from the boundary of the roof and seeks to envelop the linden, resulting in a succession of different spaces with different scales. The proximity of the skylight to the roof of the room further accentuates the elevation's deconstruction and emphasises the tree's omnipresence. Inside, the roof reveals a japonica wood structure, an economically accessible but also sustainable option since it is extracted from ocal forests whose reforestation is assured. It could be said that the comfort of this house resides in the matter and scale that goes from the isolated tree to the forest and that domestic power also rests on being aware of the inhabited place, of its specific context.

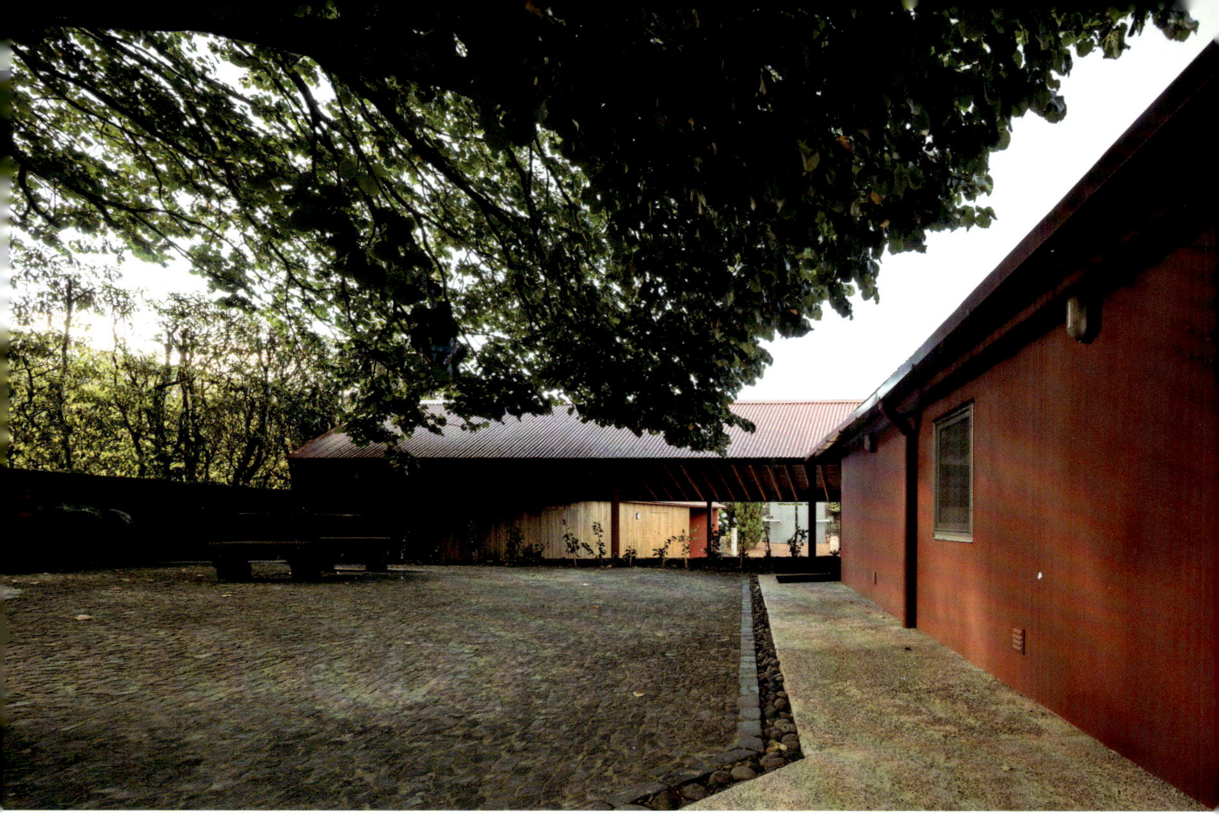

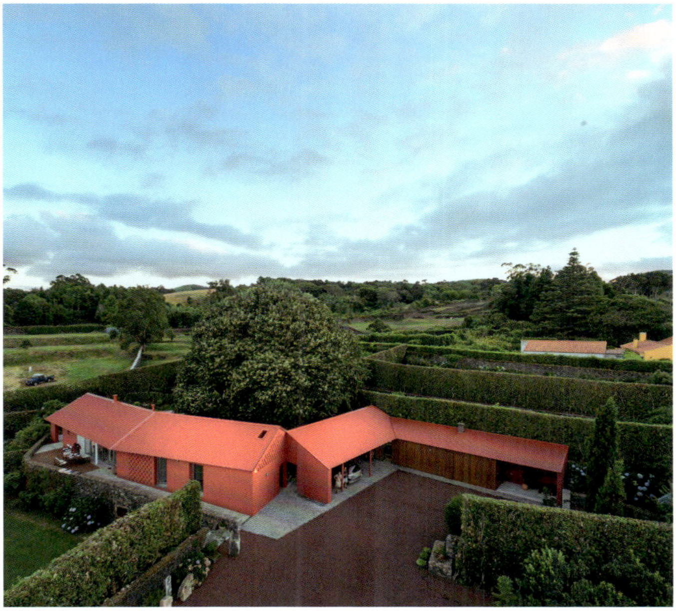

1/2 Glenn Murcutt: Marika-Alderton House, Eastern Arnhem Land
3/4 Frank Gehry: Gehry Residence, Santa Monica
5 A. and P. Smithson: Hexenhaus, Bad Karlshafen

1

2

3

1   Camilo Rebelo: Migrant Garden project
2/3 R. Bak Gordon: House in Costa do Castelo, Lisbon

CULTURAL POWER

Cultural production and consumption are gaining increasing relevance in our society. Once seen as an elitist sector, culture has democratized itself, and today we can say that everything is culture, everything is art, everything is spectacle. "Cultural industry" or "creative industry" have become buzzwords that seem to give more importance to numbers than to letters. Culture has become an event and a tourist attraction. The formal exuberance of many cultural buildings is only compatible with special budgets. But there are other questions: how are new buildings created regarding a diversified contemporary cultural production? How can cultural interests be reconciled with mass tourism, and the latter with the environment? And, last but not least, how can Architecture preserve history and collective memory?

Astley Castle Renovation, Warwickshire, United Kingdom (2012)
Whiterford Watson Mann Architects

The Landmark Trust is an institution founded in 1965 to restore historic buildings not safeguarded by government entities. Such is the case of Astley Castle in Warwickshire, abandoned after a fire in 1978. Restoration always starts from the same principle, that is, to make the building not only accessible but also able to receive guests. The Contest Program, won by Witherford Watson Mann architects, proposed the construction of a 2-4 bedroom home with a living room, dining room and kitchen. It was made clear that there would be no budget for a complete recovery of the building, and as such it was requested that whatever was considered significant to maintain was consolidated.

The intervention of the English architects creates a solution of open dialogue with the past, by taking on new materials that, while not discreet (see, for example, the contrast between brick and stone), end up emphasizing the historical fragments. Even areas only consolidated but left out in the open acquire a functional meaning that allows us to rethink the ruin beyond its romantic value. Without the fear of attributing new uses or new spatial experiences, Astley Castle is the concrete example that cultural power is in the "reminiscent sense of the monument", that is, in its permanent updating, bereft of nostalgia.

1 Astley Castle
2 Astley Castle, Lady Rose Dining Room

English perceptions of ruin are almost inevitably filtered through the elegiac sensibilities of the Romantic period. The ruin is a figure of Englishness, of reassurance in relation to change, of pleasant melancholy, the subject of countless watercolours or garden follies, where, with time, artifice and nature merge to be as one.

1

Astley Castle sits in an ancient landscape, with intense pastoral qualities. It is a ruin, the result of a catastrophic fire and years of subsequent decay and collapse. It is bittersweet - both reassuring and unsettling.

2

But there are other aspects to this rich pictorial and architectural tradition - Renaissance adorations, Baroque capriccios, and, more recently, war buildings and post-industrial landscapes. Each of these carries subtly differing moral messages: renewal, mortality, man-made catastrophe.

3

"Architecture is what makes beautiful ruins". Auguste Perret's aphorism identifies architecture with the articulation of its structure. Structures in fragile equilibrium rather than reassuring poise; spaces as porous enclosures, simultaneously transparent and contained, traces of reassuring scale erased, and interior and garden intertwined. There is much of the ruin in modernist architecture.

4

1-4   WWM: About the ruin tectonic

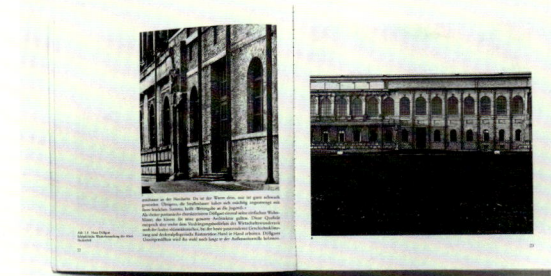

5

6

5   Hans Döllgast: Alte Pinakothek renovation, Munich
6   Diener & Diener Architekten: Renovation of the Museum
     of Natural History, Berlin

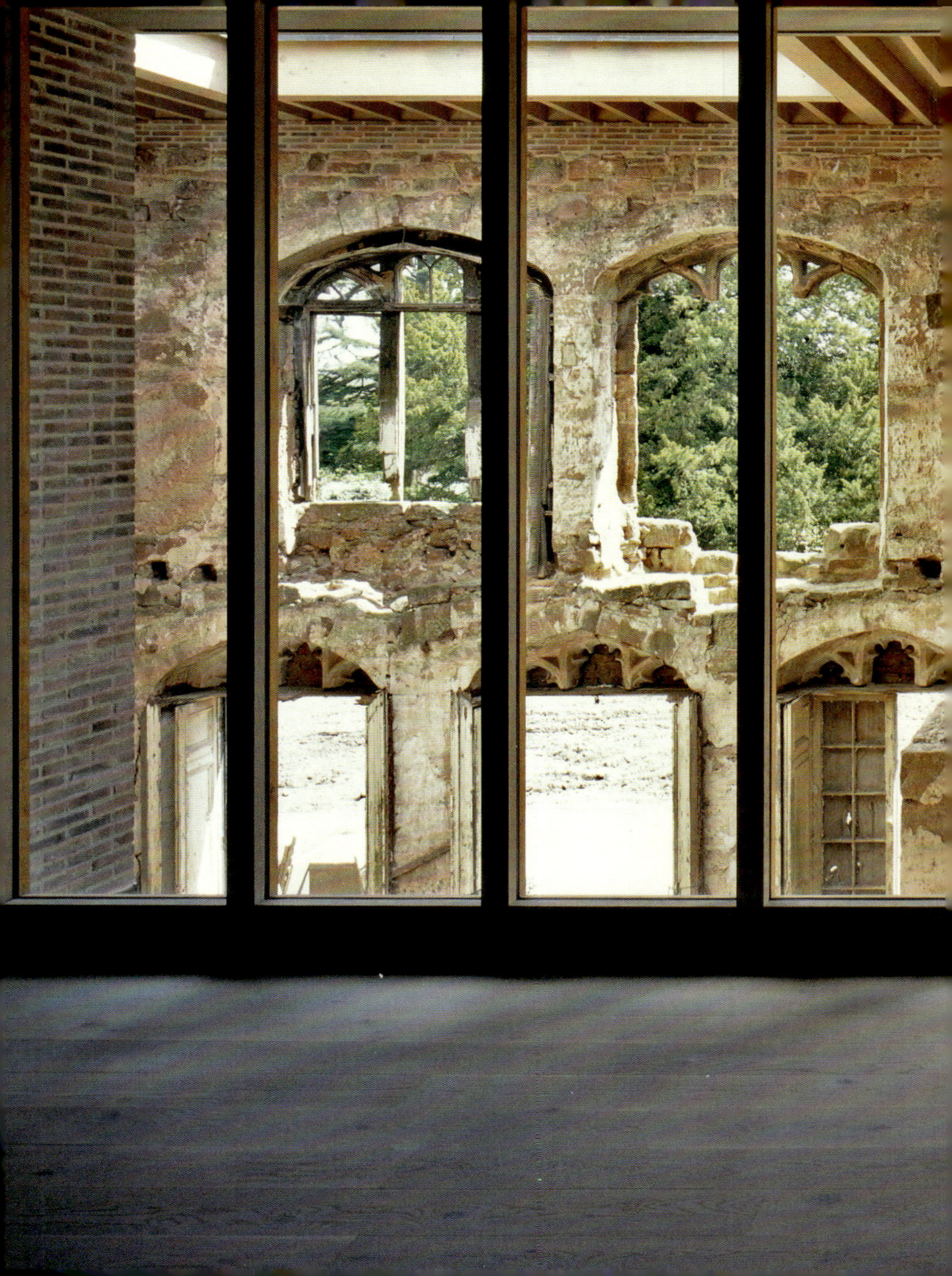

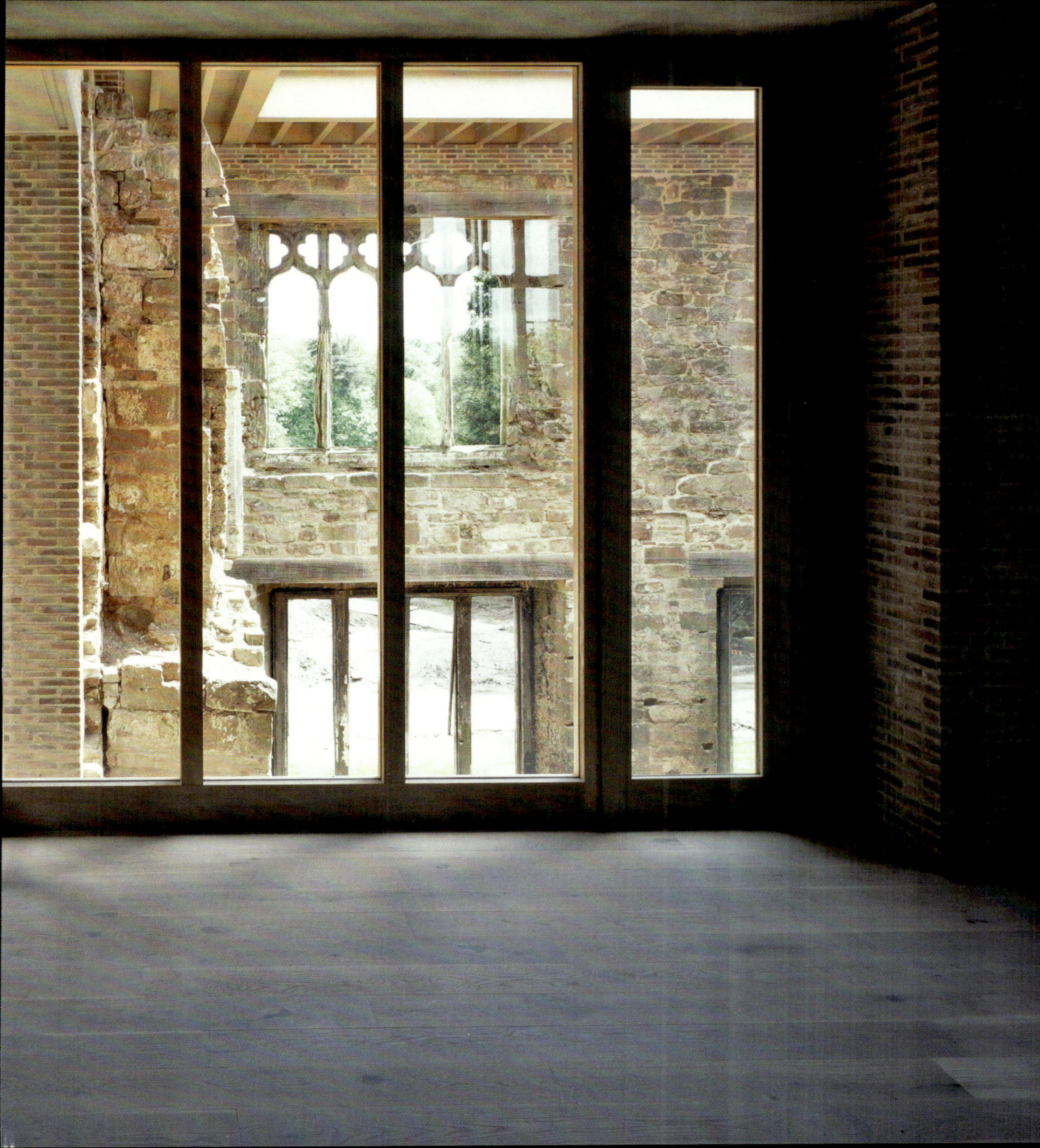

Showcase over the Camp Commander's House, Westerbork, Netherlands (2015)
Oving Architekten

The Westerbork Camp was first created by the Dutch government as a camp for Jewish refugees fleeing the Nazi regime. The occupation of the Netherlands by the German Armed Forces turned the camp into a deportation platform for more than 100,000 Jews (but also gypsies and resistance members) to extermination and concentration camps located in Poland. After World War II the camp was temporarily used as a prison for former Nazi collaborators, and during the 1950s and 1960s it received refugees from the Moluccas (formerly a Dutch colony). Deactivated and practically demolished in the 70's, the camp was designated a national monument in 1994.

The Commander's House is one of the elements that have been preserved. It is an anonymous wood building: banal and rustic. Looking at it, it's hard to imagine all the horror it served. Oving Architekten's option to insulate it inside a glass bell, as if the house were an untouchable object, expresses (albeit inadvertently) the importance of remembering and dealing with History, especially that which shames humanity.

1/2   Buckminster Fuller: Manhattan Dome, New York
3   Philip Johnson: Crystal Cathedral, Garden Grove.
5   Foster+Partners: Great Court at the British Museum, London

1   Meixner Schlüter Wendt: Wohlfahrt-Laymann House, Taunus
2-4 Adam Kalkin: Bunny Lane House, Bernardsville

Bridge, Mont Saint-Michel, France (2015)
Dietmar Feichtinger Architectes

Mont Saint-Michel's unique geographical features made it the ideal spot for a monastery during the Middle Ages: an island during high tide, but accessible at low tide. Already at the end of the 19th century, anticipating the growing tourist interest, a railroad was created over a causeway to ensure safe and permanent access. The island began to be consumed with such voracity that its entire context became threatened: aquatic ecosystems were heavily altered, as was fishing. In short, excessive tourism, aggravated by the effects of climate change, was causing the island to cease to be one. It is a territory marked by the conflict of different interests (or powers): the economic, through tourism, the cultural and the landscape / environmental.

The restoration of the balance between these interests is, therefore, a process where different areas of knowledge had to participate and engage. The bridge corresponds to the contribution of Architecture. It is the most visible face of a set of operations to restore sea level, but also to control and limit access and parking. The island's land connection became a place in its own right, a crossing for light traffic and a space of contemplation over this flooded territory.

080bis - Mont-Saint-Michel et sa baie : délimitation du bien lors de son inscription sur la Liste en 1979 et de sa zone tampon approuvée en 2007

D'après Guégan C., 2012.; Sources : Bountîles Mont-Saint-Michel, Syndicat Mixte Baie du Mont-Saint-Michel.

2   Mont Saint-Michel, silted bay taken up by a parking lot
3   World Heritage Protected Area
4   Variation on the number of visitors in 2011
5   Grande Rue, Mont Saint-Michel

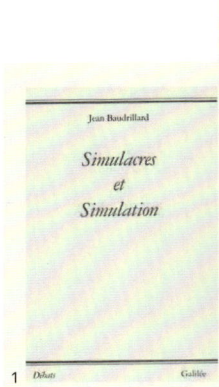

2   Disney's Shanghai Park

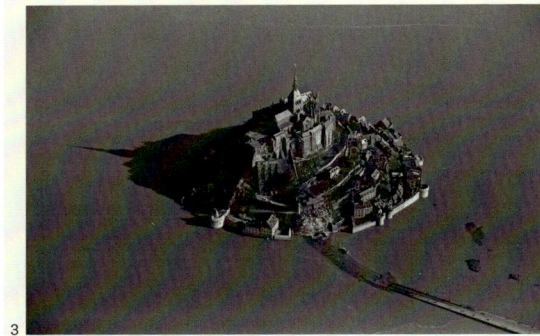

3   Mont Saint-Michel with "tide of the century"
4   Seal at Mont Saint-Michel's basin

Alhambra New Gate /Puerta Nueva, Granada, Spain (2011)
Álvaro Siza with Juan Domingo Santos

Álvaro Siza's project with Juan Domingo Santos for the New Gate of the Alhambra sought above all to "organize the access and quality complementary services, open to a large number of visitors for whom Alhambra is a myth, and the desire to visit it a truism."

Responding to an extremely demanding functional program (Alhambra receives around 8,500 visitors daily), it sought to reduce the impact of the intervention with a succession of volumes of different scales, embedded in the hillside and with the proposed use of local materials (such as Grenadine paving or the pigments and sands of La Sabika hill). The articulation with the topography, vegetation or streams also allowed to organise the flows of visitors in a set of outdoor spaces and courtyards in dialogue with walls and water tanks.

The jury (16 leaders of Spanish cultural institutions) awarded Siza's work, unanimously considering that one of its main virtues would be the subtlety of its integration in the landscape.

Paradoxically, a non-binding opinion of the International Council on Monuments and Sites (a UNESCO advisory body) considered the project too invasive, a pretext for the Junta de Andalucia to scotch it. Constant political change and the estimated budgetary impact for the work did not help in times of crisis. Subsequently, and at the request of the new direction of the Alhambra, a significant reduction of area was executed without altering the solution of the contest. Siza bet on what he refers to as a "principle of non-inhibitory continuity", albeit in a different historical context. The more conservative view on heritage that is not partial to this argument will never truly understand the architectural diversity that has built the entire Alhambra.

5 Delimitation of the zone classified as World Heritage and of the buffer zone
6 Queues during peak attendance days
7 Political propaganda against the project
8 Propaganda against the project

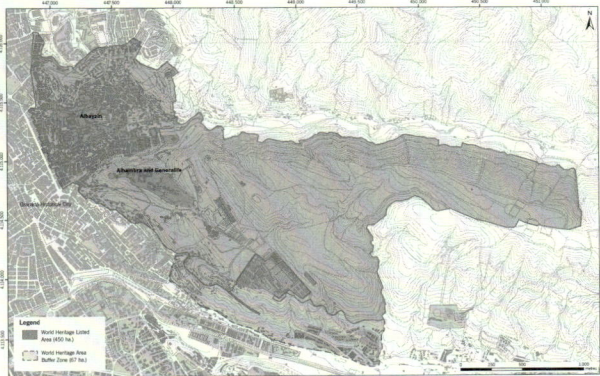

ES-314bis: Alhambra, Generalife and Albayzin in Granada (SPAIN).
Agency responsible: Andalusian Regional Government, Department of Culture.

Base map: Topographic Map of Andalusia. 1:10.000. 2007. Regional Government of Andalusia. Andalusian Mapping Agency.

Spatial Reference System: European Datum 1950, Zone 30 North.

5

6

¡NO AL ATRIO!

7

populares Granada
Juntos, más Granada

Salvemos la Alhambra, el Comercio y la Hostelería Granadina

El PSOE quiere un atrio de **16.000 m2** con un coste de **50 millones de €** "de los granadinos"

Junta de Andalucía

Palacios Nazaríes 17.000m2

Los Colegios de Arquitectos de Andalucía apoyan el proyecto Atrio de La Alhambra

El consejo andaluz pide que se realice la propuesta de los arquitectos Álvaro Siza y Juan Domingo Santos, que "tiene el visto bueno de la Junta"

El consejo andaluz de Colegios Oficiales de Arquitectos (CACOA) ha expresado esta mañana su apoyo al proyecto Atrio de La

9

1   "Initial scheme according to the competition program. Area [15,886 m2]. Subsequently, and at the request of Alhambra's new management, a reduction of area was carried out, removing part of the parking lot, the centre with the exhibition hall and auditorium, and part of the restaurant, without changing the solution of the competition. Area [8.134 m2]"

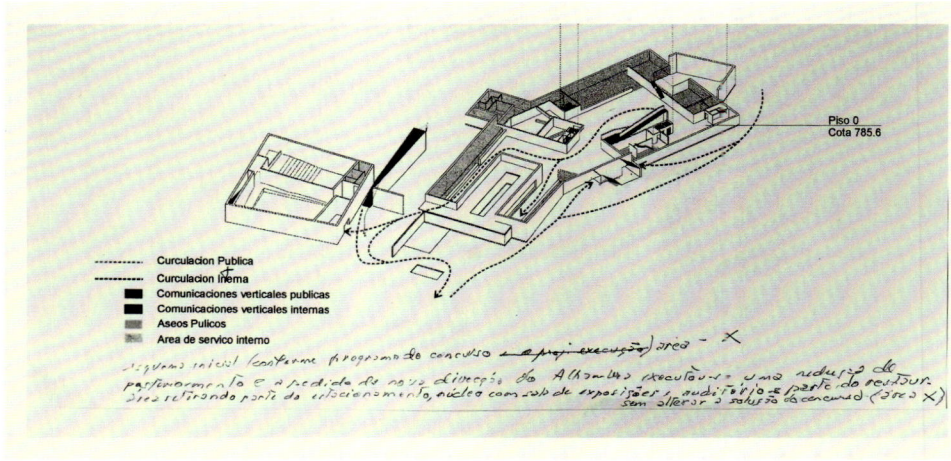

Piso 0
Cota 785.6

.... Curculacion Publica
------------ Curculacion Interna
■ Comunicaciones verticales publicas
■ Comunicaciones verticales internas
▨ Aseos Pulicos
▨ Area de servico interno

Shakespeare Theatre, Gdansk, Poland (2014)
Renato Rizzi

The Shakespeare Theatre in Gdansk, designed by Italian architect Renato Rizzi, has, as he himself says in the project's descriptive memory, two fundamental premises: one of historical character and the other of a political-cultural character. The first refers to existence of an Elizabethan theatre in the same place, in the early seventeenth century. The second premise concerns the fact that the international competition for this theatre's project was launched in 2004, the year Poland officially enters the European Union and "looks 180 degrees from east to west". Like many buildings of public and symbolic character, the Gdansk theatre imposes itself in the urban landscape by its volume and the dark colour of the massive brick. However, this monumentality, accentuated by the rhythm of its buttresses, does not yield to the recurring lightness or transparency that we find in contemporary architecture. It is the timelessness that Shakespeare represents for the theatre that the project seeks to bring to architecture. Equally striking is the contrast between the exterior and the interior of the room, built in light, soft-coloured wood. No less unexpected, despite the reference to Elizabethan theatre, is the possibility of opening the roof in two large wings that mark the city's skyline as the act of performance seeks the "sky of Gdansk, the sky of Shakespeare, the inner sky of each one of us".

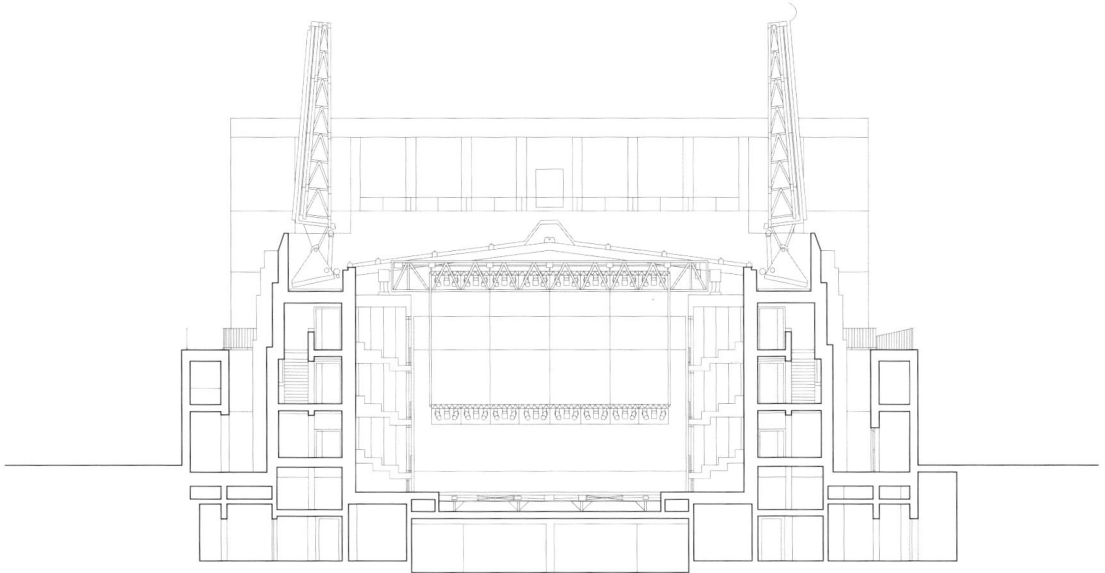

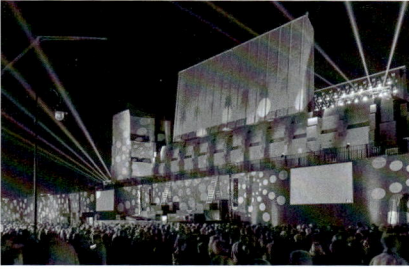

Dia da inauguração

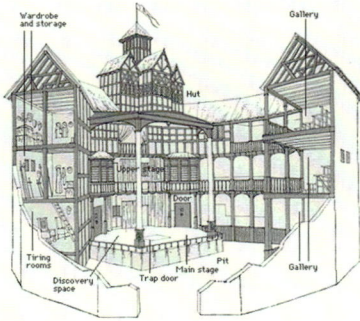

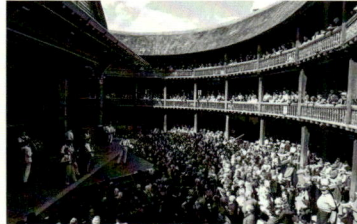

1   Globe Theatre, London
2   Shakespeare's Globe 2015 during a
    performance of Romeo and Juliet
3   The original Globe Theatre, London
4   Florian Beigel: Half Moon Theatre, London
5   Ziggurat of Ur, Iraq

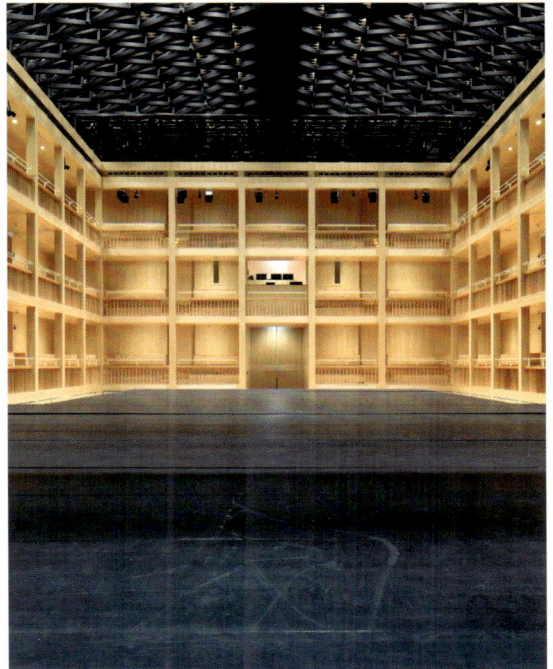

Performing Arts Centre, Taipei, Taiwan (2008- ongoing)
OMA

"In recent years, the world has seen a proliferation of performance centres that, according to a mysterious consensus, consist of more or less an identical combination: a 2,000-seat auditorium, a 1,500-seat theatre, and a black box. Overtly iconic external forms disguise conservative internal workings based on 19th century practice (and symbolism: balconies as evidence of social stratification). Although the essential elements of theatre – stage, proscenium, and auditorium – are more than 3,000 years old, there is no excuse for contemporary stagnation. The Taipei Performing Arts Centre (TPAC) takes the opposite approach: experimentation in the internal workings of the theatre, producing (without being conceived as such) the external presence of an icon." (OMA).

It is with this critical sense at the outset that Rem Koolhaas proposes a "super theatre", an ample space of great dimension and flexibility which is a result of the possibility of combining two of the three rooms of the TPAC's brief: the Grand Theatre; and the Multiform Theatre. This merger, which does not preclude the autonomous functioning of each room, allows the stage to be centered in relation to the public, abolishing the traditional hierarchy and perspective of single escape point. The TPAC also includes a Public Loop – a route that allows circulation through the spaces of production and infrastructures which are generally hidden away from the public. As always, OMA architectures' formal exuberance arises from the brief, in this case reconciling specificity with the "freedoms of the indefinite."

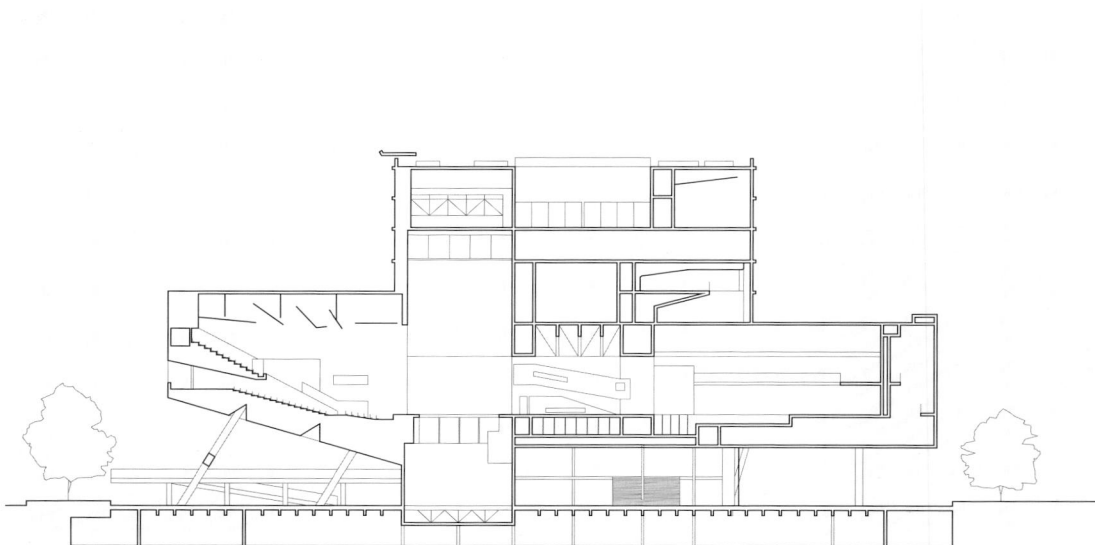

三個劇院
3 Theatres

壓縮整合
Compression

交錯聯接
Cross Connection

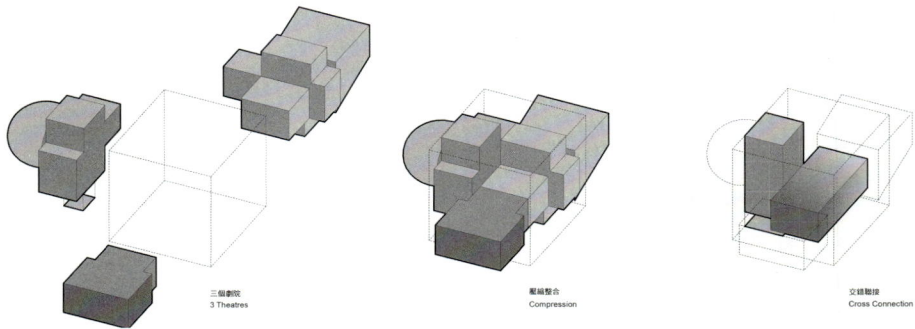

Combination of spaces

公共參觀動線 Public Loop

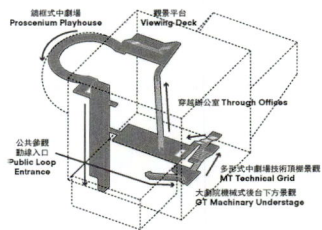

鏡框式中劇場
Proscenium Playhouse

觀景平台
Viewing Deck

穿越辦公室 Through Offices

公共參觀
動線入口
Public Loop
Entrance

多形式中劇場技術頂棚景觀
MT Technical Grid

大劇院機械式檯台下方景觀
GT Machinary Understage

Public Loop path

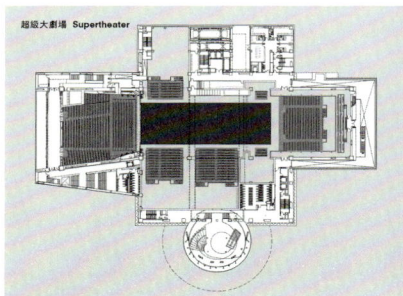

超級大劇場 Supertheater

Supertheater

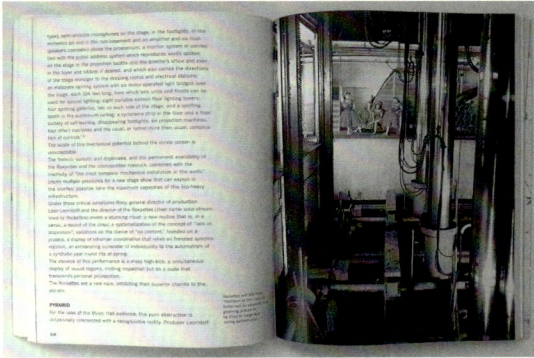

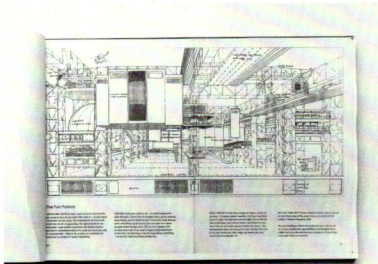

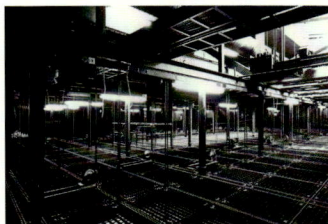

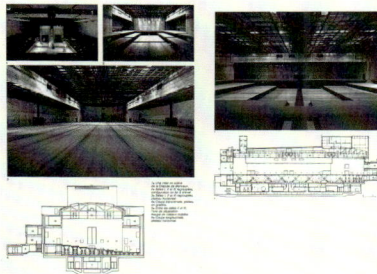

THE CINEROLEUM

Pôle Museal, Lausanne, Switzerland (2015- ongoing)
Aires Mateus

The new museum complex in Lausanne expresses the strength of cultural power in restructuring the city. With around 22,000 m2, this cultural centre represents a large public and private investment. At its origin is the desire to requalify and make accessible to the public an old zone of railway warehouses. A first stage of the intervention was awarding the project for the Musée Cantonal des Beaux-Arts to the architects Barozzi Veiga. A second phase awarded two museums (Musée du Design et d'Arts Appliqués Contemporains – MDAC, and the Musée Cantonal de la Photographie – Elysée) to the Portuguese architects Aires Mateus. With the slogan "two museums one space" the architects proposed a volume with a horizontal slit dividing the program into two. The slit is what marks the entrance, generating an artificial topography that also functions as an extension of the public space. A covered facility, it allows a multi-purpose use from which to access the two museums (from the photograph below, from the design above) and still solve its connection to the high part of the city. This fragmented and partially floating monolith is complemented by an annexed volume of support services to the museological group, unobtrusively finishing the irregular limits of the intervention.

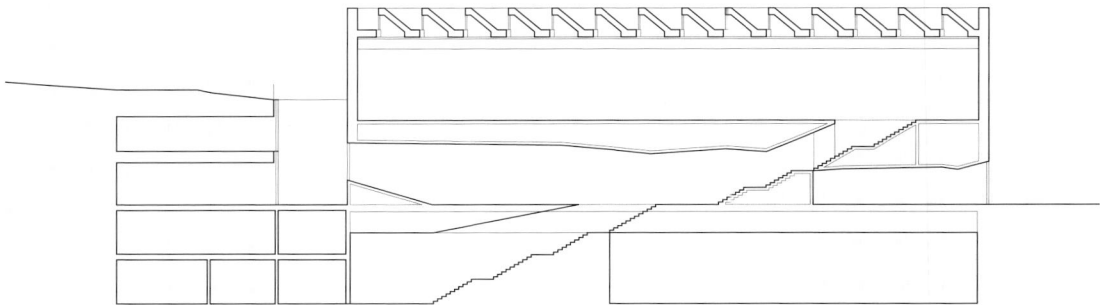

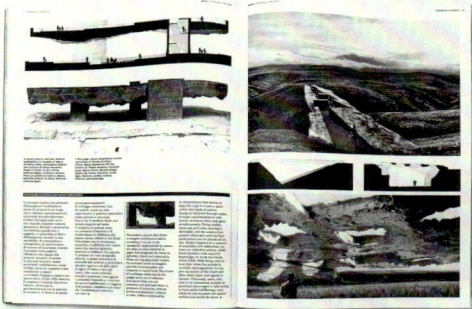

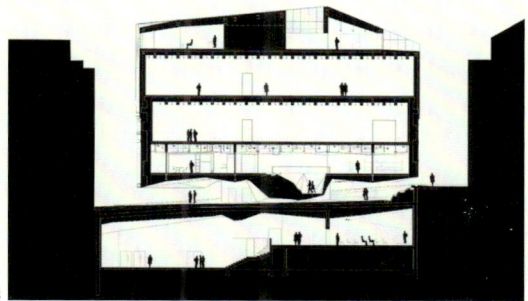

1   Aires Mateus: Mosque in Bordeaux
2   Herzog & de Meuron: Caixa Forum, Madrid
3   Caixa Forum, section
4/5   Ensamble Studio: "Tabula" Structures of Landscape, Montana
6   Ensamble Studio: "Domo" Structures of Landscape, Montana

MEDIA POWER

In the world we live in, the illusion that there only exists what is shown in the media grows ever deeper. As everything is published in social networks, the excess of information quickly gives way to indifference and ultimately forgetfulness. In the mass media, notoriety involves the notion that "a tree falling makes more noise than a forest does growing". Mediatisation is the most visible part of the different powers, and a power in and of itself – in spite of being increasingly weakened by opaque relativism and subjectivity of the image. Architecture also presents itself on this stage, which benefits as much as it harms architects. Aware of the inevitability of media power we ask: is it possible to resist mediatisation? Is there an Architecture of image? Can the speed of the media itself be compatible with architectural time? Can these factors condition our perception of Architecture?

Amager Resource Centre, Copenhagen, Denmark (2010- ongoing)
BIG (Bjarke Ingels Group)

Bjarke Ingels has shown, through a series of projects, to have a rare aptitude for mobilizing society and the media, drawing attention to Architecture's power to transform and convert problematic situations into highly qualified environments, through intelligent program management. It is a process he calls, quite aptly, "alchemy" – or, in recurring works which deal with environmental themes, "hedonistic sustainability".

The Amager Ressource Centre is one of these projects, still under construction, able to instil a positive feeling about the future. It is part of the "Climate Plan", a plan to change energy production and waste management in the city of Copenhagen. In this instance, the architects' work is to mitigate the impact on the city of a power station fuelled by urban waste incineration. Once the issues of toxic gas emission are solved, the building is then covered with a living green facade. At the top of the central, a chimney symbolically releases a ring of steam for every ton of CO2 consumed, a visual expression of an intangible reality.

But it is the treatment of the roof that makes this building unique. Denmark, as is well known, is a flat country, but one where it snows considerably. The sloping roof, which slopes down to the ground, thus becomes an alpine ski slope. Strictly speaking, there are no 100% clean energy sources that do not impact the landscape. Examples of this kind allow us to question architecture's role in helping establish a particular technological paradigm over others. Regardless, its impact on public opinion is unquestionable.

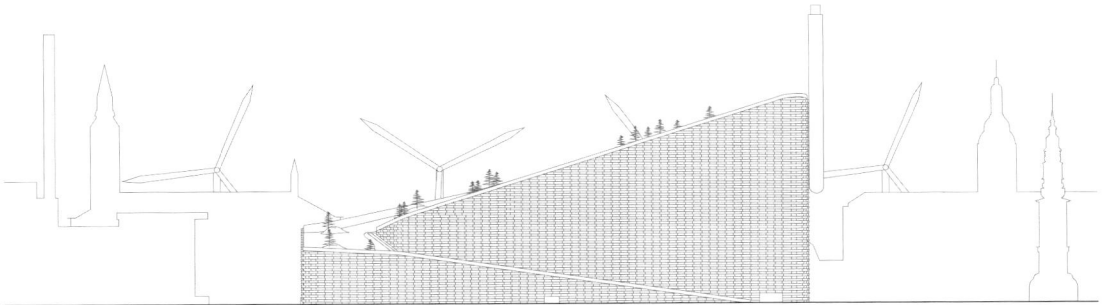

1 Gottlieb Paludan: Biomass plant, Copenhagen
2 Middelgrunden Wind Farm, Copenhagen
3 Tzannes: The Brewery Yard, Sidney
4 BBIG: Power Plant, Uppsala
5 Erick van Egeraat: Incineration Line, Roskilde
6/7 Heatherwick Studio /Arup: Garden Bridge, London

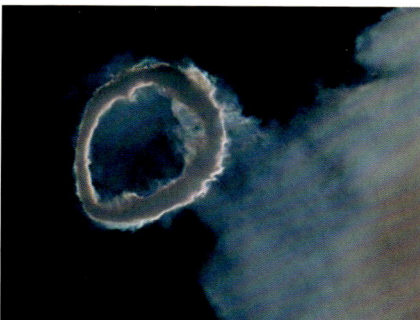

1

3

2

4

5

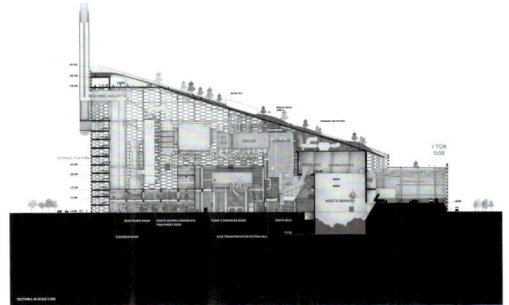

6

7

1 F. L. Wright: Guggenheim Museum, New York
2 F. Gehry: Guggenheim Museum, Bilbao
3 F. Gehry: Guggenheim Museum, Abu Dhabi
4 Guggenheim Helsinki Design Competition:
   1715 submissions
5 Zaha Hadid Architects: Port House, Antwerp
6 Herzog & de Meuron: Elbphilharmonie,
   Hamburg
7 Herzog & de Meuron: Triangle, Paris

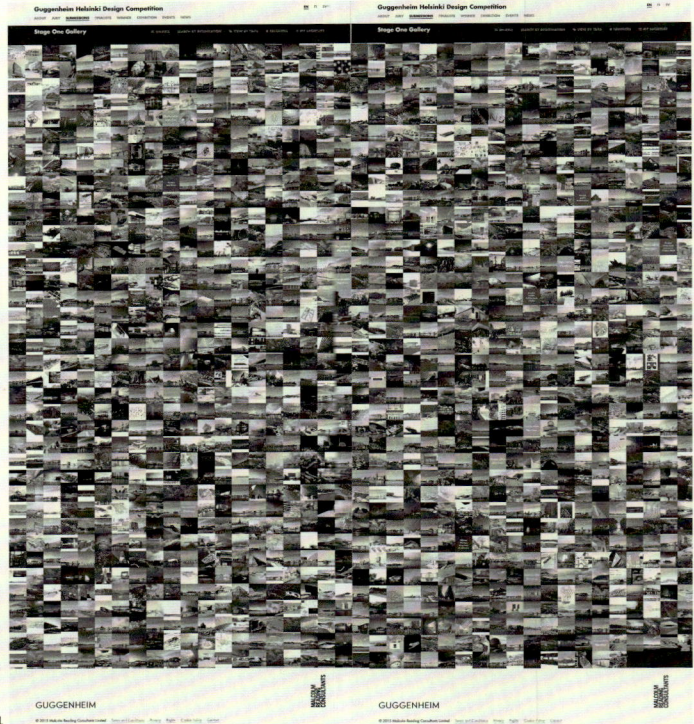

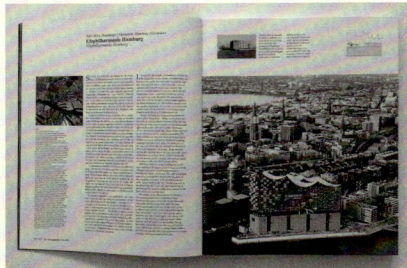

1 Bernardo Rodrigues: Voo do Pássaro House in the press
2 Voo do Pássaro House in real estate advertisement
3 Bernardo Rodrigues irony and humour

PRESS IS MORE

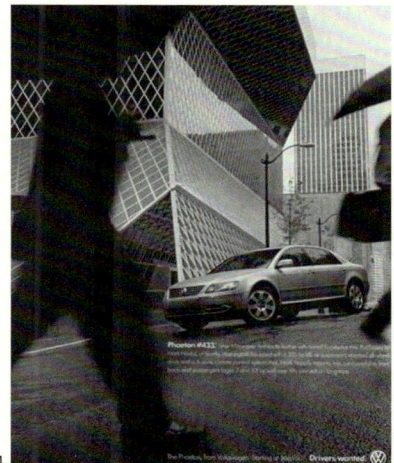

4 Seattle Library (OMA) as a backdrop to Wolkswagen's publicity

Google Search | I'm Feeling Lucky

Meet Zaha Hadid, the first woman architect to receive the Pritzker Prize

1

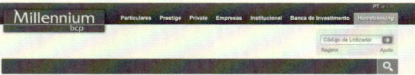

Guardian design critic named London's hottest man

Amy Frearson | 19 January 2017 | 19 comments

Guardian architecture and design critic Oliver Wainwright is "flattered speechless" after being named London's most eligible bachelor by a dating app.

Wainwright, 32, was given the title for receiving more "charms" – similar to Facebook Likes – on mobile dating app Happn than anyone else in the capital.

The app, which can be used in over 30 cities worldwide and has more than eight million subscribers, connects users when they come within 250 metres of one another.

2

Arquiteto Álvaro Siza Vieira
Terço Comemorativo do Centenário das Aparições de Fátima 1917 / 2017
Um Terço para a História

TERÇO
UM OBJETO FAMILIAR E QUOTIDIANO, UM ACONTECIMENTO, UMA ASSINATURA

No âmbito da celebração do centenário das Aparições de Fátima (1917-2017), a criação deste objeto, o Terço, ficará seguramente como um dos marcos desse acontecimento, sobretudo pela assinatura que leva consigo: Álvaro Siza Vieira.

Notas Biográficas
Álvaro SIZA VIEIRA

Álvaro Siza Vieira tem uma obra imensa espalhada por 4 continentes (Europa, África, América e Ásia) e recebeu todos os mais importantes prémios internacionais de arquitetura, incluindo o Prémio Pritzker (1992), o maior galardão que um arquiteto pode receber.

Junto da crítica e dos seus pares é considerado uma referência incontornável da arquitetura contemporânea.

Conseguir cativá-lo para esta tarefa de desenhar um Terço demorou bastante tempo, não por razões religiosas, mas por entender que é muito difícil meter mãos a um objeto tão antigo, tão minucioso, tão reproduzido e com uma carga sagrada tão forte.

A sua participação nesta obra é única e irrepetível.

Decorrem já diligências para que um exemplar seja exposto nos Museus do Vaticano.

Crédito Pessoal

O Millennium bcp disponibiliza uma solução de Crédito Pessoal M Online, TAEG 9,3%, que lhe permite adquirir esta peça. Saiba mais aqui.

TAEG 9,3%. TAN de 7,900%, com uma prestação de 72,32 € para um financiamento de 2.950 € a 48 meses. Montante total imputado ao consumidor de 3.511,19 €, incluindo juros, Imposto do Selo pela utilização do crédito e sobre os juros. Sujeito à análise de risco de crédito.

3

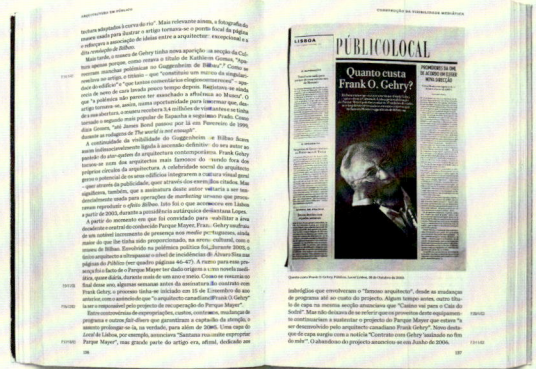

4

2 Critics are "targets" for the media too
3 Rosary by Álvaro Siza (possibility of purchase on credit)
4 "How much does Frank O. Gehry cost?"
5 "How do you answer to those who accuse you of practicing showy architecture?"

5

Pavilion of the Architecture Triennale of Lisbon 2016, Portugal

Johnston Marklee + Nuno Brandão Costa + Office KGDVS

The exhibition *Forma da Forma*, part of the programme of the Lisbon Architecture Triennale of 2016, had as its authors the architects Johnston Marklee, Nuno Brandão Costa and KGDVS studio. The project, commissioned by Diogo Seixas Lopes, mixes different spaces (fragments) of works built by the three architects resulting in a *cadavre exquis*. The result is so unexpected that it quickly pushes back to the background the selected contents of the Socks platform database. In spite of responding to a specific program, the idea prevails that the expository project had as its only consideration to think about form for form's sake, answering only to itself – an architecture freed from function, like a ruin

in the Romantic sense. There are other issues (such as the multi-author issue), but we want to emphasize the particularity of the brief: this work becomes possible in the context of an Architecture Triennale, an event that seeks the celebration, but also the media coverage, of Architecture. The installation's high costs, associated with its ephemeral duration, implies sponsor support beyond the institutional support. Everyone expects some sort of return from the media, making this work a means to other ends. Leaving aside the legitimate criticism of an architecture-spectacle, we see in this work the rare opportunity for spatial experimentation, or the essence of the difficult form of denial.

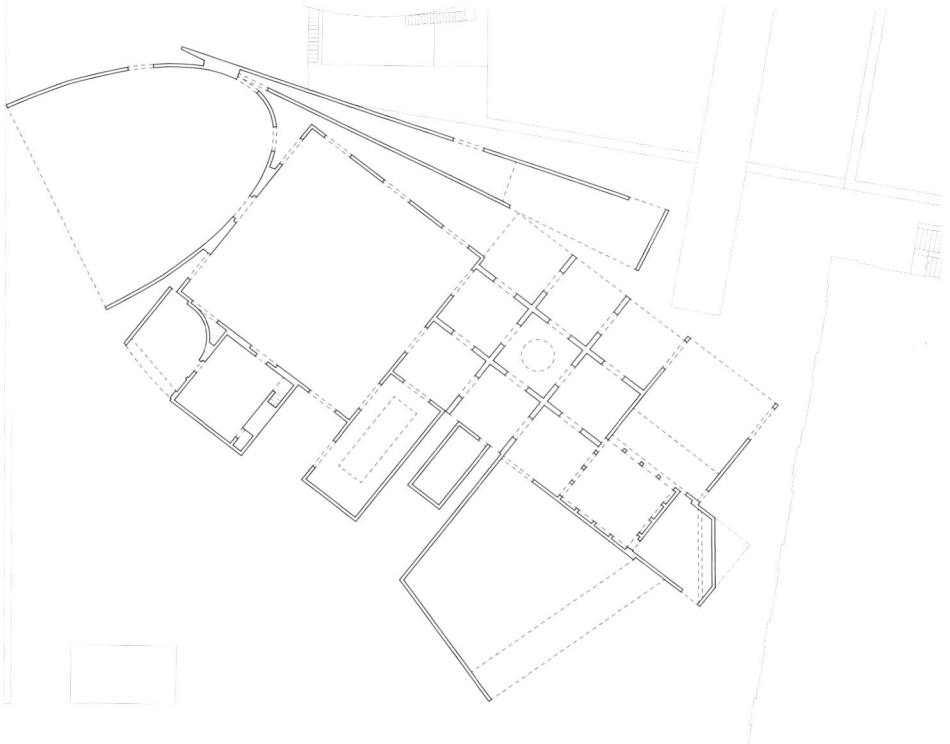

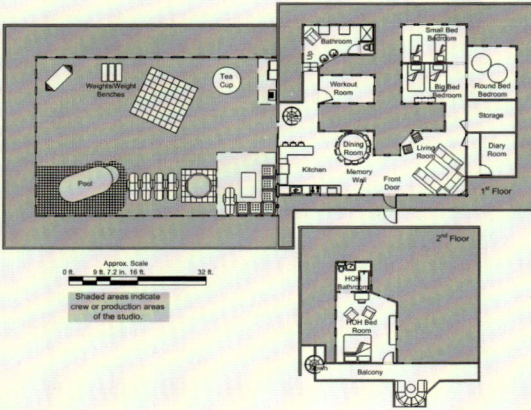

1

1 "big brother" house plans, domesticity for media
5 Big Brother House, the other side of spectacle

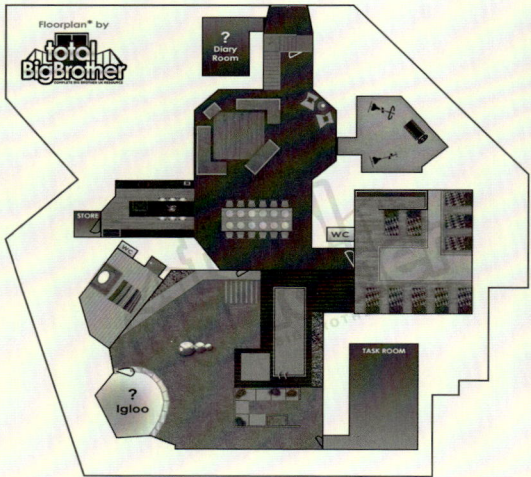

2

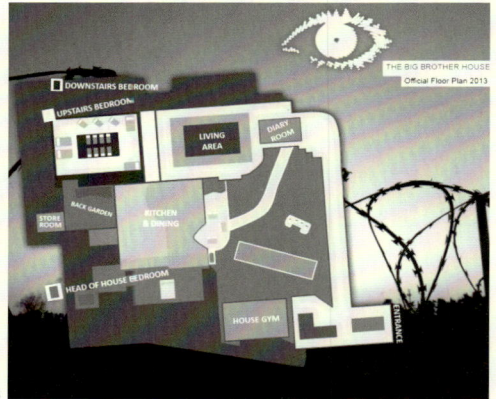

3

4

5

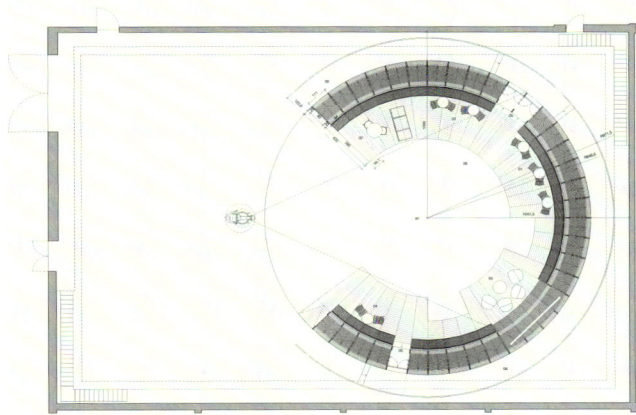

1

2

3

4

5

Jerry Seinfeld
Apartment 5A - 129 West · 81 Street
10024 New York

SEINFELD

IÑAKI ALISTE LIZARRALDE (NIKNEUK)

1-3   J. M. Ribeiro: Praça da Alegria Scenography at RTP Studios, Porto
4   Seinfeld set replica for sale
5   Seinfeld: possible plan

RITUAL POWER

Religions have played a greater role in society. The world is filled with temples which for millennia have expressed the faith and effort placed in their construction. Apparently lacking that same power today, religious cultures have fractured into micronarratives that oscillate between love and, exceptionally, barbarism. The majority of Western countries are secular states. In Europe, we have the privilege of living in cities shared by churches, synagogues, mosques and other temples. Old temples are transformed and desacralized, but new temples rise. How has religious architecture been liberated from the old canons? What is the relation between the new forms of religious architecture and the religious essence? Can architecture approach multiple creeds? Can the temple go beyond sharing a ritual?

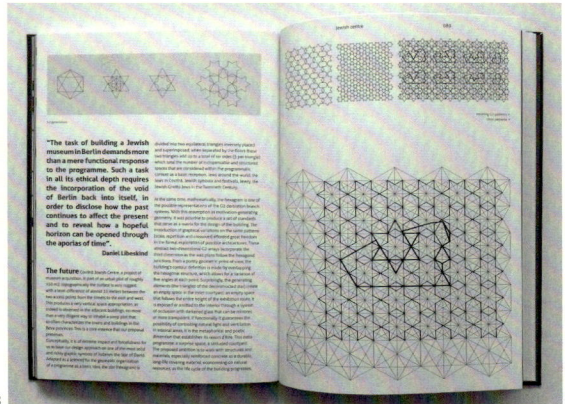

1/2 Kuehn Malvezzi: House of One, Berlin
3 The House of One: Three religions under one roof
4-6 G. Byrne, J. Laranjeira: Interpretation Center of Jewish Culture, Trancoso
7/8 Arquitectos Anónimos: Jewish Centre, Covilhã

Baitul Mukarram Mosque, Lisbon, Portugal (2016)
Inês Lobo

The Baitul Mukarram mosque, designed by Inês Lobo for the Mouraria quarter in Lisbon, aims to do more than simply offer a new place of worship to the Muslim immigrant community of Bangladesh (the existing mosque is precarious in nature, unsafe and insufficient for the number of faithful attending it). The new project is also the pretext to create a new public square and bring about the old ambition of linking Rua da Palma to Rua do Benformoso, making the neighbourhood more permeable as part of a strategy of social and multicultural cohesion.

The proposed building also has as its objective the expansion of the Municipal Photographic Archive and a flexible area for mixed uses. Wrapped in controversy, to those who seem to question the legitimacy of this facility, it is interesting to remember that Mouraria owes its origin to the confinement of the Muslim community in this area, after the Christian retaking of Lisbon. Somewhat paradoxically, it was in this quarter that *fado* (the music that symbolically represents the Portuguese soul) emerged unabashed.
It remains to be seen whether Mouraria's multiculturalism will resist mass tourism and gentrification.

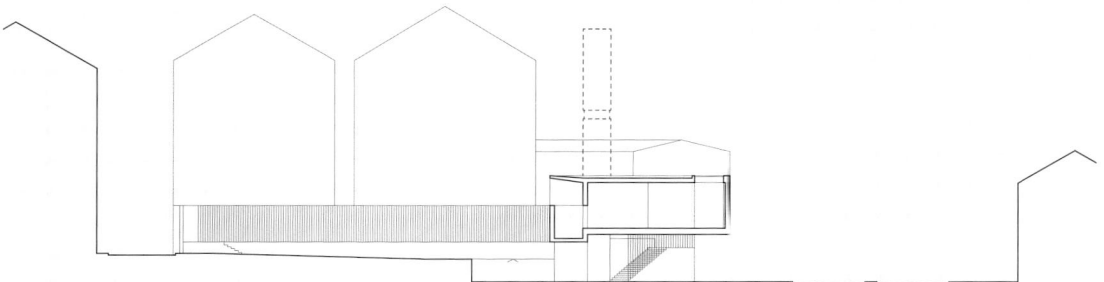

Bait Ur Rouf Mosque, Dacca, Bangladesh (2012)
Marina Tabassum Architects / MTA

The Bait ur Roufem Mosque in Dhaka, designed by Marina Tabassum and awarded the Aga Khan prize in 2016, evokes in its simplicity the search for an essence of what a mosque is in the reading of the Quran: a Muslim congregation, gathered in brotherhood, no hierarchy, between equals. The temple's plan is organised around two squares, a first one arising from the boundaries of the lot, a second corresponding to the prayer space, facing Mecca and delimited by a circle. The spaces between these geometries are the pretext for organizing functional spaces or entry points for natural light. The materials (solid brick and reinforced concrete combined with cement block) clarify the game between figures: the concrete allows for larger spans; and the brick to more discrete openings. Ventilation and light are paid special attention in this project, not only for functional but also symbolic issues. The veil-walls filter our focus and our gaze. Outside, the mosque is shaped as a simple and monochromatic volume, but the brick work, the proportion of the entrance or the elements that make up its cover impart a particular dignity to it that does not fail to refer us to the religious architecture of the Bengal region. Ritual power is also the power of continuity.

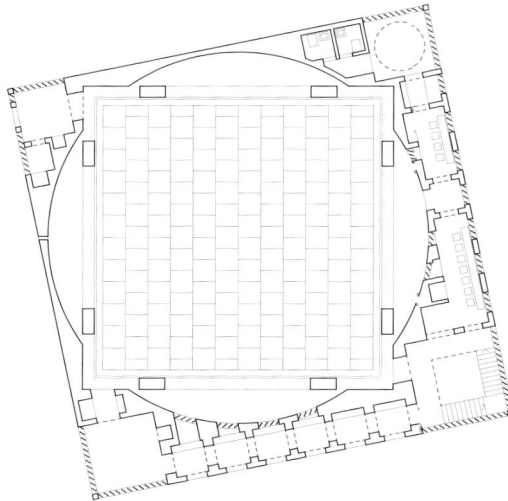

1 Choto Shona Mosque, Chapai Nawabganj
2 Sixty Dome Mosque, Bagerhat

1 Tomb of Sher Shah Suri, Sasaram Bihar
2 Basilica of San Vitale, Ravenna
3 Palace of Charles V, Alhambra and First Unitarian Church, Rochester
4 Piet Mondrian: Victory Boogie Woogie
5 John Hejduk: Diamond Museum

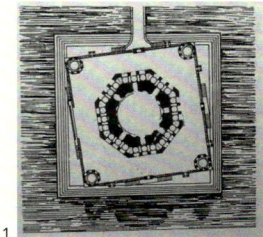

1

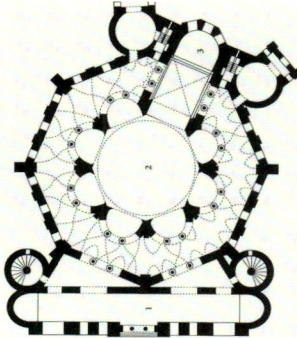

2

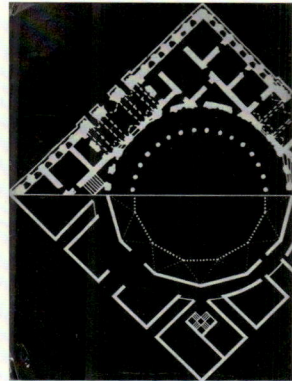

3

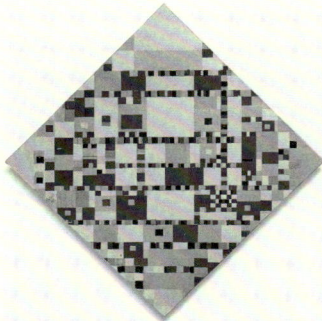

4

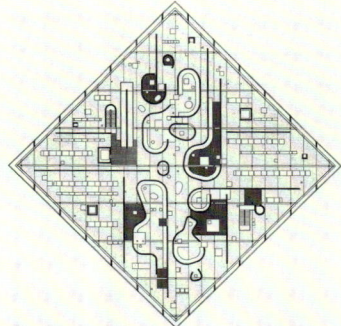

5

Anastasis Church, St Jacques-de-la-Lande, Rennes, France (2009- ongoing)
Álvaro Siza

The Second Vatican Council (1962-65) sought to bring the ritual and liturgical space closer to the faithful. Mass began being spoken mostly in the vernacular; the priest no longer had his back to the assembly (which implied removing the altar from the wall); the faithful were called to read Bible texts, etc. These alterations allowed to think the liturgical space with another freedom, e.g. by drawing away from the central axis around which the majority of the churches was organised.

The Church of Anastasis in Rennes, by Álvaro Siza, evokes this freedom. It allows the architect to separate the orientation of the assembly from the perimeter of the church itself. There are elements of perennial meaning such as the zenithal light that illuminates the altar, the pulpit, or the baptismal font. Nevertheless, the dispersed arrangement of these elements along the curvature of the nave creates a somewhat unusual peripheral circulation. The complexity obtained from pure forms (such as the intersection of a circle in a square) is for Siza the pretext for working tensions, inflections, or narratives which allow thinking about the cult as something that has to be apprehended and learnt.

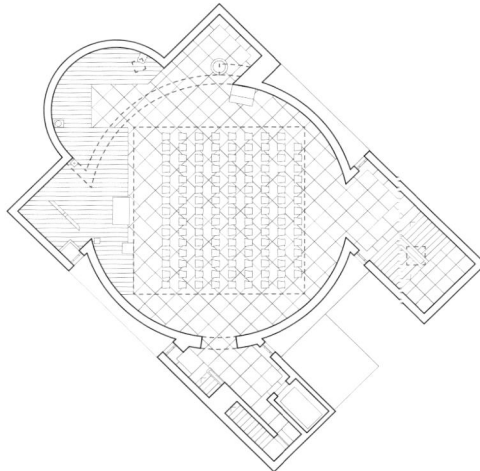

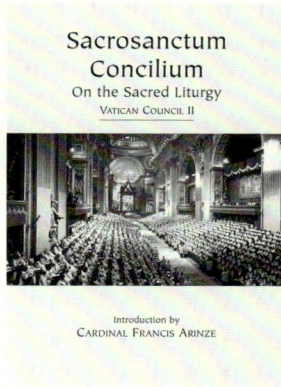

Sacrosanctum
Concilium
On the Sacred Liturgy
VATICAN COUNCIL II

Introduction by
CARDINAL FRANCIS ARINZE

1   Tridentine Mass at St. Paul's Cathedral, Münster
3   Dedication of the Immaculate Chapel, Seminary of Our Lady
    of Conception, Braga
4   Asbjørn Andresen:sculpture of Our Lady of Humility,
    Immaculate Chapel
5-7 Cerejeira Fontes Arquitectos: Immaculate Chapel
8   Cerejeira Fontes Arquitectos: Tree of Life Chapel, Braga

Santa Luzia Church, Maia, Portugal (1998)
Eduardo Souto de Moura

Before making the project for Braga's Municipal Stadium, Eduardo Souto de Moura designed the Church of Misericórdia in Maia, which was never built but, like the stadium, was based on the use of a deactivated quarry. The relationship between building and the rocky nature justifies the prone and fragmented form of the proposed volume – a gesture of humility towards its false nature. The intrusive presence of this granite outcropping inside the church, as if it were slowly-advancing lava, constrains the liturgical space, simultaneously offering something primordial –

it reminds us of the image of the catacombs and caves used as a place of worship and catechesis by early Christians. The interior lighting would be the result of the negotiation between architecture and rock. Setting the church up in this place is not easy nor its access is direct, but the difficulty is transformed into symbolism in the ritual plane. If it is ever built, this building will not erase the violence imposed by the quarry, but it will heal the wound in the territory. Ritual power is also the power of redemption.

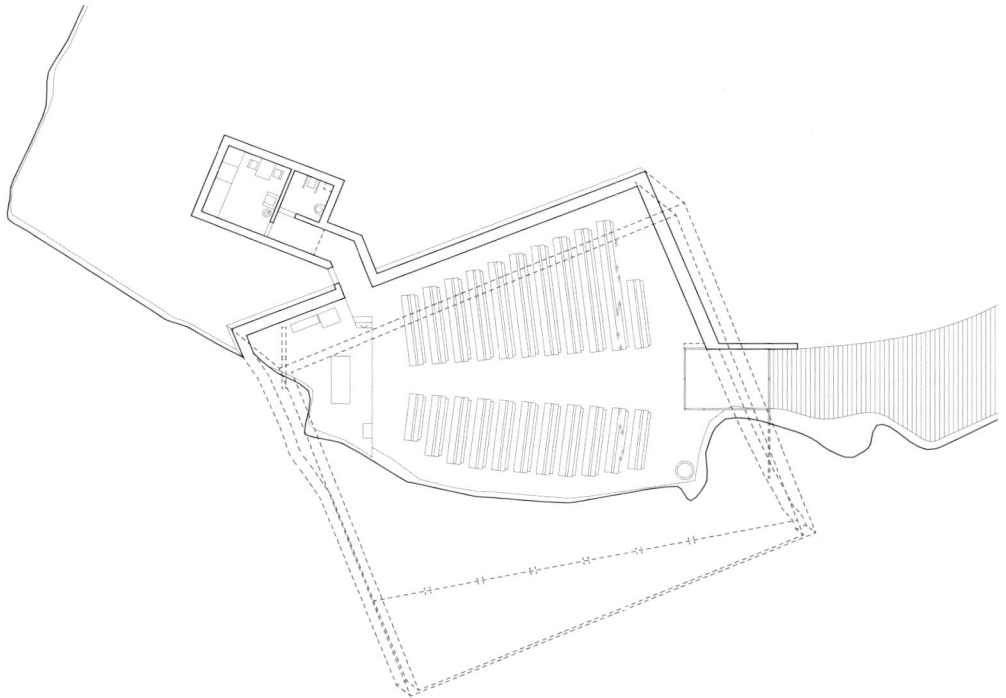

1 Santa Rosalia Sanctuary, Monte
  Pellegrino, Palermo
2 Santa Rosalia Sanctuary's Chapel
3 Cuevas de la Sombra
4 Setenil de las Bodegas
5 House in Guimarães
6 J.L. Carrilho da Graça: Church and Social
  Centre, Portalegre
7/8 Bernardo Rodrigues: Chapel of Eternal
  Light, Ponta Garça

THE CHAPEL OF ST. ROSALIA NEAR PALERMO, IN SICILY.

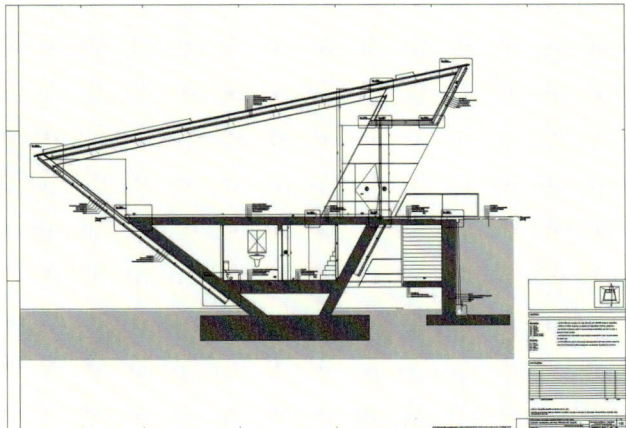

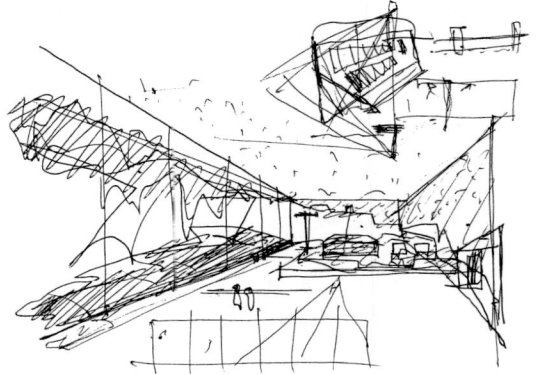

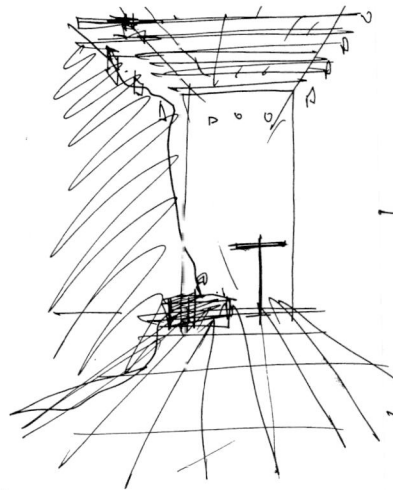
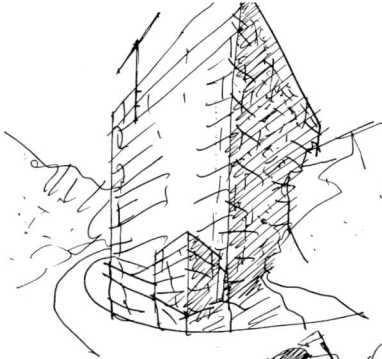
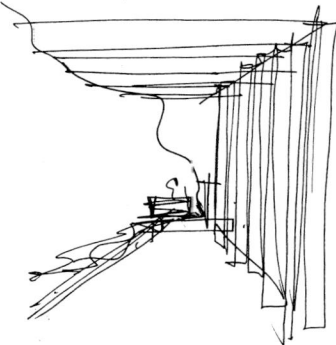

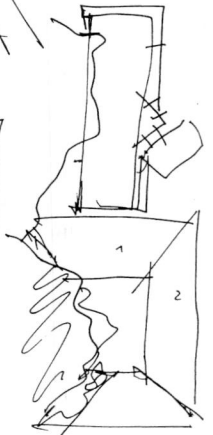

COUNTERPOWER

Architecture is almost always the expression of power. Architecture is representative. This attribute often causes Architecture to fall victim to counterpower. Attacking architecture is a symbolic way of attacking power. But power rarely exists in a convergent fashion. It has become diffused. Power and counterpower coexist in architecture just as they do in society. The architectural project is the synthesis of the relationship between every micro power represented in the different aspects of the project brief, and in its different actors and means. The project is thus the field in which all counter-powers negotiate. The great power of architecture is to dream the unacceptable compromise. Then there are the exceptions, of course, but that's another story.

Biographies

Alexandra Vougia is an architect with a PhD in Architecture from the Architectural Association – School of Architecture, London, where she has been Professor since 2012. Her research focuses on the history of architectural modernism in Germany in the interbellum period. She has worked as an architect in New York and Athens.

Andreas Ruby studied Art History at the University of Cologne. He is a Visiting Professor at the University of Kassel and founder, along with Ilka Ruby, of Texbild, a Berlin-based communication agency specializing in architecture. He is a critic and curator of architecture and art, and regularly writes about architecture. He is the current director of the Swiss Museum of Architecture (SAM) in Basel.

André Tavares is an architect with a degree by the Faculty of Architecture of Porto. He has published several books on architecture, among which "The Anatomy of the Architectural Book". He is the editorial coordinator of the Dafne publishing house and researcher at the Institute for the History and Theory of Architecture (GTA) at the ETH in Zurich. He was director of JA – Jornal Arquitectos (2013-2015) and curator general of the 4th Lisbon Architecture Triennale (2016).

Guilherme Wisnik is an architect. He is a Professor at the Faculty of Architecture and Urbanism of the University of São Paulo. He has authored books on Lucio Costa, Caetano Veloso and Oscar Niemeyer. He was also curator of the Public Art project "Margem", the exhibitions "Cildo Meireles: rio oir" (2011), "Paulo Mendes da Rocha: a natureza como projeto " (2012) and "Pedra no céu: arte e e a arquitetura de Paulo Mendes da Rocha" (2017) and the 10th Architecture Biennale of São Paulo (2013).

Joaquim Moreno is an architect with a degree by the Faculty of Architecture of Porto, and a PhD in Architecture by Princeton University. He is a Professor at the Architecture Department of the Autonomous University of Lisbon. He was curator of the Portuguese delegation at the Venice Architecture Biennale (2008) and the exhibition "On Air: Broadcasting the Modern Movement" (2017) at the Canadian Center for Architecture, Canada.

Ilka Ruby is a publisher and curator. She studied architecture at RWTH Aachen and TU Vienna and has taught at Cornell University, Berlin University of the Arts, and the Peter Behrens School of Architecture in Düsseldorf. Along with Andreas Ruby, she founded textbild, an office for architectural communication, and Ruby Press, a publishing house. Together, they have undertaken a number of curatorial projects, such as the exhibition "Druot, Lacaton & Vassal – Tour Bois le Prêtre" for the German Architecture Museum in Frankfurt (2012) and "Together! The New Architecture of the Collective" at the Vitra Design Museum (2017).

João Belo Rodeia is an architect with a degree by the Faculty of Architecture of Lisbon. He is Professor at the Architecture Department of the Autonomous University of Lisbon and at the University of Évora. He was president of the Portuguese Institute of Architectural Heritage (2003-2005) and of the Order of Architects of Portugal (2008-2013). He writes regularly about architecture and has curated several architecture exhibitions.

Moisés Puente is an architect, an architecture editor at Gustavo Gili, director of 2G magazine and founder of the architecture publisher Puente Editores. He occasionally works as a curator. He has published books on Alejandro de la Sota, Mies van der Rohe, Jørn Utzon, Philip Ursprung and Olafur Eliasson, among others, and has authored monographs on Mies van der Rohe and Alejandro de la Sota. In 2010 he received the FAD Prize for Thought and Criticism.

Nuno Grande is an architect with a degree by the Faculty of Architecture of Porto and a PhD from the University of Coimbra, where he teaches at the Department of Architecture. He was curator of the Portuguese delegation at the Architecture Bienniales of São Paulo (2007) and Venice (2016) and curator of the exhibition "Les universalistes. 50 ans d'architecture portugaise", a co-production between the Calouste Gulbenkian Foundation and the Cité de L'architecture et du patrimoine (Paris, 2016). He writes regularly about architecture.

Yuma Shinohara is a curator, author, translator, and editor in the fields of architecture and design and studied architectural history and comparative literature at Columbia University, New York. He was assistant curator for the exhibition "Together: The New Architecture of the Collective" at the Vitra Design Museum (2017). He has worked on the exhibitions "DEMO:POLIS" at the Akademie der Künste Berlin and "OfficeUS" for the American Pavilion at the 14th Venice Architecture Biennale. As a translator, he has rendered a book by Bruno Taut into English and has worked for various publications.

Jorge Carvalho is an architect with a degree by the Faculty of Architecture of Porto. In 1991 he founded, with Teresa Novais, the atelier aNC arquitectos, whose works have been awarded, published and presented internationally. He is a Visiting Assistant Professor in the Department of Architecture of the Faculty of Sciences and Technologies of the University of Coimbra. As an author, his field of interest is contemporary architecture.

Pedro Bandeira is an architect with a degree by the Faculty of Architecture of Porto, a researcher (LAB 2PT) and Associate Professor in the School of Architecture of the University of Minho. He is the author of several books on architecture: "Specific Projects for a Generic Client" (2006), "Escola do Porto Lado B (1868-1978)" (2014) – AICA 2015 Architecture Critique and Essay Award, and "Arcosanti 2012" (2017).

Ricardo Carvalho is an architect with a degree by the Faculty of Architecture of Lisbon and a PhD in Architecture by the IST of the University of Lisbon. He founded the atelier Ricardo Carvalho + Joana Vilhena Arquitectos in 1999. He is a Professor and current director of the Department of Architecture of the Autonomous University of Lisbon and was Visiting Professor at the Universities of Navarra, Spain (2013) and Carleton, Canada (2016). He writes regularly about architecture.

Illustration Credits

p. 80 Vijitha Basnayaka; 1, 2 – SLA / www.sla.dk;
3- Revista Area #43; 4 Patrick Geddes /
www.wikipedia.org

p. 81 Vijitha Basnayaka

p. 82 1- Unknown / www.travelfootprint.lk;
2- Vijitha Basnayaka; 3- Unknown / pinterest.
com; 4- Rio Helmi / www.archdaily.com.br;
5 - Unknown / www.curitiba -travel.com.br

p. 83 Vijitha Basnayaka

p. 85, 86, 87 Granby Four Streets

p. 88 1, 2- Assemble; 3- Rob Battersby / Assemble;
4- Ben Quinton / Assemble;
5- Assemble; 6- J. M. Ribeiro;
7- P. Bandeira; 8- Colectivo Há Baixa.

p.90 Roger Jardine; 1, 2- Unknown /
Andrew Makin;

p. 91, 92, 93 Roger Jardine

p. 94 1 - JasonF007/www.commons.wikimedia.
org; 2- Glass Age Development Committee,
B.T. Batsford; 3- Caleidoscópio Edição
e Artes Gráficas; 4- Unknown via
www.femmeaufoyer2011.blogspot.pt;
5- BRS Architectes / www.paris.fr.

p. 96, 97 Leonardo Finotti

p. 98 Herzog & de Meuron; 1- Jornal Fala Mãe
Luiza / www.jornalfalamaeluiza.blogspot.pt;
2- Unknown 3- Jornal Arquitectos #228;
4- Arq/A Magazine #123; Iwan Baan /
Lars Müller Publishers

p. 99 Leonardo Finotti

p. 101 Estúdio Flagrante

p. 102 1- Leonardo Finotti; 2- Hufton +
Crow / www. dezeen.com; 3- Nelson Kon /
Urdi Arquitectura; 4- Fiat Group /
www.italoamericano.org

p. 103 Matheus José Maria; Estúdio Flagrante

p. 105 1- www.ilonagaynor.co.uk;
2- Richter Verlag; 3 - www.hohensinn
-architektur.at; 4- www.theguardian.com;
5- www.change.org

p. 107 Timmerman Photography

p. 108 1- www.matthewmoore.com; 2- University
of California Press; 3- Ronald Rael, Virginia San
Fratello / www.borderwallasarchitecture.com;
4- University of California Press; 5- University
of California Press; Timmerman Photography

p. 109 1- Serge Dedina / www.sergededina.com;
2- Paul Haring / CNS / www.catholicnews.com;
3- www.sonicanta.com; 4- Unknown /
www.skyscrapercity.com; 5- Office KGDVS

p. 111 Rainer Viertlböck

p. 112 1- www.nbcnews.com;
2- www.coxarchitects. com.au;
3- www.dailydot.com; Helmut Jahn

p. 113 Rainer Viertlböck

p. 115 Carrilho da Graça Arquitectos;
Rita Burmester

p. 116, 117 Rita Burmester

p. 118 1- Público newspaper; 2- www.forbes.com
3- www.theguardian.com; 4- www.rtp.pt;
5 - www.oma.eu

p. 120 Hollan Photo / Statsbygg;
1- www.motherboard.vice.com; 2- Crop Trust;
3- Unknown; 4- Jim Lo Scalzo / European
Pressphoto Agency; 5- www.news.vice.com

p. 121 1- www.colocationamerica.com;
2 - www.af -la.com; 3 - Alan Brandt / www.pri.org;
Matthias Heyde

p. 124 Luís Ferreira Alves; 1- Unknown /
www.ip4mag.com; 2- E. Mini, C. Metz /
www.min.swiss; 3- www.serodiofurtado.com;
4 - Camilo Rebelo; 5 - Gabriele Basilico /
C. Rebelo.

p. 125 1- L. Ferreira Alves, I. D'Orey / Edições
FAUP; 2,3 - www.franekarchitects.cz;
4- Kris Van den Bosch / www.archdaily.com;
5- Luís Ferreira Alves; 6,7- PAO /
www.archdaily.com

p. 126,127 Tiago Figueiredo

p. 128 L. Ferreira Alves

p. 130 Tamás Bujnovszky; Sporaarchitects

p. 131 1- Actar / Junta de Adalucía, Consejaría
de Cultura; 2- Benedikt Taschen Verlag / MBAC
/ ING; 3- Sporaarchitects; 4- Tim Arnett / UCL /
www.boneresearchsociety.org;
Tamás Bujnovszky

p. 132 1- Hans Werlemann / www.oma.eu;
2 - www.montrealsouterrain.ca;
3,4- Miguel Figueira

p. 133 Tamás Bujnovszky

p. 135 Ralph Feiner; Bearth & Deplazes

p. 136 Bearth & Deplazes; Ralph Feiner

p. 137 1- Van Nostrand Reinhold;
2- Digital Design Media; 3, 4- AD – Made
by Robots; 5 - www.matter.media.mit.edu;
6 - www.gramaziokohler.arch.ethz.ch;
7,8- CCA / Sternberg Press

p. 139 Fernando Guerra / FG+SG; Rita Burmester

p. 140 Rita Burmester

p. 141 1- Johannes Marburg; 2, 3- www.dsrny.com;
4- Jim Henderson / www.en.wikipedia.org;
5- Dave Greer / www.davegreer.cc;
6- www.smithsonian. com;
7- Oxford Internet Institute

p. 143 Vijitha Basnayaka; 1, 2- Vijitha Basnayaka;
3- www.unisinforma.net; 4- www.asianart.com

p. 144 Vijitha Basnayaka

p. 145 1- Domus #997; 2- Seier+Seier /
www. commons.wikimedia.org;
3- Unknown; 4- Amateur Architecture Studio /
www. cfileonline.org; 5- www.patrimonio.cmpb;
6- Inês Guedes / www.paulomoreira.net

p. 148 Fernando Guerra / FG+SG;
1,2- Paulo Moreira; 3 - Fernando Guerra /
FG+SG.

p. 149, 150 Fernando Guerra / FG+SG

p. 151 1,2,3- Eduardo Souto de Moura;
4- Jornal Arquitectos #251; 5- Barbas Lopes
Arquitectos / 18:25 Empreiteiros Digitais;
6- A. Siza, G. Sheppard /
www.gabellinisheppard.com;
7- Dafne Editora.

p. 153 OMA

p. 154 1- University of Chicago Press;
2- Gius Laterza & Figli Spa / Editorial Presença;
3- AEX / OMA;
4- Tsunehisa Kimura / www.socks -studio.com;
5 - Unknown / www.stoomschiprotterdam.nl;
6- Crès et Cie / Librairie Arthaud; 7- Unknown.

p. 155 OMA

p. 156 1- The Monacelli Press;
2- Unknown / www.commons.wikimedia.org;
3- Collection of Christopher Gray /
www.architizer.com;
4- Anchor Press / Edições 70; 5,
6- Larisa Bulibasa / www.dezeen.com

p. 157 OMA

p. 158 Scagliolabrakkee; 1,2- Verlag Schnelle /
Quickborn; 3- GA / ADA Edita Tokyo Co.;
4- A+T Architecture Publishers;
5- Benny Chan, Fotoworks /
www.clivewilkinson.com

p. 160 Alp Eren

p. 161 1- Unknown; 2- John Nicholls / The Decorators;
3, 4- The Decorators / www.the-decorators.net;
5- Blond & Briggs / HarperCollins

p. 162,163 Alp Eren

p. 164 1- Chris Radburn / PA Wire;
2- Amazon / US Patent;
3- www.granby-workshop.myshopify.com

p. 165 1- Helmut Pierer / PPAG / www.pierer.net;
2- Cemal Emden; 3- Guillaume Ziccarelli;
4- Danilo Dungo; 5- Iñigo Bujedo-Aguirre.

p. 168 Iwan Baan; 1, 2- Laurent de Carniere /
www.urbanrigger.com; 3 - B.T Batsford Publisher

p. 169, 170,171 Iwan Baan

p. 173 Philippe Ruault

p. 174 Philippe Ruault; 1- www.aut.cc;
2, 4- Lancelot / Collections des Archives
de Mulhouse; 3- Editorial Gustavo Gili

p. 175 1- Editorial Gustavo Gili;
2, 3- Unknown / www.archtrace.wordpress.com;
4, 5- B.T Batsford Publisher; Philippe Ruault

p. 177 Johannes Marburg

p. 178 1- Johannes Marburg; 2- Unknown /
www.sites.arte.tv/pnb/fr; 3- Editorial Gustavo
Gili; 4- Ruby Press; 5- www.nytimes.com;
6 - Anna Puigjaner

p. 179 Johannes Marburg

p. 181 Filip Dujardin

p. 182 1- Electa / Elemond Editori Associati;
Filip Dujardin; 2- Cristóbal Portillo Robles;
3 - www.archivesdelimaginaire.epfl.ch;
4- J. A. Coderch; Filip Dujardin

Illustration Credits

p. 183 Filip Dujardin

p. 185 1- 1 Boek 2 Vylder Vinck Tailieu;
2, 3- The Monacelli Press
4- Editorial Gustavo Gili;
5- Cristina Chicau; Filip Dujardin

p. 186 1- Sasaki and Partners Structural
Consultants; 2 - Unknown; 3 - Unknown /
www.palaisdetokyo.com; Filip Dujardin

p. 187 Filip Dujardin

p. 189 Fernando Guerra / FG+SG

p. 190 1,2- Nobuyuki Endo; 3- Electa /
Elemond Editori Associati; 4- Unknown /
www.vaumm.com; 5- Unknown /
www.bdonline.co.uk; Fernando Guerra / FG+SG

p. 191 Fernando Guerra / FG+SG;
1 - Camilo Rebelo; 2 -3 Bak Gordon Arquitectos
/ G. Frias, p. Pedro.

p. 194 1- www.landmarktrust.org;
2- www.weddingtoncastle.co.uk; Helene Binet

p. 195 1,2,3,4- Witherford Watson Mann
Architects; 5 - Bund Deutscher Architekten /
Technische Universität München;
6 - Christian Richters / Accademia
di Architettura Mendrisio; Philip Vile

p. 196 -197 Helene Binet

p.198 Witherford Watson Mann Architects;
Philip Vile

p. 200 Susan Schuls

p. 201 1- Buckminster Fuller /
www.treehugger.com;
2 - Lars Müller Publishers;
3- Rizzoli International Publications;
4, 5- British Museum Press

p. 202 Susan Schuls; 1- Revista Arq /A #61;
2, 3, 4- B.T Batsford Publisher

p. 204 Jo Pesendorfer

p. 205 1- www.fr.wikipedia.org;
2- www.commons. wikimedia.org;
3- www.whc.unesco.org;
4 - Bountiles Mont-Saint -Michel / Syndicat
mixte baie du Mont-Saint- Michel /
www.cybergeo.revues.org;
5- Unknown / www.butteauxcailles.eklablog.com

p. 206 1- Editions Galilée; 2- AP / Ng Han Guan /
www.philstar.com; 3 - Jean-Claude Bertrand
/ www.jcbertrand.fr; 4- Babinet / Flickr / CC /
www.la- croix.com; Unknown.

p. 208 Á. Siza, J. Domingo Santos

p. 209 1,2,3,4- Unknown; 5- www.whc.unesco. org;
6- via J. Domingo Santos;
7- Partido Popular / www.granadaimedia.com;
8- www.sosalhambra.blogspot.pt;
9- www.ideal.es

p. 210 Álvaro Siza Vieira

p. 212 Matteo Piazza

p. 213 M. Cieszewski / www.polska.pl;
European Shakespeare Research Association /
www.esra2017.eu;

1- www.theatrelitwiki. wikispaces.com;
2- Helena Miscioscia / www.thestage.co.uk;
3- via Lenton Sands / www.flickr.com;
4- Peter Cook / www. uncubemagazine.com;
5- Unknown / www.bedwyrblog.blogspot.pt;
Matteo Piazza

p. 215 OMA / Philippe Ruault

p. 216 OMA;

p.217 1- Monacelli Press / 010 Publishers;
2- Birkhäuser Publishers for Architecture;
3- Nelson Kon / Ed. Gustavo Gili; 4- Editions du
Moniteur; 5- Unknown / www.schaubuehne.de;
6- Teatro Expandido / J. S. Cardoso;
7- José Campos; 8- Diller Scofidio
+ Renfro / www.dsrny.com; 9- Revista Arq. /
A #107; 10- www.assemblestudio.co.uk

p. 219, 220 Aires Mateus

p. 221 1- Aires Mateus / www.publico.pt; 2- A+U
Publishing Co; 3- Herzog & de Meuron /
www.herzogdemeuron.com; 4- Domus #1002;
5- Ensamble Studio / www.designboom.com;
6- Andre Costantini / www.archdaily.com;
Aires Mateus

p. 224 Rasmus Hjortshøj; Bjarke Ingels Group

p. 225 1- Gottlieb Paludan / www.dezeen.com;
2- Danish Wind Industry Association;
3- John Gollings; 4- Bjarke Ingels Group /
www.big.dk; 6- Heatherwick Studio / Arup /
www.gardenbridge.london;
7- Evening Standard; Bjarke Ingels Group

p. 226 1- P. Bandeira; 2- Mario R. D. Ortiz /
www.commons.wikimedia.org; 3- TDIC /
Frank O. Gehry / www.guggenheim.org;
4 - www.designguggenheimhelsinki.org;
5 - www.zaha -hadid.com; 6,7 - AV Monografias

p. 227 1- www.bernardorodriguespress.blogspot.
pt; 2- P. Bandeira; 3- Bernardo Rodrigues;
4 - Grupo Volkswagen

p. 228 1- www.google.com; 2- www.dezeen.com;
3- www.millenniumbcp.pt; 4- Dafne Editora /
Jornal Público; 5- EFE / www.elmundo.es

p. 230 -231 André Cepeda

p. 232 1- www.ward8online.com; 2- Total Big
Brother UK / www.twitter.com/totalbigbrother;
3- www.thisisbigbrother.com;
4- www. worldofbigbrother.com; 5 - PBM -NR /
Daily Mail Australia / www.dailymail.co.uk

p. 233 1,2,3- João Mendes Ribeiro;
4- www.seinfeldsetreplica.com; 5- Iñäki A.
Lizzaralde / www.nikneuk.deviantart.com

p. 234, 235; Tiago Casanova

p. 237 1,2- Kuehn Malvezzi; 3- Lia Darjes /
www.houseofone.org; 4,5,6- Fernando Guerra /
FG+SG; 7,8 -Caleidoscópio Edição
e Arte Gráficas

p.239 Inês Lobo; Paulo Catrica

p. 241 Sandro di Carlo Darsa / MTA; 1- Julie C /
www.tripadvisor.pt; 2- www.tourmet.com

p. 242 Marina Tabassum / MTA; Rajesh Vora;

p. 243 Hassan Saifuddin Chandan / MTA;
1- Marina Tabassum; 2- www.commons.
wikimedia.org; 3- Perspecta #9- 10 Yale
Architectural Journal; 4- Piet Mondrian /
Gemeentemuseum Den Haag / www.commons.
wikimedia.org;
5- John Hejduk / www.bmiaa.com

p. 245, 246,246 Nicolo Galeazzi

p. 248 Álvaro Siza; Nicolo Galeazzi

p. 249 1- Unknown; 2- Ignatius Press;
3,4- Edmundo Correia / www.snpcultura.org;
5,6,7 Joaquim Felix; 8- Nelson Garrido

p. 251 1- www.sicilytourist.com;
2- www. citydesert.wordpress.com;
3- E. Romero de Torres / www.imaginasetenil.
wordpress. com; J. Ortiz- Echagüe /
www.imaginasetenil. wordpress.com;
Matilde Seabra; Casabella #775;
7,8- Bernardo Rodrigues.

p. 252, 253 E. Souto de Moura

Credits

BOOK

Editors
Casa da Arquitectura

Editorial Coordination
Jorge Carvalho
Pedro Bandeira
Ricardo Carvalho

General Coordination
Jorge Carvalho

Essayists
Alexandra Vougia
André Tavares
Andreas Ruby
Guilherme Wisnik
Ilka Ruby
Ivo Poças Martins
João Belo Rodeia
Joaquim Moreno
Moisés Puente
Nuno Grande
Yuma Shinohara

Editorial Assistance and Production
Ana Pinto (Casa da Arquitectura)
Maya Ruegg (Lars Müller Publishers)

Iconographic and Bibliographic Collection
Magda Seifert
Ivo Poças Martins

Bibliographic support
Faculdade de Arquitectura da Universidade do Porto

Translation
Angela Marquito (p. 14–23, 32–37)
Anton Stark (p. 4–11, 24–31, 78–257)

Proofreading
Scott M. Culp

Graphic Design
Dobra

Re-design
Décio Nascimento

Printing and finishing
Norprint.pt

Legal Deposit: 434111/17
1st edition
Printed on (paper) Gardamatt Smooth
Typography: NB Akademie, NB Grotesk

ISBN Casa da Arquitectura 978-989-96790-6-1
ISBN Lars Müller Publishers 978-3-03778-546-1

Project dates presented are the completion dates for each project, or, in the case of non-built projects, the date of the project's design.

EXHIBITION

This book accompanies the exhibition
Power Architecture.
November 17, 2017 to March 18, 2018,
Casa da Arquitectura, Matosinhos.

General Commissioner
Nuno Sampaio (Casa da Arquitectura)

Curators
Jorge Carvalho
Pedro Bandeira
Ricardo Carvalho

Editorial Coordination
Jorge Carvalho

Editorial Assistance and Production
Ana Pinto

Exhibition project
aNC Arquitectos
   Teresa Novais
   Jorge Carvalho
   Joana Fernandes
   Inês Bastos
   Nuno Sarmento
   Beatriz Teixeira

Mapping Power/Architecture Installation Design
Bruno Figueiredo

Lighting design
Jorge Costa

Structural Design
Ana Vale

Exhibition Graphics
Dobra

Exhibition Installation
Eurowire
Outros Mercados
Interface – Produção e Cultura
(*Mapping Power/Architecture*)

CASA DA ARQUITECTURA
PORTUGUESE CENTER OF ARCHITECTURE

José Manuel Dias da Fonseca President
Nuno Sampaio Executive Director
and Chief Commissioner

ADMINISTRATION

Executive Commission
José Manuel Dias da Fonseca
President of the Board of Management
Nuno Sampaio Secretary to the Administration
Fernando Rocha Treasurer to the Administration

Members
Portuguese Chamber of Architects
represented by **José Manuel Pedreirinho**
Porto City Council
represented by **Rui Loza**
Vila Nova de Gaia City Council
represented by **Valentim Miranda**
Administração dos Portos do Douro, Leixões e Viana do Castelo, S.A.
(Management of Douro and Leixões Ports)
represented by **Emílio Brogueira Dias**
Associação Empresarial de Portugal
(Portugal Business Association)
represented by **Gonçalo Lencastre Medeiros**,
Carlos Guimarães

General Assembly
Matosinhos City Council
represented by **Eduardo Pinheiro** President
Metro do Porto, S.A. (Porto Metro)
represented by
Jorge Moreno Delgado Vice-President
Gonçalo Byrne Secretary

Executive Team
Coordination
Carla Barros
Production
Ana Pinto
Alice Prata
Claudia Rosete
Image & Design
José Pereira
Communication and Press
Margarida Portugal
Educational Service
Susana Gaudêncio
Collections
Ana Filipe
Gilson Fernandes
Financial Department
Soraia Lebre
Funding and Partnerships
Joana Ferreira
Loja da Casa
Carla Sousa
Filomena Rocha
Rita Correia Pinto
Infrastructures and IT
Paulo Silva
Main Office
Natacha Mota